PRAISE FOR *CODE NAME: LISE*

'A non-fiction thriller.' **Wall Street Journal**

'Larry Loftis has crafted a true thriller, a highly entertaining account of the most highly decorated spy of WW2. A great read.' **Alex Kershaw, *New York Times* bestselling author of *The First Wave* and *Avenue of Spies***

'Well researched, well written, and fast paced enough to keep the pages turning – this will interest fans of the history of espionage, World War II history, military history, women's history, and biography.' **Library Journal**

'Loftis tells a well-researched, novelistic story of a heroine and patriot... Swift and entertaining, Loftis's work reads less like a biography and more like a thriller.' **Publishers Weekly**

'A true-life thriller... Every chapter ends on a cliffhanger... A vivid history of wartime heroism.' **Kirkus Reviews**

'The stuff of classic World War II thrillers.' **Newsday**

'Loftis gives Sansom the epic story her experience warrants, full of spycraft, complex and important missions, incredible feats of bravery, and love.' **CrimeReads**

'Readers will not want to put this book down... A spy thriller instead of a dry biography.' **MilitaryPress.com**

'Provides a riveting account of the mayhem of the final days of WWII... Loftis' meticulous research is evident throughout.' **The Cipher Brief**

'Larry Loftis brings the past to life with a brilliantly researched and executed tale of one woman's unparalleled heroism in occupied France during ... ... of love, betrayal an... ... ...not to be missed.' M... ...**elling**

CODE NAME:
LISE

THE TRUE STORY OF THE WOMAN WHO BECAME WWII'S MOST HIGHLY DECORATED SPY

LARRY LOFTIS

m
B
MIRROR BOOKS

First published in Great Britain in 2019 by Mirror Books

This paperback edition published in 2020

Mirror Books is part of Reach plc
10 Lower Thames Street
London EC3R 6EN

www.mirrorbooks.co.uk

Published in the USA by Gallery Books in 2019
An Imprint of Simon & Schuster, Inc.

ISBN 978-1-912624-71-3

1 3 5 7 9 10 8 6 4 2

Interior design by Bryden Spevak

Cover images: Alamy, Mirrorpix, iStockphoto

*The world breaks everyone and afterward
many are strong at the broken places.*

—Ernest Hemingway

DRAMATIS PERSONAE

SPINDLE Circuit (Special Operations Executive, or SOE)

Marie-Lou Blanc (field name, Suzanne)—local operative

Lieutenant Francis Cammaerts (Roger)—head of JOCKEY circuit, replacing SPINDLE circuit

Captain Peter Churchill (Michel, Raoul)—head of SPINDLE circuit

Jean and Simone Cottet (Jean and Simone)—operators of Hôtel de la Poste

Jacques Latour (Jacques)—local operative, courier

Baron Henri de Malval (Antoine)—local operative, owner of HQ Villa Isabelle

Adolphe ("Alec") Rabinovitch (Arnaud)—radio operator

Odette Sansom (Lise)—courier

CARTE Circuit (French Resistance)

Roger Bardet (Chaillan)—Major Frager's lieutenant and courier, also of DONKEYMAN circuit

Louis le Belge (Le Belge)—courier

Major Henri Frager (Paul, Louba)—André Girard's lieutenant; later, chief of DONKEYMAN circuit after termination of CARTE circuit

André Girard (Carte)—head of CARTE circuit

Lejeune (Lejeune)—local operative

André Marsac (End, Marsac)—Marseille chief, Frager's deputy

Jacques Riquet (Riquet)—courier

Suzanne (Lucienne)—Marsac's secretary, courier

British Special Operations Executive (SOE), French Section

Vera Atkins—assistant to Maurice Buckmaster; intelligence officer

Major/Colonel Maurice Buckmaster—F Section head

Captain Selwyn Jepson—F Section recruiting officer

Pierre de Vomécourt (Lucas)—agent

British Intelligence

Secret Intelligence Service (MI6)

German Intelligence

Abwehr (Military Intelligence Service)

Sergeant Hugo Bleicher (Monsieur Jean, Colonel Henri)—field security policeman working under supervision of the Abwehr

Major Hans Josef Kieffer—Paris chief of Sicherheitsdienst

Colonel Oscar Reile—Abwehr III F Paris chief (Hugo Bleicher's supervisor)

Sicherheitsdienst (SD)—Nazi Party intelligence

Others

Gestapo (Nazi Secret Police)

Jean Lucien Keiffer (Kiki, Desiré)—agent for INTERALLIÉ and DONKEYMAN circuits

Father Paul Steinert—chaplain, Fresnes Prison

Fritz Sühren—commandant of Ravensbrück concentration camp

Trude—female guard at Fresnes Prison

PREFACE

"Be regular and orderly in your life," Flaubert had said, "that you may be violent and original in your work." Such is the prescription for spies. Odette Sansom didn't drink, smoke, or swear, and to the casual observer she was quite ordinary, perhaps even boring. Yet she was a trained killer. She feared neither danger nor dagger, interrogation nor torture. She didn't think twice about confronting German generals or commandants, and often placed principle before prudence.

Like her colleagues in the Special Operations Executive, she signed up for the war knowing that arrest (and execution) was a very real possibility—almost one in two for F Section couriers. But what her grandfather had told her as a child was set in stone: she was to do her duty when the time came.

And so she did.

WHEN I FINISHED WRITING *Into the Lion's Mouth* in 2015, I was a bit saddened because I was certain I'd never find a more thrilling story than Dusko Popov's. In my opinion, he was World War II's greatest spy, and perhaps the greatest spy in history. After all, he had more actual sub-agents (eight), was involved in more operations (ten), and accomplished more (Pearl Harbor warning, MIDAS,

D-Day deception, Yugoslav escape line, discovery of German agent CICERO, and the Monty ruse of Operation Copperhead) than any other agent.

Yet I had to find material for another book.

For months on end I scoured the UK National Archives and my World War II resources and came up empty. I looked closely at other British double agents of the war to see if there was enough material for a book. GARBO (Juan Pujol) was out because several books had already been written about him. I considered double agent BRUTUS (Roman Garby-Czerniawski), organizer of the INTERALLIÉ circuit, as he was a compelling figure and at one point had a circuit of a hundred agents. For months I dug into his story, which led me to German secret police sergeant Hugo Bleicher. I was fascinated by Hugo's penetration of INTERALLIÉ, and how he single-handedly destroyed it. When I read Hugo's memoir, *Colonel Henri's Story*, I noticed that he detailed penetration of another circuit, one involving an Allied spy named "Lise."

The more I read, the more excited I became. *This could be it*, I thought.

I followed my normal research procedure: order everything on the subject written in English, starting with the primary sources. In this case, that meant reading Jerrard Tickell's authorized biography, *Odette* (1949); Peter Churchill's three-volume memoirs—*Of Their Own Choice* (1952), *Duel of Wits* (1953), and *The Spirit in the Cage* (1954); Hugo Bleicher's *Colonel Henri's Story* (1954); Maurice Buckmaster's *They Fought Alone* (1958); all of the SOE files on Odette, Peter, and Hugo in the UK National Archives; and Odette's personal interviews with the Imperial War Museum in 1986.

I was not disappointed. This story, I realized, had more chills and thrills than even Popov's adventure, and was perfect for my nonfiction thriller style. But there was a bonus: a love story. It was almost too good to be true.

How is it possible that almost no one knows of this woman? I asked myself. After all, there had been a movie about her in 1950, *Odette*, which had been released to great fanfare in England and the U.S.

As I continued to dig, I found another shocking fact: Odette was not only the most highly decorated woman of World War II, she was the most highly decorated *spy*—male or female.

I had to tell her story.

Fortunately, because I had so much material from primary sources, I could re-create each scene from the eyewitness account of one of the principal players, and often from accounts of two or three. With the exception of about four lines, every quotation of dialogue in the book is verbatim from primary sources. In Odette's SOE files in the UK National Archives, for example, she often recites to her debriefing officer exactly what was said at the time. In the lines of exception, I rendered into a quote what was recorded in narrative for ease of reading.

So, in case you are wondering, every line of this book is true, and you can check the notes if you wish to review the source material. In many scenes, of course, I construed emotions (i.e., "Marsac stirred," "Odette shivered," "Peter paused") simply from knowing details of what occurred, and applying the natural reactions anyone would have.

My hope is that you find this work violent and original.

Larry Loftis
August 6, 2018

PROLOGUE

Shortly after ten the mist began to dissipate, leaving them partially exposed.

If it didn't come soon, someone might notice the four mounds that had not been there two hours ago. It was bitterly cold—in the low teens—but Odette remained still, shivering in her wool skirt.

Finally, they heard it. Everyone hustled into position and watched as Peter flashed the code.

Nothing back. Peter flashed again. Still nothing. The plane passed directly overhead at eight hundred feet and then vanished.

Peter scooted across the field and crept up beside her.

"I simply don't understand it," he said behind clouded breath. "He must have seen the signal."

Something wasn't right, Odette knew. It was mission feel, to be sure—the fox catching a scent it remembered as danger: men loitering around the buildings that afternoon . . . no airport activity . . . the plane ignoring their signal. The eerie mist didn't help, either.

Peter told her to stay low and crept to the end of the L formation. "Keep an eye on those buildings," he told Jacques. "I have a feeling we're in for an unwelcome interruption from that quarter."

Moving up the line, he ducked down beside Paul. "There's someone coming!" he whispered. "Lie flat on the ground."

Across the field, Odette could see the danger: two figures—

guards?—emerging from the direction of the control tower. They were headed directly toward Peter and Paul.

Ten yards.

Approaching the two mounds.

Five yards.

Odette gaped, pupils wide. Were the guards going to *step* on them?

The two figures kept walking, apparently just in front of Peter and Paul. When they were out of sight, Peter came back.

"I thought they were going to walk slap into you," Odette said. "I can't think how they missed you."

Peter cast his gaze across the field and hangars. "The plane ought to be back at any moment. If there's any danger from those buildings I shall wave my torch sideways and Jacques will come over to you and you're both to beat it over the bridge. Paul and I will make a separate retreat; better to be in two groups."

"Listen!" Odette uttered. The plane was returning. If it recognized Peter's code with the countersign, they'd turn on their lights to illuminate the landing field. If it didn't, it was German.

Peter moved back to position and Odette kept her eyes peeled. All was silent around the buildings as the drone of the aircraft grew louder.

A flash swept suddenly over the horizon and Odette froze. It was not Peter's.

It was a trap!

Some three hundred yards away—directly in line with the aircraft's flight—an Aldis lamp was flashing Morse to the tower. Barrack lights snapped on and someone shouted: "Put out those lights, you imbeciles! Wait for the plane to land and we'll grab them all."

Odette saw Peter's flashlight wave and then watched as he and Paul began racing across the field. The aircraft followed them, diving down on their heads at just six feet and then rising and disappearing.

Odette turned to take off, but she could hear the plane return-ing. Would it let loose its guns, dropping Peter and Paul like pins?

Just then, Jacques ran up.

"You make for the right," Odette called out, "and I'll meet you on the back road to Périgueux."

The Germans would expect the saboteurs to head for the only cover, but separating the posse might add confusion. Jacques tore off and Odette started to run when she heard a terrifying sound.

Turning back she saw him: an unleashed German Shepherd sniffing the area she had just left. The dog caught her scent, barked again, and was off.

Odette sprinted for the trees, adrenaline raging, but the ground was uneven and she fell. He was closing the gap, she knew. She scrambled up and dashed on.

Behind her she could hear him, the barking closer.

He would be on her in seconds.

She broke through the tree line and pushed ahead, stumbling in the darkness. It couldn't be much farther.

There was a crash as the dog lunged into the thicket where she had crossed.

Faster! Faster! She had to keep moving.

The Shepherd closed, growling and thrashing through the un-derbrush.

It was the only way.

She plunged in.

CHAPTER 1

DUTY

Spring 1942
London

Major Guthrie looked again at the photographs. The teenaged girl was tall and skinny, a bushel of thick brown hair clinging to her head like a dried-out mop. She couldn't have been more than sixteen or seventeen, but the shots appeared to have been taken ten, maybe twelve years ago. And there was something about the eyes—dark, determined . . . defiant.

If his instincts were right, this was a girl who would throw herself headlong into danger.

He wrote the letter.

BORN APRIL 28, 1912, Odette Marie Céline was the first child of Yvonne and Gaston Brailly, a banker in Amiens, France. A year later, the couple would have their second child, Louis. When World War I broke out in 1914, Gaston joined the Infantry Regiment and was soon fighting the Germans and mustard gas in the trenches of the Western Front. Brave and courageous, Gaston was promoted to sergeant and decorated with the Croix de Guerre and Médaille Militaire.

He survived the Battle of Verdun, one of the bloodiest conflicts in history, but two men from his platoon had gone missing. Gaston returned to the battlefield to find them and did—both alive but seriously wounded. Before he could summon help, however, a mortar round hit their position, killing them instantly.

Odette and Louis would never know their father, but his legacy lived on through their paternal grandparents; Gaston had been their only child. Every Sunday afternoon they would take Odette and her brother to place flowers on Gaston's grave at La Madeleine. "In twenty or twenty-five years' time, there is going to be another war," Grandfather would say, "and it will be your duty, both of you, to do as well as your father did."

Odette would never forget these words.

YVONNE BRAILLY HAD TROUBLE enough as a single parent, but further difficulty arose with a turn in Odette's health. Always a sickly child, she contracted polio at the age of seven, leaving her paralyzed for more than a year. Worse, just before she turned eight the disease stole her sight. Over the next three years Yvonne took Odette to every specialist and medical expert she could find, but to no avail; Odette would have to struggle through life in complete darkness.

Lest Odette despair or feel sorry for herself, her grandfather encouraged her not to use blindness or pain as an excuse or handicap, but to be as clever as possible; there were many things she *could* do, and she should focus on those. Odette heeded the instruction and, as Hemingway put it, became strong in the broken places.

She couldn't see, but she could hear, and soon her thoughts were captivated by Beethoven, Chopin, and Mozart. In piano and strings and waltzes, Odette would lose herself. Her blindness, it seemed, had opened a light of felicity previously unknown.

Yvonne Brailly, though, would not give up on Odette's sight. She took her to see an herbalist—a witch doctor if you asked the medical community. The man was old, unkempt, and surprisingly dirty for a health practitioner. But Yvonne had exhausted all other options so the risk from a little herbal magic seemed negligible.

The man examined Odette and gave Yvonne a solution to bathe the child's eyes. When Odette begins to see again, he said, gradually expose her to light. Yvonne followed the treatment and two weeks later Odette's vision started to return. They continued the application and after two years Odette's sight was fully restored.

A miracle, it seemed.

But no sooner than that malady had been beaten, Odette was struck with another: rheumatic fever. She spent a summer mostly in bed and the disease dissipated, but not before leaving her weak and partially paralyzed.

Yvonne was at her wit's end. What her daughter needed was the strong air of Normandy, she felt. With Louis enrolled in the lycée in Amiens, Yvonne moved with Odette to St. Saëns, a small village some twenty miles inland from Dieppe, and from there farther east to the coastal city of Boulogne. Odette was enrolled in a local convent and when Louis visited for holidays, the siblings would spend hours walking the coast and marveling at the arriving ships, especially those with sailors of the strange English accent.

When Odette graduated high school, the nuns sent Yvonne a final report. Odette was intelligent and principled, they said, but possessed a volatile and petulant streak.

It would prove useful in due time.

Fascinated with the neighbors across the Channel, Odette determined to marry an Englishman and soon after her eighteenth birthday her wish came true: she met Roy Sansom, a Briton who was the son of an old family friend. They married a year later, in 1930, and lived in Boulogne. Their first child, Francoise, was born in 1932, and shortly thereafter the couple moved to London, where they had two more girls: Lily in 1934, Marianne in 1936.

From the security of her new home, Odette observed the progression of her grandfather's prophecy. Adolf Hitler had become chancellor of Germany in 1933 and a year later ascended to head of state upon the death of President Paul von Hindenburg. Germany soon occupied the Rhineland, and in '38 it annexed Austria and occupied the Sudetenland. In 1939 it invaded Poland and the prophecy was complete: France and Britain declared war.

Roy enlisted with the British army and left on deployment soon thereafter. But as Odette was about to discover, England itself was scarcely safe; the Battle of Britain began the following summer, and in September the Luftwaffe began lighting up London.

Odette had no choice: she moved with her girls a hundred miles west to the safety of Somerset. The quaint village was a haven and refuge but had a surprising disadvantage: the countryside and rolling hills—fresh with apple orchards, blackberries, and dahlias—were so enjoyable that Odette began to feel guilty. Countless others, she knew, were sacrificing greatly for the war.

One afternoon in the spring of 1942, Odette heard on the radio

Odette Sansom and her girls: Marianne, Lily, and Francoise. MIRROR/PA

a plea from the Royal Navy asking for photos of the coast of France. From her time in Amiens and Boulogne, Odette had several she could send. They were quite useless, she thought, since they were of her and her brother on the beaches around Calais. In her accompanying letter, she noted that her parents were French, and that she knew the coastal area well. Mistakenly, however, she mailed her package to the War Office instead of the Admiralty.

A week or so later she received correspondence from a Major Guthrie asking if she could stop by the War Office at three o'clock the following Thursday. Odette assumed the purpose of the meeting was to return her photos, which she was eager to receive back. Over tea the silver-haired major asked about Odette's childhood in Amiens and Boulogne.

Odette explained why they had moved and reiterated her knowledge of the area. She offered to sketch the Boulogne Fish Market if the major liked. Guthrie said they probably had something in the file and came to the point.

"Has it occurred to you, Mrs. Sansom, that your knowledge of France and, of course, of French, might be of use in some job or other? The War Office might possibly be able to find one for you."

Odette replied that she had three children and they needed a lot of looking after, but she wanted to help. "If I can be of any use to do some translations," she said, "or adopt two or three French soldiers, or send alouette[1] to a few, I would like to be able to do something. After all, I am French born, and I was brought up in France. My family has always lived on the battlefield of world wars, my father was killed thirteen days before the armistice in the first one, my brother is in this one, my mother is in France, suffering with the Germans, so I would like to be able to do some little thing."

Guthrie said he understood; three children were quite a responsibility. He mentioned that there might be some part-time jobs and asked if he could send her name along to someone he knew.

---

1   Cheese spread.

Odette agreed. She went home assuming that was the end of the matter, but was disappointed she hadn't received back her photographs.

Shortly thereafter she received a notice from the Red Cross informing her that her brother had been wounded and was in a military hospital in Paris, and that the Nazis had taken her mother's home. Odette was grief stricken; this was the second time in her mother's life that she had been forced to leave her home and had lost everything to the Germans. On top of that, a number of Odette's friends were already in captivity.

She struggled with the situation. Here she was in the safety of Somerset, playing with her girls on the majestic rolling hills, while others suffered and died to secure her and her children's freedom. Was she to accept this, Odette wondered, the sacrifice others were making, without lifting a finger? She reminded herself that as a mother of three she was somewhat exempted from the war, but she was tormented.

On June 28 she received a letter from a Captain Selwyn Jepson[2] asking her to visit him at room 238, Hotel Victoria, Whitehall, on July 10. Major Guthrie had not mentioned anyone by that name, but perhaps this had something to do with a part-time job, Odette thought.

Jepson, it turned out, was the recruiting officer for F (France) Section of SOE—Special Operations Executive—a new sabotage outfit that Prime Minister Winston Churchill had tasked to "set Europe ablaze."

Its origins and objectives were predictable. Hugh Dalton, Minister of Economic Warfare, believed that Britain needed something more than the existing military to fight the Germans—something secret, something subversive. On July 2, 1940, he sent a letter to Edward F. Halifax, Foreign Secretary, outlining his idea:

---

2 Before and after the war, Jepson was an accomplished novelist. Many of his thrillers were later made into movies, including Alfred Hitchcock's *Stage Fright* (1950), adapted from Jepson's *Man Running*.

"We have got to organize movements in enemy-occupied territory comparable to the Sinn Féin movement in Ireland, to the Chinese Guerillas now operating against Japan, to the organizations which the Nazis themselves have developed so remarkably in almost every country in the world. This 'democratic international' must use many different methods, including industrial and military sabotage."

But fighting a guerilla or dirty war was not something any branch of the military would take on, Dalton knew. What was needed, he explained, was "a new organization to coordinate, inspire, control, and assist the nationals of the oppressed countries who must themselves be the direct participants. We need absolute secrecy, a certain fanatical enthusiasm, willingness to work with people of different nationalities."

Halifax presented the idea to Churchill and the prime minister agreed. SOE was born and Dalton was tasked to coordinate its development. Churchill gave the organization two directives: (1) to create and foster a spirit of resistance in Nazi-occupied countries, and (2) to establish an underground body of operatives who would perform acts of sabotage and assist in liberation when British forces landed.

From its founding, the organization was shrouded in secrecy; even other military branches working with it had no idea what it was. To the War Office, it was MO 1 (SP); to the Admiralty, NID (Q); to the Air Ministry, AI 10; to others, the Inter-Services Research Bureau, the Joint Technical Board, or the Special Training Schools Headquarters. Its officers and operatives called it "Baker Street," after its address at 64 Baker Street. Money, too, was hidden: its operating budget was covered largely by siphoning expenses from other ministries, with remaining costs paid from a secret fund.

Operating in the shadows of ill intent, its agents were referred to by many names: spies, saboteurs, commandos, Baker Street Irregulars, and Churchill's Secret Army. Indeed, they were spies, but the role of Baker Street was not one of spymaster—that was MI6's field—but to be masters of mayhem.

The Germans called them *terrorists*.

This purpose, though, led to direct conflict between SOE and the Secret Intelligence Service; the latter wanted to eavesdrop, the former to be a bull in the china shop.

So Odette found herself in the bowels of the Ministry of Ungentlemanly Warfare, but the only secret she knew was that someone was hoarding her photos. Once again, she assumed that she'd been summoned to pick them up and, perhaps, to set up some part-time translating.

Captain Jepson was nothing like what she expected. Instead of a rigid officer in crisp khakis, she found a man who looked like a high-priced barrister. He wore a grey suit, dark-blue tie, and beautiful shoes. His eyes were intelligent and shrewd, and he came across as kind and generous. What kind of military outfit would have a captain like this? she wondered.

Jepson explained that they had made inquiries about Odette in England and France, and were very satisfied with what they found.

Odette was appalled. She had simply provided some photos and here they were traipsing around two countries digging about her business.

"Why did you have to make inquiries about me?" she asked. "What do you think I am?"

What she was, in Jepson's mind, was the one in a million who could pull it off. F Section's biggest recruiting hurdle was the language; few native-born Britons could speak French without an accent. As a result, anyone born and raised in France who happened to be in England at the time—like Odette—was a jewel not to be missed; agents who went to France without this language skill typically did not return.

Jepson gave her the minimum: "We train people here. We send them to their country of origin, or if they speak a foreign language very well we send them to that country. We think women could be very useful, too."

What Jepson couldn't tell her was that SOE desperately needed women to counter the Nazis' Service du Travail Obligatoire[3]: the rounding up of able-bodied Frenchmen for forced labor in Germany. F Section women, who would be used as couriers, could move about France more easily and with far less suspicion than men.

He asked her how she felt about the Germans, and she said, "I hate them. I mean that I hate Nazis. For the Germans, oddly enough, I have pity."

"I thought you might separate Germans and Nazis. It was not the Nazis but the Germans who killed your father."

Odette blinked. Jepson had done his homework.

She looked at the captain. "Yes, but they were driven then as they are driven now. I think the Germans are very obedient and very gullible. Their tragedy—and Europe's—is that they gladly allow themselves to be hoodwinked into believing evil to be good. Last October a German major was shot in Bordeaux. You know that?"

Jepson nodded.

"The Nazis took one hundred hostages and shot fifty of them. You know that too?"

He nodded again.

"Well, it's not only because of that that I hate Nazis. It's because theirs is a humorless creed and a damned creed, and because they make men despoil other people's fields and carry misery and fear wherever they go."

Sensing he had touched a nerve, Jepson let Odette continue.

"I do hate Nazis," she went on. "But it's not much good hating people, just like that. I'm a woman and I can't do anything about it."

Jepson heard what he wanted. "Yes," he said, "it must be most unsatisfactory for you." He paused a moment and then asked, "How

---

3 While the rounding up of French citizens began earlier, the Vichy law requiring compulsory labor in Germany for Frenchmen between the ages of twenty-one and thirty-five was enacted in September 1942. The law was extended to all Frenchmen in February 1943.

would you like to go to France and make things unpleasant for those despoilers of other people's fields?"

Odette found the suggestion preposterous. "You may or may not be aware that the Germans have conquered France and that the Channel boats are no longer running. I understood from Major Guthrie that there was a possibility of some part-time work. Could you please tell me about that?"

Jepson assured her that there were other ways of getting to France.

"You mean that the War Office can send people to France—in spite of the Germans?"

"Never mind how these things are arranged, Mrs. Sansom. Accept the fact that the journey to France *could* be arranged and tell me how the idea appeals to you."

Odette said it didn't appeal at all, that she was the mother of three children.

"Yes. Three daughters. Francoise, Lily, and Marianne."

"It's not possible. It's absolutely not possible. My children come first. I mean, I want to do everything I can for this country, which is my adopted country and the country which has adopted me. My children are English and I have a French family, and all my roots are in France; I have two reasons for wanting to help, but I can't do that. Furthermore, you've got the wrong person. Certainly you must be of a certain type to do this kind of job. I am not it. I haven't got the brain for it, I haven't got even the physical things that are necessary for the job. So, no."

Jepson ignored the finality of her answer and returned the conversation to France. He spoke with the familiarity of a Frenchman, bringing up Baudelaire and the Bistro, Pau and Pétain. And did Odette know about the Stavisky affair?

"This is where people like you come in, Mrs. Sansom. People who know and love France, people who can move about freely and not be noticed." He emphasized that the work was very dangerous and that some who went failed to return.

"My view is that you could be of very great value to us," he added. "I do not say that because of your more obvious qualifications but because of the singleness of purpose which I believe you possess."

Odette sighed. "Captain Jepson, you must know that I am a very simple, ordinary woman. Believe me, I am not very intelligent or well informed. I do not know about politics or governments or movements. I am a housewife and as good a mother as I can make myself. Sometimes that's not very good, I'm afraid. Frankly, I don't think I'm the right sort of person to undertake this work."

Jepson nodded. "Possibly not—but I think you are." He explained that there was some training and that if Odette participated, everyone would know for certain whether she was fit for the job. He said he didn't need an answer right away.

Odette stood and Jepson saw her out. "Thank you for seeing me," she said. "I think . . . I think I shall say 'no.'"

He gave her his number and asked that she call sometime.

Jepson returned to his desk and made a final notation at the bottom of Odette's dossier: "*Direct-minded and courageous. God help the Nazis if we can get her near them.*"

Odette contemplated the matter all day and mentioned it to Roy that night. He said the decision was hers to make, but primary sources reveal no more. Was their relationship strained at this point, such that a husband and wife would both go to war, risking not only the loss of a spouse but also possibly orphaning their children?

We don't know.

Odette struggled with the decision for months. "If everybody thinks my way," she asked herself, "what is the future going to be for all of those children everywhere? If I were in France, with children, I could be like some of other people who've already been captured, even with their children in concentration camps. No, because I'm here, I have a great excuse for not doing anything more than staying put with my children."

She saw only one solution: to do the training and show Jepson that she was not the right person. That way she could come back saying she had tried and wasn't right for the job, and her conscience would be clear.

She found a convent—St. Helen's, in Brentwood, Essex—where the children could board during the school term. For holidays, Odette made arrangements for them to live with an uncle and aunt.

She notified Jepson and he set up a meeting with a man soon to play an important role in her life: Major Maurice Buckmaster, head of SOE's F Section. Buckmaster was an Eton man and an Oxford scholar who had moved to France after college to take a position as a reporter for *Le Matin*. He became fluent in the language and at age thirty switched careers to become a manager with the French division of Ford Motor Company. It was this position which provided Maurice with tremendous knowledge of French towns and roads. Four years later, in 1936, he was promoted to a managerial position in England.

Although he was doing well, Buckmaster wasn't satisfied with business. In 1938 he joined the reserves as a captain, even managing a short course with the Secret Intelligence Service. When war broke out, he was assigned to the British Expeditionary Force and was soon fighting the Germans in Béthune and Arras. On June 4, 1940, he would catch one of the last boats out of Dunkirk.

The British saw in Buckmaster a natural leader and he was promoted quickly, becoming an acting major in December. He spent three months with Admiral Cunningham's fleet and was then reassigned to the Africa Campaign as an intelligence officer. Before leaving for Libya, Maurice told his commanding general that he didn't speak Italian and asked if there was an assignment where he could utilize his French. The general said he'd look into it.

On March 17, 1941, Buckmaster was transferred to SOE and six months later, in September, was appointed head of F Section.

THE MEETING WITH ODETTE was held entirely in French, and Buckmaster began by asking for a brief summary of her background.

When she mentioned her children, the major blurted, "Good God, you look like a child yourself!"

Odette had just turned thirty but looked years younger. She finished her thought and Buckmaster gave her an overview of the work of SOE, noting that she'd probably be a courier. First, however, was the training, which would begin at a country house in New Forest. But before the training, the major wanted to make certain that she understood the risks.

"In many ways it's a beastly life," he told her. "It will be physically hard. More than that, it will be mentally exhausting, for you will be living a gigantic lie, or series of lies, for months on end. And if you slip up and get caught, we can do little to save you."

"To save me from what?" Odette asked.

Buckmaster shrugged. "Oh, from the usual sickening sort of thing; prison, the firing squad, the rope, the crematorium; from whatever happens to amuse the Gestapo."

As one agent put it, what Buckmaster offered was quite simple: death.

But a useful, heroic death.

CHAPTER 2

JINXED

Death, particularly the kind slow and painful, is a potent deterrent. The major asked if she wanted to reconsider, given the danger, but Odette shook her head.

"No. My mind is made up."

It will be your duty . . .

Buckmaster explained that Odette would need an alias during training and asked what name she'd like to use.

"Would Céline do?" she asked, suggesting part of her real name: Odette Marie Céline.

Buckmaster confirmed that they didn't have a Céline, and it would be fine. "I'm going to introduce one or two people to you and then turn you over to a very nice woman in the FANYs,"[4] he added. "She'll tell you about the Corps and how our section of it functions."

Odette was fitted with a khaki uniform, complete with military

---

4 Founded in 1907, First Aid Nursing Yeomanry was an all-female voluntary service within which SOE couriers were registered. While its members wore a military-style uniform, FANY was not part of the army or reserve.

Odette in her FANY uniform. *IMPERIAL WAR MUSEUM*

belt and beret, and at home she looked long at herself in the mirror. There was something special happening to her. It wasn't just a uniform; there was more. She seemed to have taken on a dignity of unique privilege: a Frenchwoman who had been given the honor of representing England.

The following day, July 18, Odette strode confidently in her crisp uniform to London's Portman Square. As she turned a corner, two British soldiers in battle dress saw her and saluted.

Odette blushed. She had entered a new life.

CANDIDATES FOR SOE WERE processed in four stages, the last two of which sometimes had an inverted order: preliminary school, paramilitary school, parachute school, and finishing school. Female candidates who would be serving as couriers, however, sometimes skipped the paramilitary training, and it appears that Odette did so. Each stop was designed to weed out unsuitable candidates, and only those who passed continued on to the next course. By the end of the training, up to 80 percent would be disqualified.

The preliminary school was a two-to-four-week course at Wanborough Manor, a country house near Guilford, England, to assess a candidate's character and potential for clandestine operations. The training focused on three areas: physical development, weapons, and field craft. Candidates learned how to fall, subdue a sentry, and roll down a flight of stairs. Afternoons brought weapons and explosives. Trainees would fire and become proficient with virtually every weapon found in Europe: pistols of all varieties—German Luger, British Enfield and Webley, American Colt and Smith & Wesson, Canadian Browning, and their Italian and Belgian counterparts—as well as the assassin's silent single-shot Welrod; submachine guns such as the Sten, Schmeisser, Tommy Gun, and M-3; and automatic rifles like the Czech Bren and American Browning.

And Odette learned a different method of shooting. Instead of the common practice of firing a pistol with two hands, aiming down the sights at stationary targets, SOE candidates did just the opposite: combat shooting.

"You will always fire from the crouch position," the SOE training manual instructed, "you will never be in an upright position. You will have no time to adopt any fancy stance when killing with speed. You have no time to use the sights. Any method of firing which does not allow for all these factors is useless. Gun fighting at close quarters is a question of split seconds."

Utilizing a one-handed grip, Odette fired with "instinctive pointing" at moving and bobbing targets, at varying distances and heights. She fired from inside buildings, sometimes in poor lighting and sometimes in total darkness. She practiced spinning right, left, and by grabbing a gun from a table.[5]

Explosives were a specialty of SOE, and Odette had to master their use and detonation.[6] She learned how to put a detonator into a primer, and the primer into the explosive. Fuses[7] of all types also had to be mastered so that the agent wasn't derailed before the train. And since operatives might be caught in compromising situations, Odette also learned how to use close-in weapons: the Fairbairn-Sykes fighting knife, the pen pistol—which could fire a bullet or an asphyxiating gas cartridge—and the ultrathin lapel knife.

In the evenings, Odette was introduced to field craft: Morse code, ciphers, map reading, Aldis lamp signaling, and night compass navigation.

Students who passed stage one were then sent to the paramilitary school in Arisaig, Scotland, a three-week course to expand all

---

5   SOE's shooting and training methods were validated in the field time and again. One radio operator, upon returning to England after escaping, shared his story. Not long after arriving in France, his cover had been blown, and he was arrested by the Gestapo. The agents searched him but failed to find the .38 he'd hidden in a concealed holster. He was handcuffed and hustled into the back of a car. Three Gestapo joined him, one in the back and two up front. As they sped down the Route Nationale, the operative unbuttoned his shirt and slid a manacled hand over his weapon. Per his training, the pistol was cocked, with only the safety catch on. Pushing down the lever, he whisked out the gun and delivered two rounds to the back of the driver's neck. The car flipped, and he shot the other two. He escaped, still handcuffed.

6   The boys at the Frythe's Station IX, a former hotel in Welwyn Garden City, and the Firs, a mansion in Whitchurch, invented and developed an unusual assortment of "dirty tricks." The Royal Arsenal had already invented plastic explosive, so rigging a bang inside a lump of coal, a log, a Chianti bottle, or a flashlight was relatively simple. The most devious of these small explosives was the rat charge. Skinned and hollowed, the carcass was stuffed with explosive and sewn back together. With a time-pencil fuse up the tailpipe, the incendiary was undetectable.

7   The impact fuse—used famously in the "beanbag" Gammon grenade—was a particularly innovative invention from the mad scientists at Frythe and Firs. It was this very explosive that had been employed by SOE-trained Czech agents to assassinate Reinhard Heydrich in Prague only months earlier.

aspects of training. Here, candidates continued to practice with pistols and submachine guns, but now added live hand grenades and machine guns: the British Vickers, and the German MG 34 and 42. By all accounts, though, the memorable part of stage two was William Fairbairn, the Arisaig combat instructor better known as the Shanghai Buster. Widely considered the father of hand-to-hand combat, Fairbairn had spent twenty years with the International Police Force in Shanghai—a lawless city in those days—and his arms, hands, and body bore testimony of his knife fights with thugs, gangs, drug dealers, and criminals. At fifty-five, he was one of the most dangerous men in the world.

His specialty was silent killing. Without weapons.

While Odette was not required to attend Arisaig, her future circuit leader, Peter Churchill, excelled here, as enemy soldiers would soon learn.

FROM WANBOROUGH ODETTE PROCEEDED to finishing school at Beaulieu. After showing her identification at a front-entrance checkpoint, she was driven to a charming New Forest country house set on a small lake, behind which was a deep wood.

The irony was striking. Here, in a setting of paradise, Odette would learn the fine arts of espionage and, again, killing.

In the morning she awoke to the clatter of activity in the kitchen and moments later a servant appeared. He politely let her know that she was required to be on the tennis courts—in gym shorts and sneakers—at eight o'clock sharp. Physical training, he said.

While slim and in arguably good shape, Odette wasn't particularly fond of fitness training, especially during the breakfast hour. She finished her morning tea, donned the gym clothes, and trudged to the courts. There, a young Adonis led the group through exercises, and Odette discovered that she wasn't nearly as fit as she had imagined; her muscles were on fire.

"Now we'll just have a breather and a few questions," the instructor said as the women gasped for air. "Céline!"

It took a moment for Odette to remember that Céline was her alias here, and she finally looked up.

"I'm so sorry. Yes?"

"Suppose a big SS man came for you; what would you do?"

"Er . . . how big?"

"Very big," the instructor said. Six foot one and broad shouldered.

Odette pondered the scenario. "I would run away in the opposite direction," she finally muttered, "as fast as I could."

"Suppose he caught up with you?"

"Then I would pinch him."

The instructor restrained a laugh. "Oh, you'd pinch him, would you? Anything else?"

"I'd pull his hair."

"You'd pinch him and pull his hair. Poor chap. My heart bleeds for him." The instructor focused his tone.

"Ladies, it will be my unwelcome and embarrassing duty to teach you other and less refined methods of disabling would-be masculine aggressors. It comes in a later lesson and I very sincerely hope that you will take it in the spirit in which it will be dished up."

He then told the group to put their hands on their hips, and the exercises continued.

While there would be more weapons practice, the main purpose of Beaulieu was to teach prospective agents spycraft: radio and house security, losing a tag, dealing with border controls, and handling the ubiquitous inspection of their papers. Simple questions such as "Why haven't you drawn your tobacco ration for the past two weeks?" could spell doom for the hesitant.

More than anything, agents had to learn to play the part: to *be* the person indicated by their cover. Survival depended on not only having their story straight—memorizing every detail provided by F Section—but also being able to improvise convincingly when questions strayed from the script.[8]

The Beaulieu staff also monitored the students while they slept. Did any talk in their sleep? If so, in what language? Some nights, male candidates would be sent to a local bar or cafe to meet a contact. After a drink or two, there would be a chance meeting with Christine Collard, a stunning blonde who was supposedly a French journalist. The contact would invite her over, introduce her as a helpful former acquaintance, and then invariably be called away, leaving the two alone. Christine would be quite amorous—to the point of suggesting that they leave for someplace more comfortable—and ply the recruit for indiscretions. Her real name was Marie Christine Chilver—"Fifi," as Baker Street called her—and she was an SOE agent provocateur. A number of otherwise promising recruits failed this test and were rejected; candidates who had mastered countless weapons and explosives, survived punishing fitness regimens and twenty-mile mountain treks, memorized Morse, and perfected compass night marches, only to be felled by Fifi.

While in France, it was critical for an agent to be able to distinguish the uniforms of Vichy and Axis police, as well as Gestapo, SS, Wehrmacht, and Luftwaffe soldiers, and to identify their ranks and credentials. During one class, the instructor called on Odette and pointed to a uniformed German on a wall chart.

"What's this chap, and what do his badges of rank mean?"

"He's a *Feldwebel* in the Luftwaffe, and he's wearing the Iron Cross, Second Class."

The instructor nodded and pointed to another.

"He's an *Oberleutnant* in the Panzer Grenadiers," Odette said,

---

8 One instructor who knew a thing or two about playing a part was Kim Philby, a Soviet spy who later worked for MI6 and fled to Russia after the war. He recalled a night training exercise where a group of candidates was called to breach an upstairs room in a house that had been set with alarms and booby traps. They each also had to get past patrolling guards played by Philby and other staff members. They did, although Philby said later he could have sworn that no one got through.

"and I don't know what his medal ribbons mean. I consider the medal ribbons to be of no importance."

"Your opinion is not shared by the staff, Céline," he replied. "I must insist that you pay attention to what we *know* to be of importance."

At the map-reading class, Odette was quizzed on the field requirements for landing Lysanders and Hudsons. She gave the proper measurements.

"Right," the instructor said. "What is the Morse sign for the letter 'L'?"

Odette paused and then said, "Dot, dash-dash, dot."

"Wrong. Think, Céline."

"But it *is* that."

He assured her that it was not.

Odette frowned. "Of course. 'L' is dot, dash, dot-dot."

"Good. But you must think calmly before you answer. The lives of an aircrew depend on accurate signals."

On the gun range, candidates continued to practice with various weapons, and Odette displayed her newfound skills. When it was her turn to fire at a target with a Sten submachine gun, she sent a quick blast and waited for the marker's response.

"All on," he yelled. "Three bulls. Next please."

Beaulieu students also trained for the downside: arrest. A number of times throughout the course, Odette and the others were roused in the middle of the night and hustled before men in German uniforms for interrogation. Recruits were stripped and forced to stand for hours facing blazing lights; shock and awe when cobwebs clouded memory and judgment.

When the intelligence work was over, Odette learned how to canoe, navigate by the stars, poach, steal chickens, and trap and cook a rabbit without removing the skin. She was also introduced to agents who had returned from France and candidly explained what had happened to others who didn't.

The stories only made Odette more resolute and it was here, at Beaulieu, that she went all in on her commitment to go to France as an SOE agent. So committed was she emotionally that the make-believe of the exercises began to irritate her, a response not missed by the school's instructors.

On August 25 Lieutenant Colonel Stanley Woolrych, the commandant of Beaulieu, sent Buckmaster the school's final evaluation of Odette:

> *"She has enthusiasm and seems to have absorbed the teaching given on the course. She is, however, impulsive and hasty in her judgments and has not quite the clarity of mind which is desirable in subversive activity. She is excitable and temperamental, although she has a certain determination. A likeable character and gets on well with most people. Her main asset is her patriotism and keenness to do something for France; her main weakness is a complete unwillingness to admit that she could ever be wrong."*

Buckmaster was torn. Odette had the fighting spirit he was looking for but exhibited glaring weaknesses in vital areas. He drove to New Forest to speak with her before making a decision.

"Well, Céline," he began, "I've had your report."

The tone of Buckmaster's voice wasn't cheerful, and Odette could feel impending rejection. "I hope it is satisfactory."

"Not altogether. It's . . . mixed."

Odette took a breath, and Buckmaster waited a moment before continuing.

"I am very much exercised about you, Céline. The work I had planned for you to do is so desperately important and so . . . so interlocking that we can only dare to send people who are cool in their judgment and who have a crystal clarity of mind. I believe you to be single-minded, loyal, and tenacious. But, let's face it, there is the question of this mercurial temperament of yours which comes out every now and again like a nettle rash."

He looked at her—now pale white—and asked if she would be very disappointed if he said no.

Odette was at a loss for words. The evaluation was spot-on, she knew, but the thought of failing before she had even set foot in France—of not doing her duty as grandfather had urged—was crushing.

"Major Buckmaster," she finally said, "I would never let anybody down."

"That I know. It's very difficult."

Buckmaster cast his eyes off in the distance and pondered the decision. Impulsive. Hasty. Temperamental. Arrogant. Yet she was French, had a tenacious determination, and was a born fighter.

He went with his instincts. Odette would continue the training.

Parachute Training School
Ringway, Manchester, England

"NOW, LADIES AND GENTLEMEN," the Ringway major barked, "the mental reaction to one's first parachute jump has been likened to that of a man who decides to commit suicide by jumping off the top of the *Nelson Column*—with the strong possibility that the attempt will fail. In Ringway, the attempt will *positively fail*. You will float through the air with the greatest of ease, like daring young men— and women—on the flying trapeze."

Odette sighed, and the major went on explaining the training. There would be four jumps, he said, two from a balloon, two from a twin-engine bomber nicknamed the Wimpey.

"You will enjoy every moment of it!" he boasted.

Odette took it with a grain of salt and did her best to quickly gain coordination. Buckmaster's words had troubled her, and she knew that the slightest failure here would destroy her goal to fight the Germans on her home soil. She focused her efforts, rolling softly on the coconut mats, swinging gracefully on the rungs, bending her knees properly in the Japanese roll.

After several days she was cleared for her first balloon jump. That afternoon, however, the instructor decided there was time for one more practice jump before the real thing later that day. It was a simple exercise: an eight-foot drop from a mock-up Whitley bomber.

"We'll have just one more jump," he said, "before we break off. Now don't forget to keep those knees together, Céline."

Odette paused. "May I be excused from this one? I've done several this morning and I particularly want to be fresh for this afternoon."

"Be excused? That's a word we don't welcome at Ringway. You've been doing very well," he told her, "and this is the last jump. Have a crack at it, ma'am."

Odette went up the ladder into the fuselage and jumped awkwardly from the hole.

Her weight had been too far forward and her feet had hardly touched the ground when her face crashed into the matting. Burning sensations flashed through her body—her right ankle, right knee, and face seemed to be on fire. She tried to stand but couldn't.

At the medical clinic she was told that she had a concussion and a badly sprained ankle, perhaps even a cracked metatarsal. The swelling in her face had closed one eye, and she was sent to London's Ophthalmic Hospital for treatment.

When the injuries healed, she was back in Buckmaster's office. The major asked if she was willing to return to Ringway to complete the training.

"Certainly, if you think it is necessary. I don't *want* to go again," Odette admitted, "because it's uncomfortable and tiring and indeed a bit frightening. But if I am to land in France by parachute, then of course I must return to Ringway."

Buckmaster asked how she felt about being sent by submarine and Odette winced.

"That's like parachuting in reverse. I don't suppose I should like traveling in a little metal box under the sea any better than I would dropping down from the sky clutching a silk umbrella. But again, if that's the way you want me to go, I'm quite prepared to risk the claustrophobia."

Buckmaster smiled and mentioned they might use an alternate

form of insertion. He suggested that she get her children settled as the office was preparing her identity cards and mission plan. She would be leaving soon.

ODETTE BROUGHT HER CHILDREN together and did her best to explain that she would be leaving for a while.

"Good-bye, Francoise. Look after Lily."

"You will write to us, won't you, Mummy?"

"Yes. I'll write. Good-bye, Lily. Look after Marianne."

"I will, Mummy, where are you going to?"

"A place called Scotland. Good-bye, Marianne. You'll look after Francoise and Lily for me, won't you?"

"Yes, Mummy. Where's Scotland?"

"It's a long way away, Marianne. And you'll all be good girls until I come back."

"When *are* you coming back, Mummy?"

"As soon as I can."

"Are you going to the war, Mummy?"

"Yes, I'm going to the war. But I'll try to come back soon."

Dropping her children off at St. Helen's was excruciating and heartbreaking. There was nothing the Gestapo could do to her now, she felt, since it would be only physical.

This was the ultimate torture.

BEFORE ODETTE SET FOOT in France, Hitler gave new orders to the military and Gestapo regarding spies and commandos. On October 18, two weeks before her arrival, he decreed: "I therefore order that from now on, all opponents engaged in so-called commando operations, with or without weapons, are to be exterminated. It is immaterial whether they are landed for their operations by ship, or aeroplane, or descent by parachute."

The follow-up directive was worse: "It must be made clear to the enemy that all sabotage troops will be exterminated, without exception. That means that their chance of escaping with their lives is nil. Under no circumstances can they be expected to be treated according to the rules of the Geneva Convention. If it should become necessary for reasons of interrogation to initially spare one man or two, then they are to be shot immediately after interrogation."

And Hitler was an equal opportunity killer, without regard to nationality or gender.

ON THE MORNING OF September 14, Buckmaster gave Odette an identity card for her new persona—"Odette Metayer"—and asked her to recite her "life story." Odette parroted the details of her birth and life growing up in Dunkirk, her father's name—Gustav Bédigis—and his work as a bank official at Crédit du Nord. Her mother's maiden name, she said, was Lille Lienard.

Reciting the actual death of her real father—woven seamlessly into the Metayer story—she spoke of her marriage to Jean Metayer, his employment at the Hernu Peron et Cie Shipping Agency, and his untimely death in 1936 due to bronchitis. They lived at 73 Grande rue in Boulogne, she said.

Buckmaster nodded and handed her a ration card. "You happened to be in Cannes at the end of December 1941, and you exchanged your ration card on the twenty-fourth. You were then living at the Hôtel Pension des Alpes, 15 rue Dizier. Coupons for September have been cut out." He explained that her code name within SOE—in the office and in the field—would be "Lise," and that her operation would be identified as CLOTHIER.

Maurice then paused. "There is one matter, Madame Metayer, which you have omitted to mention in telling us the story of your life. Have you any children?"

Odette paused a moment, and then her eyes went dead.

"No, Monsieur. I have no children."

Buckmaster nodded and read Odette the final instructions for Operation CLOTHIER, including contacts, addresses, postboxes, codes, and overall mission. She was to be stationed at Auxerre, he said, forming a small network and acting as a courier to Paris. She'd be given 50,000 francs and would be instructed later about receiving more. She'd depart for Gibraltar the following day, September 17, and should be in France roughly ten days later. She was to memorize the instruction pages overnight and return them to him in the morning.

"Have your clothes been checked?" he asked.

"Yes. Every stitch I have on is either French or has a French dressmaker's tab. I picked out a dark grey coat and skirt," Odette added, "so as not to show the dirt in prison."

Buckmaster held her gaze. "Do you think you're going to prison?"

"I don't know. But it's as well to be prepared."

The major nodded and handed her several small pills. "One of these will incapacitate your enemy for twenty-four hours," he said, "by giving him or her a violent stomach ache and its attendant disorders. If you want to feign illness yourself, take one. It won't be comfortable but it'll fool any doctor."

He handed her a second batch. "Now these, on the other hand, have the reverse effect. They are stimulants and should only be taken when you're damned tired and have to make a special effort. They are guaranteed to keep you going, mentally and physically."

Odette put them away and Buckmaster gave her a third set. "If you slip one of these little chaps into anyone's coffee, it will knock him out completely for six hours—with no aftereffects."

She nodded and the major held up one more, a small brown tablet. It was called an "L" tablet, he said, for lethal. "If you get into the sort of jam where there's absolutely no way out, swallow this and you'll be out of the jam permanently."

Odette added it to her bag and Buckmaster grinned. "That's not a very pretty going-away present, I'm afraid, so we've decided to give you another. Here you are, Lise, with love from the French Section."

He handed her a small item wrapped in tissue and Odette opened it and smiled. It was a beautiful silver compact.

She was now ready. Diarrhea pills, speed, sleep dope, lethal pill, and beauty aid. Bring on the Germans.

Buckmaster asked if she had any final questions and Odette said she didn't, but requested a favor. She had written a batch of letters for her children, she said, all undated, and asked if he could post them one week at a time.

Buckmaster said he would and Céline–Lise Clothier–Odette Metayer was off.

THE FOLLOWING DAY, ANXIOUS to see her beloved France and begin her work, Odette boarded a Whitley bomber. The plane taxied to the end of the runway and stopped to wait for the landing of an incoming aircraft. Odette peered through the window and started.

The landing plane was coming straight at them.

There was a violent collision of metal as the plane clipped the Whitley's starboard wing. The pilot immediately cut both engines and the shouting began. Someone opened the door and Odette tumbled out. Fortunately, the plane didn't ignite and no one was injured.

On September 27 a Lysander became available and Odette again headed to the airfield. As the plane was warming up, however, Baker Street received a cable stating that the Gestapo had arrested her contacts; three had been summarily executed, the rest soon to be.

Odette returned home, and Buckmaster told her to sit tight while he coordinated other contacts and searched for another plane.

A week later he called and Odette caught a train to Plymouth, where she was to depart by seaplane for Gibraltar. As she sat in the Mountbatten Airport, she watched the *Catalina* bobbing in the water as high winds jerked its moorings. Sheets of rain followed, and it appeared that this mission, too, would be jinxed. After several hours, an officer from the Royal Air Force came in and confirmed what Odette expected: the weather would not allow departure.

She returned to London.

The War Office scheduled another flight five days later and instructed Odette to report to Redruth in Cornwall. From there she was escorted to a hotel and told to get any sleep she could. An attendant would wake her at 0100, they said, for a 2 A.M. departure from Newquay Cornwall Airport. Odette drifted off, and promptly at one someone knocked on her door with a cup of hot tea.

It was raining.

At the airport she was told there was a slight delay: the Whitley's starboard engine had a fuel stoppage, someone said, and mechanics were addressing it while the luggage was stowed. They'd be under way shortly.

Finally, the craft was cleared and Odette climbed aboard. There were no seats, she saw, and the fuselage was crammed to the hilt with cargo. Finding a small spot on the metal floor, she arranged herself against a wooden crate and tried to stretch her legs. It wouldn't be the most comfortable ride, but at least she was finally leaving.

The engines revved up and they taxied to the runway. Odette sat back. It had been a long process: the guilt at Somerset, worry about leaving her children, the training, the injuries, the false starts. Now at last she could fulfill the duty her grandfather had encouraged so many years before.

The Whitley lifted off, dipping for a moment and then resuming its trajectory. Another dip. Odette swung her eyes to the cockpit. The pilot was trying to gain altitude, but the bomber was responding by rising and sinking. Up and down, up and down it went, a sluggish battle with gravity.

The airframe began to shudder.

Cargo creaked as it slid, then a thunderous burst as the starboard engine went.

Odette braced herself.

They were going to crash.

CHAPTER 3

MISSION TO MARSEILLE

A sense of weightlessness and then falling, a thirty-three-thousand-pound coffin screaming down. The Whitley slammed the earth, freight crashing forward, and Odette covered herself as a tidal wave of cargo rained against her. The bomber skidded along, dragging itself over sodden turf and rock, and lurched to a stop.

Odette heaved a wooden crate off of her and heard someone trying to yank open the door.

It was jammed.

"Get out everyone quickly!" someone shouted. "She may go on fire."

The door finally gave way and Odette scrambled over the scattered freight and jumped out. Miraculously, the plane didn't ignite and she ran ahead of it a few yards and froze: they had stopped ten yards short of a cliff that fell a hundred feet to the Celtic Sea.

BACK IN LONDON, MAJOR Buckmaster asked once more if she still wanted to go to France. Odette said she did, but suggested that it might be best if she went by *sea*.

"You *are* going by sea," he replied. "This country can't afford to write off any more bombers on your behalf."

IN THE MIDDLE OF October a troopship leaving from Gourock finally transported Odette to Gibraltar. While the British colony was the logical staging point for an Allied insertion into France, "the Rock" was a less than ideal waiting station. Situated on the tip of neutral but pro-Axis Spain, the area was closely monitored by Abwehr (German Military Intelligence) agents. J. C. Masterman, chairman of the Double-Cross Committee of the Security Service, or MI5, called it "one of the most difficult and complicated places on the map." And since it was the launching point for convoys operating in the Mediterranean, it was bombed by the Italians and its port raided by commando frogmen from their Tenth Light Flotilla. In July 1940 Vichy France had even attacked it in retaliation for the Royal Navy's assault on the French fleet docked in Mers-el-Kébir, Algeria.

Here Odette waited, holed up in a safe house. For two days she heard nothing, but on the third, a young man in naval uniform showed up at her door. His name was Jan Buchowski, an impetuous but brave Pole who, at twenty-three, had already won a Virtuti Militari. He was one of two Polish seamen who were captaining a pair of twenty-ton feluccas[9] on the Gibraltar-to-French-Riviera run. Poland's General Wladyslaw Sikorski, in describing the young bucks to SOE's General Colin Gubbins, said that they were "too rough even for the Polish navy."

Depending on weather, the trip would take ten to eighteen days,

---

9   A traditional wooden sailboat commonly used in the Mediterranean.

and the quarters were tight. The boat would travel under several flags, and when another craft was in sight, the passengers had to be herded below. Rough seas were a constant and German patrols, surface or U-boat, were always a risk. As everyone at Baker Street knew, the job required hardy, confident men; if they were a little rough around the edges, so be it.

"I am the commander of the felucca *Dewucca* and I am ordered to take you to France," Jan told her. Before Odette could reply, he added: "I must now refuse to carry out this operation."

"Why?"

"You are a woman. I will not take a woman, a young woman such as you, to this . . . this business. A man—yes. A woman—no. The matter is finished. May I have a drink please?"

Odette poured some whiskey and Jan raised his glass.

"Your health, Madame. You will possibly permit me to invite you for some dancing when I return to Gibraltar?"

"When you return to Gibraltar, you will already have landed me in France. It is an order of the War Office."

Jan smiled. "The War Office is very far away, Madame."

Odette poured another drink and explained that it was her fifth attempt to get to France. If she had to *swim*, she told him, she was going to get there.

"Madame would look most beautiful in a bathing dress."

"I demand that you take me to France."

"All over. I will not take you. I am Polish and I will not take a lady like you in my small and dirty boat. The conditions are bad, very bad. It is no good. All over. When I return, I will invite you for dancing. To travel to France is no good for you but only foolish. I refuse to take you and I spit in the face of the War Office. Finished."

The luck. Odette had finally made it to Gibraltar, only to be thwarted by a Polish Don Quixote. She kept the drinks flowing and eventually, highly intoxicated, Jan relented.

They set sail October 23 and at long last Odette's espionage career began. Jan was earning his keep, she saw, as he had four men and three women[10]—apparently only one of whom he considered a lady—aboard the *Dewucca*.

About the fourth day at sea, Jan began to tease Odette. "Did they give you a big pistol to take to France?" he asked, grinning. She replied that she could have taken one but that they were noisy and cumbersome.

"You prefer the more subtle, more quiet, more feminine methods of killing people?"

Odette paused and measured her response. "Have you a pistol, Jan?"

He handed her a .38 revolver.

"If you throw up an empty bottle and I hit it, what will you give me?"

Jan chuckled. "You hit a bottle! You are foolish. As well, this pistol makes a very big bang. Not a bang for small girls. When we return, I will invite you for dancing in Gibraltar."

"What will you give me?"

"If you hit a bottle, I will give you anything you ask. I will even dance the tango with you—in Gibraltar."

Jan grabbed a bottle and flung it far into the air. Just as it touched the water, Odette fired and the bottle exploded.

Jan gaped. "My God."

Odette asked for his fifth of whiskey and tossed it into the sea, chiding him for being obnoxious when he drank. Her Beaulieu evaluations were being confirmed, it seemed, even before she set foot in France.

That night Odette slept on deck, under the lee of the galley as she had been doing, but the temperature dropped significantly before sunrise. Sometime after dawn, she woke peacefully. She could feel the chill on her cheeks, but she was not cold. Glancing down, she saw why: Jan had draped his sheepskin coat over her while she slept.

---

10 Including Major George Starr, organizer of the WHEELWRIGHT circuit; Marcus Bloom, radio operator for the PRUNUS circuit; Mary Herbert, courier for the SCIENTIST circuit; and Marie-Thérèse Le Chene, courier for the PLANE circuit.

BEFORE DAWN ON NOVEMBER 2, the *Dewucca* slid quietly into the harbor at Cassis, a small port on the southeastern edge of Marseille, and dropped anchor. Odette stood on the bow, staring at the shore and listening to the soft lapping of waves.

France. *Her* France.

And her war with Germany, now commencing. She was neither anxious nor nervous. Instead, she was calm and resolute, almost detached.

She was ready.

She said good-bye to Jan and watched as a dinghy motored out to meet them. On board a man named André Marsac, head of a Resistance group in Marseille, greeted her and the others and said he would escort them to Cannes.

When the dinghy reached the water's edge, one of the men in the reception committee took her suitcase and Odette stepped ashore. Even with her eyes closed she could have determined that this was France: the smell of pine and lavender, mimosa and thyme, garlic and perfume could be found nowhere else.

Marsac delivered the group midmorning to the Villa Augusta, a flat owned by a trusted Resistance member, Marie-Lou Blanc, who was code-named "Suzanne." Inside, Odette met her contact, Captain Peter Churchill.

He was tall, she noticed, and extremely handsome. He wore glasses but behind them were confident brown eyes. His face was chiseled and tan, and from the way he moved and the muscles in his forearms, she could tell he was athletic.

The son of a British consul but no relation to Winston, Peter Churchill had graduated from Cambridge with a degree in languages and was fluent in French, Spanish, Italian, and German. His reputation as a remarkable athlete was well deserved: he had captained the Cambridge ice hockey team—one of the finest players the university had produced, they said—and was a first-class skier, diver, and six-handicap golfer. Following in his father's footsteps, he had served in the British diplomatic corps in the Netherlands and Algeria before becoming undersecretary of the Home Office Advisory Board in September 1939.

With his languages, athleticism, and diplomatic calm, Churchill was a natural for the Special Operations Executive, and Odette couldn't have asked for a better supervisor. He had aced all aspects of SOE training and had already made two tours of France. Dropped by submarine at Antibes in February, he had delivered two million francs to Resistance groups in Cannes, Lyon, and Marseille. After sneaking across the Pyrenees to Spain, he made his way to Madrid and then hid in the trunk of a diplomat's car to slip into Gibraltar. A second trip at the end of March was equally successful, although Peter narrowly avoided death when a French destroyer running with its lights off came within a hair of ramming the surfaced sub he was on.

Captain Peter Churchill. *ALAMY*

In every respect Peter Churchill was the consummate leader: intelligent, quick witted, and even-tempered. His cover identity was "Pierre Chauvet," but he was to be addressed as "Michel" or "Raoul" when among network agents. Unbeknownst to Odette, Peter had already earned somewhat of a reputation at Baker Street. He was "here, there and everywhere," Buckmaster said of him, "testing our methods of introducing our men into France, recruiting new units and encouraging existing ones—in short, doing the work of ten men."

Peter made a few remarks to the group and then instructed Marsac to take the men to the Villa Isabelle, a luxurious residence owned by Baron Henri ("Antoine") de Malval,[11] temporary headquarters for SPINDLE, the code name of Peter's circuit. Introducing the ladies to Suzanne, he suggested that they freshen up and join him for lunch. In the meantime, there was wine and cake in the kitchen, he said, for a small reception party.

As the women mingled and made their way to the kitchen, Peter considered the recruits: a grey-haired woman of about fifty-two who spoke too much English for his liking; a woman around twenty-seven who seemed too refined for the business; and the one called Lise, whom he estimated to be twenty-five. She had fair skin, light-brown hair, and discerning eyes. She also had a determined look about her, suggesting that she feared neither the Gestapo nor the concentration camp. This could be a problem, he thought, if her iron resistance led her to skip precautions necessary to avoid arrest.

But what captured his gaze were her hands; hands such as he had never seen before. They were long with slim, capable fingers, and as he watched her holding a wineglass, he noticed the expanse between her thumb and forefinger; it was a sign denoting extravagance, generosity, and impetuosity.

After lunch Odette waited until the other women retired to

---

11 A former French naval attaché in London. Prior to the arrest of Peter's predecessor, Francis Basin, Baron de Malval had allowed Basin to use Villa Isabelle as the circuit's headquarters.

bed and then approached the handsome captain. The reception was nice, she said, but she was anxious to get on with the job and go to Auxerre, her first stop.

Peter acknowledged Odette's assignment, but told her that crossing the border was no mean feat. The demarcation line was heavily patrolled by German guards, he said, often with dogs, and she would need a *passeur*: a guide who specialized in helping people cross. Unfortunately, one wouldn't be available for a day or two. He told her to relax for a while and suggested that maybe she should nap with the other women.

"I don't need any rest, thank you."

"Well, I'm afraid I have one or two things to attend to, Lise, so you'll have to excuse me."

Peter played the part of the strict commanding officer, but it was difficult; there was no denying that this young woman was attractive and alluring.

Before heading off to Antoine's to visit the men, Peter went to see his radio operator to have a message sent to London. Adolphe Rabinovitch—code-named "Arnaud"—was a twenty-six-year-old Russo-Egyptian Jew with the temperament of a wolverine. As Leo Marks, SOE's chief cryptographer and cypher instructor, put it, Arnaud could and did swear in four languages. His angry eyes and cynical mouth warned that he didn't suffer fools lightly—or anyone, for that matter—and that the slightest offense would trigger his wrath.

And Arnaud was built to deliver: he reminded Peter of a Hercules who moved with the ease of a panther. To be expected, Arnaud had a background in fighting, having been a junior wrestling and boxing champion. When he and Marks disagreed during cypher training over heavyweight boxing champ Joe Louis's best punch, Arnaud had sought to settle the matter by demonstration. "Rabinovitch swung his giant fist at my jaw," Marks recalled, "and pulled it up a microdot away just as Buckmaster walked in."

After transferring from the French Foreign Legion to the SOE, Arnaud had been parachuted in September near Grenoble with orders to proceed to Paris; his Polish pilot, however, missed the drop zone by twenty miles. Arnaud hid at a local farm and eventually connected with a Resistance agent, who took him to Cannes and introduced him to Peter.

When they first met, Peter had looked beyond Arnaud's gruff personality to see a man who was highly competent, fearless, and deeply committed to the cause. Peter suggested that Arnaud work for him, and the blunt radioman said London would never approve it. Peter asked if he would care to bet and they did, to the tune of 50,000 francs. London approved, and Peter now had one of the best wireless operators in France

Adolphe (Arnaud) Rabinovitch.
IMPERIAL WAR MUSEUM

Peter told him of the arriving felucca and Arnaud asked what the new agents were like.

"Very tired," Peter said. "One of them—Lise—disapproves of the whole setup. She is like an angry gazelle."

THE FOLLOWING DAY PETER returned to Suzanne's flat. He knew Lise would be disappointed when he told her that he couldn't borrow a guide from André ("Carte") Girard, leader of the adjacent CARTE circuit, and wasn't surprised when she asked for something to do.

He thought a moment. First assignment for the angry gazelle.

"I want you to go to Juan-les-Pins," he said. "When you get there, leave the Provencal Hôtel on your right and go straight up to the top of the hill. Just over the brow you'll find a sharp right-hand turn. Take it, and four hundred yards down on the left you'll see a villa called Les-Jonquilles. Ask to see Carte, tell him who you are—he'll recognize you from my description. Give him these messages, which you must hide on you, and wait for the answers. It's about seven kilometers each way."

He asked her to repeat the instructions and Odette recited them virtually word for word. He asked if she could ride a bicycle and she said that she could. There was a bike downstairs, he told her, and Suzanne could tell her the best way out of town.

Odette left and another agent, Jacques Riquet—a twenty-five-year-old former French air force sergeant—came in. As they were conversing they heard a loud crash, followed by the feeble ring of a bell.

Peter looked to the door. "What was that?"

"That," Riquet said as he peered through the window, "was Lise and her hoop. She's dusting herself off . . . She's dabbing her knee with a handkerchief . . . Blood! . . . She's gripping the handlebars sternly . . . We're off! . . . We're on . . . We're off! . . . We're on again. She's swaying . . . she's round the bend."

In the afternoon, Arnaud came by and began lingering by the window.

"Very restless today, aren't you, Arnaud?" Peter asked. "You've been hanging around that window as though you expected the Queen of Sheba to pass."

"And so I do. I can hardly wait to see this Lise."

"You may have to wait several days if I'm any judge of trick cyclists."

Arnaud asked if she was staying with the group and Peter said that he knew very well that she was going to Auxerre.

"I seem to remember I was going to Paris, once," Arnaud said, grinning. He peered again through the window. "My God! There's a walking dead coming through the gate and trailing a heap of scrap iron."

Peter glanced out. "The Queen of Sheba herself. Arnaud, don't go all goosey when she comes in. I tell you, this girl's dynamite. One moment of weakness and she'd have any man climbing Everest for a sprig of edelweiss."

Odette came in and the men pretended to be preoccupied. "Ah, Lise," Peter said. "You're back all right, then. Lise, this is Arnaud. He works the radio."

Arnaud mustered up a charming smile and offered his hand. "*Enchantè*, Lise."

Odette went to change her torn stockings and over lunch asked for another job. Peter mulled the request. It was clear that his clumsy but fearless courier would take any assignment, regardless of danger, and would likely be insulted if the task wasn't somewhat complicated.

He had in mind a job—a dangerous mission even for a man—which wouldn't be for the faint of heart. But should he send Lise out on such an assignment so fast? he wondered. He tossed the idea around in his head a day or so and on November 6 called her in.

"I want you to take those four new men to Marseille tomorrow," he told her, "and see them on to their connections. Three of them are English and naturally feel a bit strange out here.

"Now, Lise, Marseille at the moment is an ugly town, full of traps, raids, and other disagreeable surprises. You'll find the Gare St. Charles swarming with whole companies of the Afrika Korps, but you needn't pay any attention to them. The people you must be on your guard against are the armed Vichy troops in blue uniforms who stand by the exits with German uniformed soldiers of the Security and RTO Units. However, these uniformed men fade into insignificance beside the glowering gentlemen in civilian clothes who are liable to be checking papers. These are the Gestapo."

Odette nodded. "Fine."

"Having got rid of your charges," Peter continued, "walk along the side of the station until you come to a vast flight of steps leading down to the town. Go down them on the left side and stay on the left-hand pavement so as to avoid the Hôtel Splendide opposite. It's the H.Q. of the Gestapo. Go down to the Canebière—the main street—and turn right. Stay on the right-hand pavement, and after passing some stalls you'll find the Hôtel Moderne. Go up to the first floor where there's a fat, blowsy woman sitting inside a glass cubicle. Ask her if Monsieur Vidal is in."

Peter didn't mention that "Monsieur Vidal" was General Charles Delestraint, a recently retired commander who had led the counterattack against the Germans at Abbeville in 1940, and who had been chosen as commander in chief of de Gaulle's secret army.

If Vidal was in, Peter said, Odette was to give him the password greeting: *Je vous apporte des nouvelles de Monsieur Ternier, Monsieur Ternier de Lyon.*" In return, Vidal would ask, *"C'est de Monsieur 'Jean' Ternier que vous parlez, Madame?"*

Odette asked if this was the man she had seen at the felucca reception with Marsac, and Peter confirmed that it was.

He explained that Vidal would have a suitcase full of clothes and that she was to bring it back. "When you've got all that tied up, I want you to go back into the Canebière, turn left along it until you reach the Vieux Port and then right, where you'll find a glass tram terminus. Catch the No. 3 tram. It goes to Aix-en-Provence, twenty-nine kilometers away. When you get there, you go to the Boulevard Zola which is road 96, and almost on the corner is a blue-painted garage. Ask for Monsieur Gontrand."

Odette blinked. This was her first field test: memorizing a massive amount of information upon hearing it once. But it was the life of the courier, she knew, and lives—particularly her own—depended on accurate and instant recall of details.

Peter handed her 50,000 francs—petrol money for Gontrand to hold five hundred liters—and asked her to repeat the instructions. Odette fired back with the speed with which he had delivered and missed only a couple details. Peter corrected the discrepancies and Odette was ready. She left with the men the following day and they arrived in Marseille without incident.

MARSEILLE WAS INDEED DANGEROUS, as Peter had warned, but it presented tremendous opportunity. A valuable port city with an unruly population of a half million, Marseille had a tradition of rebellion and an extensive underworld. In addition, Baker Street had just posted three agents there for sabotage and training, including H. M. R. Despaigne, Peter's backup radioman.

With her companions discharged, Odette went off in search of Vidal. She followed the serpentine directions and found the Hôtel Moderne. As Peter had said, the blowsy woman was at the reception desk, but Vidal was out. The lady said he'd likely return about six o'clock, and Odette said she'd come back then. The schedule would be tight, she knew, since the last train to Cannes left at 7:10 P.M. If she missed it, she'd have to find a hotel and be off the street by curfew at ten.

She left and found Gontrand at the garage and gave him the petrol money. Now free until six, she took in a movie and strolled through town to kill time. On every street corner, it seemed, were German warning posters. In French, they read:

> It is forbidden to conceal, befriend or aid in any way persons who are part of the Army of the enemy (particularly members of air crew, enemy parachutists and enemy agents). Whoever contravenes the above order exposes themselves to being brought before a military tribunal and there they will be punished with the utmost severity, in some cases the pain of death.

Pain of death. Marseille, however, was a warren, and the Resistance rabbits had long since gone to ground.

Catch us if you can.

Shortly after six Odette was back at the hotel, but Vidal had yet to arrive. The receptionist said he was expected at any moment and Odette took a seat in the hall. At a quarter to seven a tall man in a dark suit came in.

Odette stood. "Monsieur Vidal?"

"*Oui*, Madame."

"*Je vous apporte des nouvelles de Monsieur Ternier, Monsieur Ternier de Lyon.*"

Vidal paused and then asked, "*C'est de Monsieur 'Jean' Ternier que vous parlez, Madame?*"

"*Oui*, Monsieur. *Précisément.*"

He nodded and asked if she'd join him for a drink. They strolled to a nearby cafe, and Odette placed a folded newspaper on the table and mentioned that it was money from Raoul.

Vidal quietly thanked her and slipped the paper into his pocket. He said that one of his couriers—a man named Bernard—was meeting him at the cafe, and if Odette could wait a few minutes, it would be helpful if they could meet.

Odette inquired about finding a hotel where no questions would be asked, and Vidal said that Bernard could recommend such a place. The man arrived moments later and suggested that they order dinner. Odette asked again about a hotel, and Bernard said it would be no problem; after the meal he'd take care of it.

At nine o'clock—one hour before curfew—Odette reminded Bernard about the hotel. He apologized and said he'd do it now and slipped away. Fifteen minutes later he returned and said that all of the hotels were booked. Not to worry, though; he knew of another place where no questions would be asked and she would be safe.

They walked toward the Vieux Port for several minutes and Bernard abruptly stopped.

"Here I leave you. It is better that I come no farther. Go down this street until you come to the sixth house on the right. Push the door and it will open. Inside is a woman. Tell her that you come from Monsieur Bernard and that you want a room for the night—a room with a key in the lock. She will understand."

Odette wondered why Bernard couldn't come with her. "What is the place where I am to sleep?"

"It is the only house where you will be absolutely safe in Marseille tonight. I am sorry, Lise. It is a German soldiers' brothel."[12]

Odette asked if it would be possible to sleep in the waiting room at the train station. Bernard acknowledged that she could, but that it would be unsafe. The Nazis had a habit of raiding the waiting rooms,[13] he said, and transporting the passengers to petrol factories in Germany.

It was an understatement. France was now Germany's vassal, and the suzerain regularly plundered the country for livestock, steel, textiles, corn, coal, and wine to feed and supply the fatherland. In similar fashion, it requisitioned homes for German officers and was deporting millions for forced labor in Germany.

Bernard assured her the brothel would be safe and said good-bye.

Indeed, brothels for Germans were considered the safest of safe houses because they were never searched; who would be found at a German brothel but Germans? At some, a room or two would even be kept vacant for escaping agents or aircrews.

It was now minutes before ten and the streets were deserted and dark, like a necropolis at midnight. Odette made her way down the sidewalk, counting houses. Everything was quiet save her footfalls, which echoed as a ticking clock. At number six she pushed the door and it opened. A middle-aged woman sitting at a table looked up.

---

12 Each brothel contained a notice stating whether it was requisitioned for German soldiers or "open to civilian gentlemen."

13 In Holland, these raids—the *razzia*, they called them—were conducted in neighborhoods to snatch young men between sixteen and thirty.

"Que désirez-vous, Madame?"

"I come from Monsieur Bernard. He said that . . . he said that I could have a room here tonight, a room with a key."

The woman stared at her. "You know what manner of house this is?"

Odette said she did.

The madam gave her a key and assured that she would not be disturbed.

Room 10 was decrepit but seemed safe enough. Tired lace curtains hung before closed shutters and a tarnished brass bed with a single grey blanket stood in the middle. A divan rested against the wall next to a wardrobe and armchair. Beside it was a small cabinet, on top of which was an ashtray with a stubbed-out cigarette and three hairpins. There was a smell Odette couldn't place—maybe a cheap Parisian perfume—and a dirty dressing gown rested inside the wardrobe.

Odette dragged the divan in front of the door and placed the chair on top of it. Turning out the light and taking off her shoes, she reclined on the bed fully clothed and dozed off.

VOICES.

It was three in the morning and there was a clatter of boots around the building.

The brothel door opened and a man entered, followed by several more.

German military police, the captain told the madam. They were looking for an army deserter, he said, and would be conducting a room-to-room search.

Moments later they were standing before room 10.

CHAPTER 4

THE BRIEFCASE

Strange, Peter thought. *Odette should have been back by now.* He was concerned but not overly worried; she had an iron will, after all, and he was confident she could handle most any situation. She'd be back in the morning, he told himself.

By eleven o'clock the next day, though, she had yet to arrive. He sent lookouts to meet all of the inbound Marseille trains and then left for a meeting with Carte.

When he returned, Arnaud was waiting.

"Where's Lise?"

Peter feigned unconcern. "Search me."

"Where did you send her?"

"Marseille."

Arnaud scowled. "Fancy sending her to that —— pit of Sodomy before she's had time to catch her breath."

"What d'you expect me to do with her? Stick her in a glass case? If she were my courier she'd have to go wherever I sent her."

"You're a callous bastard," Arnaud bellowed. "I always knew it."

He stomped out, slamming the door so hard that a picture fell from the wall.

Peter poured a glass of wine and drained it. He tried to tell himself he'd made the right decision in sending her to Marseille, but his conscience haunted him. *Remember when you were there last January . . . Remember that raid when they cordoned off the street . . . Remember all those women and children they hustled off to Germany . . . Remember the French police they trapped at the stadium and sent off . . . Remember how those spivs shook you down for twenty-five thousand in a backstreet . . . This is the gay resort from which Lise has not yet returned.*

He went to the window and checked the time: 6:25 P.M. There were two more trains for the day: the 7:53 and the 11:37. He arrived at the station at 7:48 and relieved the lookout. The train was on time, and he strained to examine every face as passengers streamed through the gate.

No Lise.

He had no appetite for dinner, so he biked back to the flat and wrote a report to London about his visit with Carte. Dealing with the zealous circuit leader was delicate, to say the least. On the one hand, Carte had a vast organization which covered much of Vichy France and penetrated even parts of the occupied zone. He also had at his disposal, he claimed, a band of some three hundred thousand guerillas which could be brought to bear at the appropriate hour.

On the other hand, Carte was overbearing, arrogant, and lacked all notions of security. He kept in his study a list of more than two hundred agents in his network, including names, addresses, descriptions, telephone numbers, experience, specialties, and, in some cases, photographs. If that wasn't enough, Carte didn't like Arnaud and wanted nothing to do with him. In short, Peter warned London, Carte was going to be a problem.

The distraction of preparing the message lasted only minutes, and for the next two and a half hours Peter agonized over Lise. Was Arnaud right? Had he given her too much, too fast? He headed back to the station and joined the crowd waiting for the 11:37. Chain-smoking, he paced back and forth before the luggage office.

The crowd murmured at the rumble of the train and Peter slid to the back to have a full view of the platform and exit. As the first disembarking passengers hurried through, he scanned them. Dozens, perhaps hundreds, traipsed past but no Lise. After a few minutes he was about the only one left; two or three stragglers, and then the area was clear.

His mouth went dry and he put his hand against the wall to steady himself. "Oh, God," he muttered, "give me strength."

He passed his eyes across the platform one last time and there, dragging the large suitcase, was Lise. Swallowing the lump in his throat, he slipped through the shadows and came up behind her, snatching the case and putting his arm through hers. Odette jumped, and then relaxed with a tired smile.

They went to a restaurant still open—the Chez Robert—and over a midnight dinner, Odette recounted the trip. She told him about the men she escorted to Marseille, and the one who lost his nerve and returned to Cannes. She moved on to picking up the suitcase and meeting Vidal, followed by the surprise visit of Bernard.

Next came the brothel story, followed by the harrowing events later that night. The place had been raided by the German military police, she said, and she was saved from having her room breached only by the quick-thinking madam. When the police arrived at room 10, the woman told them that it was occupied by her niece, who was suffering from smallpox. It worked, and the police moved on.

Peter didn't comment on her incredible bad luck with the raid or ask why it took so long for her to return. He congratulated her on a first-rate job and asked how she liked working in Cannes.

"Cannes has nothing to do with the real France," Odette said, "the France I came to find. I expected a hard, resentful, smouldering France, and I came to live and work in that France. It is my misfortune that I came to the one bit of my country where the war doesn't go on. I wanted very much to be with my true compatriots and to fight the Germans."

She paused and then added: "But if you ask me if I like working in your group and with you, the answer is 'yes.' I think that you work very hard and I know that I could do much of that work and leave you free to get on with the more important things."

He asked if she liked Cannes in general and she said she didn't.

"It's easy and silky and sophisticated. I am none of those things. The thing I seek is reality—and I don't think it is to be found in this . . . this decadent sunshine. Please don't think that when I use the word 'reality' I mean danger. I don't particularly want to get into danger. If I did, I should be weak and frightened. I am far better at blowing little girls' noses for them than sleeping in Marseille brothels. I am a much better cook than I am a British agent. I prefer bouillabaisse to Bren guns. I am a very ordinary woman."

Peter said he disagreed. "No very ordinary woman would have set out along the Corniche on a completely unfamiliar bicycle, fallen off, cut her best silk stockings and her knees to ribbons—and completed her journey. Why didn't you tell me that you didn't know how to ride?"

Because, she replied, he seemed to take for granted that everybody was as competent as he was. "It is most irritating."

Peter shook his head and admired his angry gazelle. One in a million.

"Lise, this Auxerre business, why don't you drop it and stay here?"

Odette said she wanted to be in a place of action, like Marseille, but even if she agreed to stay in Cannes, London would never approve it. Peter said it was up to her but that with her and Arnaud on his team, there'd be no stopping them.

Odette again mentioned London, saying she'd bet anything they'd never allow it.

Peter grinned. He'd played this game before. He said he'd take her bet.

"How much?" Odette asked.

"Fifty thousand."

"Make it one hundred thousand."

Peter agreed and had Arnaud send the request. The following day, London replied:

SEND LISE TO AUXERRE AS ORIGINALLY PLANNED
STOP SURELY CARTE CAN PROVIDE MEANS OF CROSS-
ING DEMARCATION LINE.

Peter sent an immediate response—LISE INDISPENSABLE—
and met with Odette that afternoon. He said that she had won the
bet, but would she give him another twenty-four hours?

She agreed.

The following day, Arnaud brought London's reply:

OH VERY WELL.

SPINDLE was set. Peter had his handpicked team—Arnaud
and Odette—and the pair now officially owed him 150,000 francs.
The danger, he realized, was that his affection for Odette could
impair his judgment, something he'd have to be vigilant to watch.

Paris
March 1943

WHILE THE SPINDLE TEAM was being approved by London, the
Germans were preparing a formidable counter.

Sergeant Hugo Bleicher was amazed that he had become some-
what of a celebrity among the Geheime Feldpolizei—German
Secret Police—operating in France. Throughout the Gestapo and
Abwehr, word had spread that in just four months he had almost
single-handedly dismantled the largest Allied espionage network:
INTERALLIÉ.

His prominence as a super spy-catcher seemed most unlikely.
He had been born in Tettnang, Germany, a small village on the
northeast side of Lake Constance, five miles from the Austrian
border and across the lake from Switzerland. His father owned a
successful cycle shop and had encouraged Hugo to join the business. After graduating from the gymnasium, however, Hugo had
other plans.

He tried to join the navy but failed due to poor eyesight. After that, he became a banker's apprentice at a firm in nearby Ravensburg. During World War I, when Hugo turned eighteen in 1917, he was drafted into the German army as an infantry private and sent to the Western Front near the Somme. Almost immediately he was captured by the British and interned as a prisoner of war in a camp near Abbeville. Displaying uncanny skills, he escaped on four occasions but was recaptured each time.

Two years later he was repatriated to Germany and apprenticed with a Hamburg export company, working for them in Tetuan, Spanish Morocco, from 1925 to 1928. Promoted to senior clerk shortly thereafter, he returned to Hamburg.

"There had been nothing unusual about my life," he recalled years later. "I was a business man and I liked my occupation. I had a steady income and a regular life, with a little villa just outside the city. My work kept me fully occupied. I had no time for political matters and it was always languages in which I sought to perfect myself. Although a South German, I was glad to live in Hamburg. It was a city of wide horizons and a pulsating life of its own with its many foreign connections. I felt at home there and my life seemed to lie in a well-regulated vista in front of me."

The following summer, August 11, 1929, Hugo married and settled down to a homebody routine. Ten years later he and his wife, Lucie, had their first child, a son, and Hugo's well-regulated vista seemed bright.

His sedate life took an abrupt turn, however, on August 20, 1939. Only twelve days before Germany invaded Poland, the Hamburg Chamber of Commerce placed a circular in the morning paper soliciting personnel with knowledge of foreign languages. Wartime censorship readers were needed, the advertisement said. Since the export industry would disintegrate during war, Hugo thought this would be a splendid opportunity and he applied.

For several months he heard nothing. Then, in November, he received military call-up papers indicating that he was to report to the Hindenburg barracks "for uniform." Still thinking that he would be instructed in censorship, Hugo was perplexed when he was not only fitted for uniform but also given a pack, sidearm, steel helmet, and gas mask.

In December he was sent to Duisburg for training and told that he would be part of a secret police force working in the occupied countries of Europe. It all came too fast.

Was he a soldier or a policeman? he wondered. He had no qualifications for the duties and enjoyed no aspect of the work. But what else was he to do? It was wartime and he had to obey.

Before Hugo knew it he was part of the Geheime Feldpolizei and stationed in Caen, France. Here he was, an undercover cop who spoke French but had no training in police work, and he wasn't quite sure what he was supposed to do. Caen had little need for occupation police, it turned out, so he was reassigned to Cherbourg, a hotbed of Allied espionage.

In October 1941 he was asked to interrogate a man who had been arrested as a suspected spy. The man turned out to be Jean Lucien Keiffer, code-named "Kiki," an agent for a Resistance net operating out of Paris.

Kiki was in Cherbourg to find a patriotic fisherman who would act as a courier to England, he told Hugo. He stated that their network was called INTERALLIÉ and was run by a Polish captain and his French assistant. It was a large group—perhaps as many as one hundred agents—comprised mostly of freelance spies. Within hours, Hugo had convinced Kiki to work for him.

Such a fast turn seemed unthinkable, but occasionally happened. J. C. Masterman, chairman of the committee that supervised Britain's double agents, explained the delicacy of the game: "Every spy who is sent into enemy territory must be alive to the possibility of capture and, in the event of capture, of saving his life not merely by full confession but by returning with messages couched in a form approved and perhaps dictated by his captors."

Kiki had not been tortured, however, or even threatened with torture, but Masterman knew the type. While a majority of spies could commit treachery under pressure, he wrote in his final MI5 report, "there are others who have a natural predilection to live in that curious world of espionage and deceit, and who attach themselves with equal facility to one side or the other, so long as their craving for adventure of a rather macabre type is satisfied."

Kiki was this type. His duplicity began by giving Bleicher the INTERALLIÉ headquarters address in Paris, which allowed Hugo to arrest its key leaders: Roman Czerniawski, Lily Carré, and Renée Borni. Bleicher immediately turned Carré and Borni, and, with Kiki, the trio assisted Hugo in the arrest of some sixty agents.

Sensing they had found a gifted agent, the Abwehr claimed Hugo for their own and relocated him to Paris; he was still part of the Geheime Feldpolizei, but would now operate under their supervision.

Administration of German law enforcement, intelligence, and counterintelligence was complicated, though, even for those in it. The Nazi Party, under the leadership of Heinrich Himmler, conducted all of these operations within the sister organizations Gestapo and Sicherheitsdienst (SD). Overlapping these same tasks, however, was the military's Geheime Feldpolizei—Bleicher's group—and the Abwehr's counterintelligence division.

No love would be lost between the Nazis and the military.

Summoned to the Hôtel Lutétia, Hugo met his new boss, Colonel Oscar Reile, the agency's counterintelligence head in Paris. A former chief of police, Reile was a prototype German officer: forty-six, intelligent, well groomed, and athletic. His speech was measured, slow, and direct, but he didn't speak French—another reason he desired the services of Hugo Bleicher.

Hugo would be undertaking a new, broader assignment, Reile told him, arresting British spies and Resistance saboteurs throughout the country. "We are fighting against bitter enemies who do us immense damage," he said. "It is our duty to fight them with every available weapon, but I want our methods to remain clean; for our coat must remain clean, too. No violence in interrogations, no third degree, which does not really produce good results. No threats, please, and above all no promises that cannot be kept."

Hugo was fully aware that the instruction was to operate in a fashion exactly the opposite of the hated Gestapo, filled as it was with thugs and criminals. The Abwehr, as a military organization, expected discipline, civility, and professionalism.

With Bleicher's INTERALLIÉ success, Reile gave him complete autonomy and access to agents and assistants as needed. Hugo could travel anywhere in the country, and did. His perfect French served him well; when traveling he was "Monsieur Jean," and, if need be, he could converse in English or Spanish.

Sergeant Hugo Bleicher ("Monsieur Jean"). *WILLIAM KIMBER*

Germany could not have found a better bloodhound. A fearless policeman with the cunning of Sherlock Holmes, Hugo was relentless in his work.

He was a worthy opponent for SOE's best.

Throughout the fall of 1942, Bleicher paid careful attention to the Resistance groups growing along the Côte d'Azur—Nice, Cannes, and as far west as Marseille—and two events later that year greatly enhanced his work.

On November 11 Germany scuttled the terms of the 1940 armistice—which had allowed a "free" section of France (Vichy)—and declared all of the country occupied, with the southeastern portion to be governed by the Italians. All of France was now open game for arrests, and Hugo planned accordingly. He had heard that Resistance agents were regularly traveling by train from Marseille to Paris and alerted the Abwehr to be on watch.

Days later Marsac himself was making this very trip. Trains were the only way to travel any distance for most people and the crowd mitigated the risk for Resistance workers. Since food was rationed at a level of only 1,800 calories a day, the black market flourished. An allocation of only six and a half ounces of meat a week meant that people in the city would constantly travel to the countryside to bargain for beans, carrots, poultry, eggs, cheese, and beef. With papers in proper order to board, the danger was slight unless your name was on a list and there was a check of passengers at a stop.

Marsac's papers were solid and he settled in for the long journey. In his briefcase next to him was Carte's list of network agents, some of whom knew the SPINDLE trio and their hideouts.

The slow, mundane rocking of the train had the effect of a sedative, and after a while Marsac dozed off. When he awoke, he stirred.

The briefcase was gone.

CHAPTER 5

CONTROL

Marsac's decision to carry incriminating evidence in his briefcase violated every rule of espionage. Spies generally carried no papers or even notes which would reveal their work. For SOE agents, communication with other operatives was accomplished by couriers, and wireless messages to and from London were disguised within codes. But Germany, too, had its code breakers and cryptographers, so any cables sent to Baker Street had to be well hidden within labyrinthine formulas.

To begin, all messages had to be at least two hundred letters long. And since SOE expected captured operatives to be tortured for their codes, each agent had to have a unique platform, or all messages to all agents would be broken.

During training, radio operators and circuit leaders were asked to provide a favorite poem or quotation that would be their coding framework. Shakespeare, Keats, Tennyson, Poe, and the Bible were among the favorites. Once in the field, the agent would code messages by choosing at random five words from the poem. Each letter of the words would be assigned a number and the group of numbers jumbled to conceal the intended text. The rub, however, was human error. If the agent made a mistake in the Morse, or misspelled a word, the code collapsed to gibberish. These flawed messages—often up to 20 percent of traffic—were identified as "indecipherables" and given to FANY women at the Grendon Underwood wireless station to try to unscramble. Few jobs in intelligence were more secret, more important, or more stressful. And the average age at Grendon was twenty.

To prepare the women for the weighty task, chief cryptographer Leo Marks broke them in gently. They were herded into a Norgeby House[14] basement with no heating or chairs and told that someone in Codes would be with them shortly. For an hour the girls were kept waiting, freezing. What they didn't know was that the room was bugged, and that they were being recorded.

When Leo finally arrived, he started the meeting by broadcasting what had been secretly taped. *Where was their instructor?* a voice asked. *Why was he so late?* The girls debated the issue for some time before reaching a consensus: Marks was late because he had been "having it off" with one of the FANY girls—in a variety of specified positions—although they were undecided whether she had kept on her brigadier's hat. They would decide when they saw him, one of the girls said, whether the transpositions had been single or double.

The discussion moved on to why there were no chairs. Apparently, said one, it was because Marks didn't realize that FANYs had fannies.

Leo turned off the recorder. All eyes were averted.

"You've been kept waiting in a cold room," he began, "to make you tired and irritable because when you're tired and irritable you grow careless, and when you're careless you're talkative. Next time you feel like talking, remember that the Germans have recorders too.

"You're going to be told about things you shouldn't know," he said, "but we can't help ourselves, we have to trust you. Every department has its secrets—you in Codes will read all the secrets of all the departments. If you talk about any of them, a man will die. It's as simple as that.

---

14   83 Baker Street, next to SOE's main offices at 64 Baker Street.

"You think you're tired, don't you? Then imagine how tired an agent feels who's had no sleep for three nights and has to encode a message. The Germans are all around her so-called safe-house. She has no supervisor to check her coding. All she has is a vital message which she must transmit. Now, I'm going to put a question to this house. Hasn't that agent a right to make a mistake in her coding? And, if she does, must she pay for it with her life? Must she come on the air again to repeat her message, whilst German direction-finding[15] cars get her bearings?

"There's an indecipherable down there with your names on it. It's from a Belgian agent who's completely blown. He's sent us a message telling us coordinates—that is, where he can be picked up. A Lysander is standing by to get him out. The message won't budge. At ten o'clock this evening he's due to come on the air and repeat it. If he does, those cars will close in. We will lose that man—just as a few weeks ago we lost a young Norwegian agent named Arne Vaerum, code-named 'Penguin.' The SS shot him while he was re-transmitting an indecipherable message."

Marks had made his point. Security. Gravity. Urgency.

On some occasions, an indecipherable was so difficult that the Grendon girls couldn't crack it. Those rocks were passed on to Marks himself, the last best hope of unscrambling the inscrutable.

In mid-November 1942 the Grendon girls had been tasked to unscramble eight indecipherables. They managed to solve seven and reluctantly passed the Gordian knot to Marks.

The culprit was Peter Churchill.

His poem-code was fairly simple:

I danced two waltzes
One fox-trot
And one polka

---

15 The Germans inserted "direction-finding" vehicles—which could trace the location of SOE wireless transmissions—in the unoccupied zone in July 1942.

With no partner
That they could see
And hope I did not tire you.

I glided round
The other ballroom
The one called life
Just as alone
And have to thank you
For giving me
The sprinkling of moments
Which are my place at the table
In a winner's world.

Keep a space for me
On your card
If you are dancing still.

Marks recalled that during Churchill's training, Peter had a habit of transposing columns in the wrong order. Unscrambling Peter's message would require mathematical surgery, Leo knew, and he sharpened his scalpel. Starting with the assumption that Peter had "hatted"—misaligned—some columns, Leo made a few calculations.

His guesses were right. He excised the coding cancer, and Peter's message to Buckmaster floated up. It was a complaint about Carte; the man's incompetence and lack of security, Peter said, were causing significant difficulties for SPINDLE, and something had to be done.

Without knowing the details, Baker Street had to decide if it was merely a personality clash, or if Carte had to be cut off and his work reassigned. What they were soon to learn was that it wasn't just Peter; Carte's own men were fed up with him. Carte's number two, Henri Frager—code-named "Paul" or "Louba"—had come to Peter and Odette asking if he and his colleagues could work with them; they were finished with Carte. And after being on the job for only a few weeks, Odette had also made it clear that she wouldn't work with Carte because his security was nonexistent.

Buckmaster decided to settle the matter by bringing Peter and Carte to London to sort it out. London notified Peter that he needed to set up a flare-path landing for a soon-arriving Hudson. The plane would be picking up Carte and him, as well as four French generals, they said. Peter notified Carte, who said that he would find an appropriate field.

The location one of Carte's men found was ideal in the sense that it was remote: the Luberon Regional Nature Park, fifteen miles northeast of Aix-en-Provence. The actual landing area, however—a small farm on the banks of the Durance—was the size of a postage stamp. The field markings would have to be perfect or the pilot would land in water or crash into a foothill. Per the SOE standards for night drops and landings, the site would have been rejected outright.

When Peter asked to inspect the field beforehand, Carte rebuffed him. "My dear Raoul," he said, "there is no need whatsoever for you personally to inspect the field. My subordinates—all of whom are distinguished aviators, have already satisfied themselves that it is in every way suitable for the reception of a bomber."

Peter didn't want to create an unnecessary rift, but he didn't want to trust hearsay, either. "How long is the field?" he asked.

Sixteen hundred meters, Carte replied.

Peter asked how wide and Carte said eight hundred to nine hundred meters.

And the surface?

"The surface, my dear Raoul, has been examined by my aeronautical subordinates. It is flat, as flat as a grilled sole, and as hard as the heart of a well-bred Englishwoman."

With Carte's assurance, Peter concentrated on other details. The petrol that Odette had purchased from Gontrand during her mission to Marseille would be used for two cars on the drive from Marseille to the field: one with Peter, Odette, and Gontrand, the other with Marsac and his men. Carte and the generals would meet them there, the Frenchman had said; everything was ready, and Peter need only arrange the lights upon arrival.

Before they left Peter had Odette pack extra flashlights and two bottles of Armagnac, which would help to offset the bitter cold. The landing window, London had said, was between ten at night and two in the morning. The parties met in Marseille and then set out for the short drive.

After a few minutes they saw lights ahead and everyone grew quiet.

Odette's scalp crawled. To be caught without papers or permits after curfew—particularly at a Control stop—was almost a death sentence.[16]

Gontrand pulled over.

"Your papers!"

Gontrand handed him his driver's license.

"I don't mean that, I want your permit for this journey."

Gontrand said he didn't have one.

The gendarme looked at Peter and Odette. "In that case I want to see all of your identity cards. And I shall require you to come along with me to the station."

"Oh, officer, this is a perfectly innocent journey," Gontrand said. "I'm only obliging this young couple by driving them to Manosque for private reasons. You know how long it takes to get these permits. I told them I'd take them at my own responsibility. You'll see us coming back presently. You simply must trust me."

As the gendarme mulled the feeble excuse, Peter steamed: an entire operation in jeopardy because Gontrand had failed to get a permit beforehand.

Inexplicably, the officer consented and let them pass.

----

16 Of the thirty-eight female SOE agents sent to France, sixteen were caught and executed, or died in captivity—a 42 percent fatality rate. On the Allied side, only Bomber Command had a higher death rate—45 percent.

AT THE FARM ADJACENT to the field, Peter and Odette met Carte and the generals, along with Marsac and his flare-path crew: Jacques Riquet, courier Jacques Langlois, a man named Bernard, a pilot, a farmer, and a museum curator. With Peter and Odette, they would make up the nine lights directing the Hudson. Carte, as Peter had anticipated, had forgotten flashlights.

Peter distributed his set and assigned each person to a spot along the L formation. There was to be no smoking or flashing of lamps, he said, and no noise. At nine thirty they began setting up.

While counting off the meter intervals between lights, Peter stopped. Here, running diagonally across the field, was a five-foot-high ridge—a hazard which would destroy a heavy bomber hitting it at ninety miles per hour.

"Where are the 1,600 meters of length and 800 meters of width which I explained were the minimum essentials and that you promised were here?" he asked Carte.

Carte pointed to the airman who had selected the field and Peter asked what planes he had flown. Potez 43s, the man said.

Peter grimaced. The ancient French utility plane—which had a top speed of 103—was so small and light that it could land about anywhere. As he blistered the pilot, they heard the Hudson approaching. It was ten fifteen.

Peter had no choice: he couldn't signal the landing. The plane came low and circled, waiting for lights, but none came. As they left the field and headed back, everyone stopped in shock. Before them lay an abandoned airfield two thousand meters long. How Carte's pilot could have missed it was beyond belief.

Peter, Odette, and Gontrand stayed at the Pascal Hôtel in Manosque that night, and Odette called Suzanne to get in touch with Arnaud. The landing would be rescheduled for the following night, he was to tell London.

The rendezvous was confirmed, and the landing party repeated the drill. With everyone in place at ten o'clock, they waited. The temperature dropped below zero, but they couldn't move. For four hours, everyone shivered in darkness.

No Hudson.

At 2:15 A.M. Peter called it off and they returned to the Pascal. It was a drill he and Odette would repeat often.

The following day London cabled and said that the operation would be rescheduled for "December Moon" in Chanoines, Arles, forty miles west of Aix. Since each month had five or six days on either side of the full moon, they had a window of thirteen days. Per SOE procedure, once a date was given the reception committee would have to stay in the area up to five nights if the aircraft could not be sent or encountered problems.

Peter gave the reconnaissance job to Odette, telling her to take Jacques Latour to Arles the following day to lay out the field. Gontrand, he said, would take care of the travel permit.

Over dinner that night Peter did his best to break the chain of command and have a personal, informal conversation. "You're an odd one, Lise," he said, only half joking, "you don't smoke, you don't drink, and you don't swear. All that'll have to change, you know. You can't belong to this crazy racket without even biting your nails."

"None of these things will ever change, Michel. I simply don't like alcohol or tobacco and the word *zut*[17] has served me well for many years."

Peter asked her to tell him about herself and she said there was nothing to tell.

"Come off it, Lise. Let your hair down."

Odette said that she was the mother of three little girls and Peter's jaw dropped. "Good God! How on earth could you have left them?"

Odette pondered how to answer. How does one explain to a commanding officer—one to whom you have an undeniable attraction—that you are unhappily married and heartbroken over leaving your children, a decision that you struggle with every day, every hour, every minute?

---

17 *Zut* is the French equivalent of "heck."

"It's a long story," she finally said.

"Lise, it's going to be a long war, so get weaving with the first installment."

Odette explained the London raids, Somerset, and how easy it would have been to spend the war shielded by motherhood while others suffered under occupation. Peter asked about the girls and Odette explained that they were in a convent in Brentwood and were looked after by two aunts and an uncle. She intentionally didn't mention Roy.

And their ages?

"Marianne's seven, Lily nine, and Francoise ten."

"And where is their father?"

"He's in the Army. But don't imagine he could have stopped me in doing this job. I'm inclined to arrange these things on my own."

Peter said he wasn't surprised, but now here she was under the command of a complete stranger.

Stranger, Odette thought. If only she could keep it that way. She and Peter seemed to be drawing closer toward each other by the hour. Was it the danger, the espionage? Peter's charm and commanding presence? Or was it her failed marriage? A combination of all three, perhaps?

"No one's a complete stranger who's doing this job," she replied.

ODETTE LEFT FOR ARLES the next day and got off in Marseille to stop by the Resistance headquarters in the rue St. Bazil. There a Frenchman introduced himself as a member of the team. Odette thought he looked like a ruffian but kept it to herself.

His name was Kiki.

While Odette was gone Peter returned to Cannes to try to ameliorate the growing rift between Carte and Arnaud. The radioman was livid when he heard that Carte had botched the Hudson landing; if Peter had asked him to strangle the Frenchman in a dark alley, it would have been done before dinner.

Peter settled into a safe house at 20 Quai St. Pierre, and it was fortuitous. That afternoon Antoine called with some disturbing news: two police inspectors had come by his villa, he said, asking if a Pierre Chauvet lived there. He confirmed that Pierre did live there, and the officers asked to see him. Pierre was in Paris, Antoine told them, but would be back in four days.

Peter told Antoine to contact Suzanne and to be ready for his move to another flat.

That night Peter's doorbell rang. He wasn't expecting anyone.

Peering through the peephole, he saw that it was Suzanne and opened the door.

"Michel," she whispered, "I don't think it's safe for you to stay here any longer. Two inspectors from the prefecture called at the Augusta only half an hour ago. They asked a lot of awkward questions about the purposes for which the flat was used. I played the injured innocent role quite easily and they pretended to swallow it; however, my intuition tells me there may be some tie-up in their minds between the two places. There's something very queer in the air."

Arles

PERMIT PLEASE.

Odette looked at the sergeant and drew a breath. She and Peter had just dodged a bullet with Gontrand days before, but she didn't have the luxury of a "lovers' trip" ruse now. To beat a Control check, she knew, you had to maintain complete composure, stick to the cover, summon all your wits, and hope for a little luck.

She wasn't traveling during business hours, however, which brought scores of travelers to process, but during the forbidden curfew. What alibi would be credible in the middle of the night?

She told the sergeant she didn't have a permit.

Wait here.

Odette's heart pounded. The end of the road.

The guard summoned the duty officer.

CHAPTER 6

THE KISS

The inspector's questions at the Augusta flat were the tail of an investigation trail, Peter realized, and the SOE handbook was clear: in the event a hideout came under suspicion, a second should be ready, complete with underlying cover. He had neither.

He tossed his things on his bicycle and set off for a safe house owned by a woman named Catherine. She wouldn't mind a temporary boarder, he thought; she was quartering Odette and a Hungarian refugee, and was accustomed to agents being washed up by the night. Since Lise was in Arles, Catherine placed him in her room and he went to bed early. Morning came and Peter cracked his eyes to see Odette staring back at him.

"Where the devil am I?" Sleep in his voice.

Odette gazed into his eyes, almost close enough to kiss him. "While I talk my way through half a dozen Italian Control Posts, in the curfew, you're sleeping in my bed, *mon cher.*"

Peter cleared his head and sat up. There was something in Odette's face, something beautiful yet defiant. It was lovely. She was no longer an angry gazelle; more like a determined angel. *His* angel. He wanted to go over details of the landing field, but hearing that she had been up all night, he suggested that she get a bath, fill him in on essentials, and then sleep all day.

Odette wasn't interested in sleep. After breakfast she brought up Arles. "It's a peach of a field," she said. "The surface is perfect."

He asked about trees and she said there were none in the way.

And what was this business about driving all night? Peter asked. That should have been unnecessary.

Gontrand's permit was no good after 11 P.M., she explained, but she had wanted to chance it to get back by morning. When the Control guard brought out the duty officer, she told him it was an emergency: she was traveling through the night to see her very sick child in a Cannes nursing home. The duty officer seemed unmoved, so she played the ace: "I turned on a few tears and that fixed him."

ON DECEMBER 12 ARNAUD heard the BBC transmission, *"Deux et trois font cinq"*—London's announcement that the Arles-Chanoines operation was moving forward. Peter contacted the landing party and they were off to the station. The December moon would peak full on the 22nd, the lunar calendar showed, so the operation would have sufficient lighting anywhere from the 17th to the 28th.

Trains throughout France were a microcosm of espionage. In addition to Control checkpoints at most stops, Abwehr and Gestapo agents, as well as German officers, were often in the coaches. The danger, though, was little deterrent for SOE and Resistance operatives. Messages were passed, for example, one circuit to another, by placing the paper inside a lavatory sign. On a seemingly innocent trip to the restroom, the receiving courier would unscrew the sign, retrieve the note, replace it with her own, and reattach the sign.

Agent rescues were almost as foolproof. When a captive was being delivered from one city to another, a rescue team would board the train and assume positions by the lavatory and behind the escorting German guards. At the appropriate moment, a team member would flash the prisoner a sign, indicating it was time for a restroom visit.

Once the guard uncuffed the prisoner and escorted him to the lavatory, the ambush team went to work; the guards suddenly felt pistols poking their stomachs or kidneys, and the captive was spirited away.

THE ARLES TRIP WAS not without its own drama. At lunchtime Odette and Peter joined couriers Jacques Riquet and Jacques Latour in the dining car. As they took their seats they noticed a number of German and Italian officers around various tables. Voices low and conversation light, the SPINDLE spies enjoyed themselves as ordinary travelers. After the meal Peter paid the bill and set out eight francs—two per diner being customary—next to the children's Winter Relief Fund tickets, a tax paid by French nationals to assist orphans of parents killed during the war.

Odette looked at the tickets. Had her family stayed in France, those orphans could have been her own children. She felt herself growing hot.

Snatching one of the tickets, she stood.

"I know the very person who should be paying for this slight offering."

"Now, Lise," Peter said, "for goodness' sake don't start anything stupid."

Odette marched down the aisle until she came to a German general. Placing the stub before him, she said, "I think that you, who are instrumental in bringing about the need for this fund, should pay for this ticket."

The dining car fell silent as the general glanced at it. With the snap of a finger he could have had her arrested and sent to a labor or concentration camp. He motioned for the waiter, who—thinking he had mistakenly set it before the German—began apologizing. Handing the server the ticket and a two-franc coin, the general turned to Odette with a silent, patronizing look. She said nothing and returned to her table.

Peter held his fire until they made their way back to the coach. As they passed between platforms, he said, "An admirable performance, Lise, and I understand your feelings, but for God's sake lay off that kind of thing. It's quite dangerous enough as it is."

THEY ARRIVED IN ARLES without further incident and Peter, Odette, Riquet, and Latour checked into the last four rooms at the Grand Hôtel Nord Pinus. The town was crawling with occupation troops and the other rooms, it turned out, were occupied by senior German officers. To compound matters, Carte and Paul—sensing that Cannes had become too hot—had moved to Arles; Resistance agents summoned for meetings in cafes would be mingling now shoulder to shoulder with Wehrmacht soldiers.

While they waited for London's signal, Peter and Odette decided to blend in as tourists. Arles is a city whose gates and ruins protest its modern insignificance, and even the most culturally deaf could appreciate the Roman baths, Barbegal aqueduct, and history of van Gogh's ear. By day it's a museum of monuments, of ancient glories past; by evening, a tapestry of cafe terraces and starry nights over the Rhône.

They visited the Amphitheater—a coliseum built for thousands to watch gladiator fights, the first-century Gallo-Roman theater, and the Romanesque St. Trophime Church. It seemed appropriate. They were, after all, fighting for their lives in the arena, wearing the masks and playing the parts, and, when the curtain fell, praying that they'd exit the stage as peacefully as they'd entered.

Days later, however, still nothing from London.

On December 23 Peter began to worry; the moon would provide sufficient light for only five more nights. The following day, he received news of the apparent obstacle: antiaircraft batteries. One of Carte's men had collected details on the locations of batteries and night fighter squadrons throughout France, and the problem for the

Chanoines operation—which London might have heard—was that an AA battery had been installed less than twelve hundred yards from the landing site. Peter sent the information just in case.

As Christmas approached the mood was festive. December had brought heavy snow and the town—locals, visitors, occupiers, and saboteurs—seemed to harmonize in the holiday spirit. On Christmas Eve the reception committee gathered at the hotel to celebrate. Someone brought cake and a dozen bottles of Côtes du Rhône, but one thing was missing, Odette felt: a piano. She inquired with the hotel proprietor and was told that the Germans had moved it to their dining hall. She went there and found three officers eating.

"*Bon-soir*, Mademoiselle," a major greeted as he stood.

"Gentlemen, please forgive this intrusion. The fact is that it is Christmas Eve and, though this terrible war has separated many friends and families, I am fortunate enough to have around me tonight some of the playmates of my childhood. If you are indeed as generous as one occasionally hears, you could do us a very great service tonight."

The major said the German Reich sought to be friends of France and asked how he could be of assistance. Odette noted the piano in the corner and said that among her guests was a pianist. It would give her group great pleasure, she said, if he could play songs of Christmas and France.

The major bowed. "Mademoiselle, my colleagues and I will be very pleased for your friend to play the piano—in view of the German policy of cooperation and because it is Christmas Eve."

Not exactly what Odette had in mind. She politely explained that her friend would not experience the appropriate nostalgia unless he played *only* to his compatriots.

"You wish the piano to be moved upstairs, Mademoiselle?"

"Please."

"Very well, Mademoiselle. Though it would have pleased us to hold the concert in this Mess, the piano may be taken upstairs—provided it is returned by eight o'clock tomorrow morning."

Odette thanked him but that wasn't quite sufficient, either. Her friends, she told him, no longer had the physical vigor to move a heavy piano.

The major stiffened. "Am I to understand, Mademoiselle, that you wish to suggest that my brother-officers and I carry the piano upstairs?"

"Gentlemen, you are more than kind."

The Christmas party of the Resistance saboteurs—complete with piano accompaniment—began moments later.

Grand Hôtel Nord Pinus, Arles, 1943. SUDWALL SUPERFORUM

ON CHRISTMAS DAY THEY waited for London but heard nothing. No word came until the 27th, when they heard *"Deux et trois font cinq"* on two of their three radios. The cars did not have enough space for Odette to go, so she said good-bye to Peter at the hotel. She asked that he deliver presents for her daughters, and he agreed.

"And you will come back, as you promised, won't you, Michel?"

Odette's words echoed back to her. She and Peter were at a critical stage, she knew. The passion in her own marriage had expired long ago, but she remained a married woman. Yet it was clear—if Peter took her hand, there would be no turning back.

Peter said he would return, and that she should take care of herself meanwhile. "I want to find you here when I get back, so don't go out of your way looking for trouble."

"I promise you that, Pierre."

Peter noticed the subtle change; it was the first time Odette had used the French translation of his real name. He wanted to kiss her, but that would have been highly inappropriate for a commanding officer. But he couldn't walk away. Not with Odette's overture . . . *I promise you, Pierre*. Never had his name sounded so sweet. It was a bouquet of promise and more, much more, and it demanded a reciprocal token of love.

Seconds hung as he wondered how to respond. Unconsciously, he reached for Odette's soft, elegant hands and gazed into her eyes.

He had to leave. *Now*.

He brought Odette's hand to his lips, kissed it, and walked away.

THE FLARE-PATH TEAM AND generals were waiting at Carte's house when Peter arrived, but there was an eerie silence. A German motorcycle unit of forty men and machines, Paul Frager said, had just camped down two kilometers from the Chanoines landing spot. Coupled with the nearby AA flak post, he said, this made the operation too dangerous.

The men looked at one another, all trying to determine the odds and the next man's resolve.

Captain Roland, a French infantry officer, countered that the speed of the pickup would catch the Germans off guard and that the line of retreat would be into the Camargue, where they could spend the remainder of the night. Peter objected, saying that he couldn't risk an aircraft in such harrowing circumstances; the chances of getting ten men and their luggage away would be slim.

Carte was unmoved. "I have listened to all points of view," he announced, "and my decision, despite all the dangers is that we must tackle these heavy odds. We can't expect to glide through this war with all our cards in our favor so will all those who agree raise their hands?"

All hands went up other than Peter's and Paul's.

Peter relented and they crammed into two cars and were off for Chanoines, flak battery and motorcycle unit notwithstanding.

By 10:20 P.M. Peter had everyone in place. Once again they huddled silently in the cold waiting for the drone of a Hudson. The hours passed and they heard nothing. At 2:00 A.M. Peter suggested to Carte that they give the plane another half hour. Carte agreed, but by 2:35, they still had heard nothing and left.

When they were just over a mile away, they heard a faint hum. It was the sound of an aircraft. Could be a German plane, Peter thought. In any case, they were too far away to race back and re-align the lights. Moments later they watched as the aircraft flew directly toward the field.

It was the Hudson. The *only* Hudson available to SOE during the war.

WHEN ODETTE AND PETER arrived back at Cannes, a message was waiting. London wanted them to land SOE's only Lysander during the same moon period at Bassillac, six miles west of Périgueux. Peter checked the map—it was *five hundred miles* to the place; they'd have to change trains in Marseille and again in Toulouse. Once in Périgueux they'd have to book a hotel, find transportation to Bassillac, and then reconnoiter the field. Either Buckmaster had downed one bourbon too many, or the operation was too difficult or dangerous for a closer, lesser team.

Marsac met them at the Marseille station and gave Odette a portable radio to pick up the BBC broadcast; the coded message for the operation was *"Les femmes sont parfois volages."* In Périgueux, they took the last two rooms at the Domino Hôtel and settled in for the night. At six in the morning there was a disturbance—pounding and rumbling down the hall.

The police were arresting someone.

Peter and Odette sat tight in their rooms, surrounded by incriminating radio equipment. The voices disappeared and the danger passed, although every close call brought them one step closer to exposing their cover.

After lunch they hailed a *vélo-taxi* to Bassillac and, arm in arm like newlyweds, strolled through the village and around the abutting airport. Being "a couple" was their cover, yet each held the other's arm as if it were true. Perhaps it *was* true. Were they a couple?

The field had only one strip, they saw, a large and small hangar, a block building—perhaps a barrack—and a control tower. On the side opposite the buildings, the open field ran some six hundred yards and was bordered by a line of trees and then a small river. In the northeast quadrant there was a bridge, beyond which the road splintered in four directions.

Odette and Jacques Latour would take the lower portion of the lighting pattern, Peter decided, close to the trees if trouble arose. Since he and Paul were boarding the craft, they would align themselves along the top of the L and clamber aboard when the plane stopped. If all went well they'd be in the air ninety seconds from touchdown.

As Peter and Odette moved about the field, they saw two or three men loitering but no aircraft activity. If the airfield was inactive, they wondered, who were these men?

They walked back to Périgueux and Odette radioed Arnaud that they were ready. Paul and Jacques met them later at the hotel and suggested that Odette join them for dinner at the Fénélon Hôtel, where Paul was staying. In the meantime, Peter would remain at the Domino and listen for the BBC broadcast. If nothing came, he'd join them; if it did, they'd be off.

That evening, Peter fiddled with the radio trying to get a clear signal, but also trying to keep the volume low. When he'd arranged the dial, he heard it: *"Les femmes sont parfois volages."* Slipping the radio into a cardboard box, he grabbed his rucksack and hurried into the freezing night. Minutes later he was at the Fénélon, and by eight they were off for the hike to Bassillac. They reached the airfield at a quarter to ten and found that it was blanketed by four feet of mist; if it didn't clear, the pilot would have to manage a blind landing.

With everyone huddling behind an embankment, Peter assigned flashlight positions and then slipped away to set handkerchiefs where he wanted each person—150 yards apart along the long bar of the L, with Jacques positioned 50 yards at the right-angle tip.

He returned and they ate some smoked ham Odette had packed and washed it down with Armagnac. Then something strange happened: the mist began to scatter even though there was no wind. Good for the pilot, bad for them. The control tower and barrack, fortunately, were quiet.

Around ten thirty they heard it—the faint droning of an aircraft—and everyone hustled into position. Odette huddled in her wool skirt as the chill seeped into her—the temperature was now in the low teens—and watched as Peter flashed the code.

The plane didn't countersignal. Moments later, it passed overhead and then vanished.

Peter came alongside and told her to stay low. Moving to the end of the light formation, he told Jacques, "Keep an eye on those buildings. I have a feeling we're in for an unwelcome interruption from that quarter."

Peter continued on to Paul's position and then ducked down. "There's someone coming!" he whispered.

Across the field, Odette watched as two men walked from the direction of the tower directly toward Peter and Paul. She didn't see flashlights, but if they continued in that line there'd be a party soon.

She held her breath as the men patrolled directly in front of Peter and Paul but apparently didn't see them. When they were out of sight, Peter came back. The plane would return, he said, and if there was any danger from the control tower or barrack, he'd wave his flashlight and she and Jacques were to run for the trees.

Suddenly Odette heard a distant buzz. The plane was returning. Peter moved back into position and everyone waited.

After a minute or so a flash—not from Peter—swept across the horizon.

It was a trap!

Odette found the source across the field: an Aldis lamp was flashing Morse to the tower. Lights suddenly flooded the grounds and someone shouted, "Put out those lights, you imbeciles! Wait for the plane to land and we'll grab them all."

Peter waved his flashlight and Odette turned to take off, but she could hear the plane returning. Just then Jacques ran up and Odette suggested that they escape in different directions. He tore off to the left and Odette started to run right when she heard barking. Gazing back, she saw a German Shepherd sniffing the area she had just left.

The chase was on.

She bolted for the woods and made it past the tree line when she heard the Shepherd closing, growling and thrashing through the underbrush.

It was the only way.

She plunged in.

CHAPTER 7

PEARL OF THE FRENCH ALPS

The icy L'Isle snatched her breath as she sank waist deep.

Wading through the current as fast as she could, Odette reached the opposite bank and quietly pulled herself out. Across the river she could hear a man calling after the Shepherd. "Frizi, Frizi!"

Shivering, she wrung as much water as she could from her skirt and shook it from her shoes. The imminent danger now was not the dog, or even the Germans, but freezing to death.

PETER AND PAUL STOPPED under some trees to catch their wind. They had been running for three miles.

"I wonder how Lise and Jacques got on," Peter said between gasps.

They were fine, Paul assured. They had a head start, after all.

They continued until they reached the edge of Périgueux and Peter pulled up. Germans were crawling all over the place, he said, and likely had set up a blockade. Better to head in at first light.

They moved away from the road and cleared an area in a thicket. Each taking a long pull on the Armagnac, they curled up next to each other and let sleep come.

Peter awoke as dawn seeped through a milky sky. It had been only four hours since he'd closed his eyes and frost was everywhere, including where Paul was supposed to be. He looked around and saw his companion pacing to keep warm. Paul had been doing so for two hours.

Straightening their hair and cleaning their shoes, they headed into town at half past seven and ordered coffee at a cafe. In theory, Odette and Jacques would be doing the same. Peter and Paul looked around, but no sight of the pair. When they finished a cup, they went to another cafe. Again, one cup and the bill. By nine o'clock they had hit every cafe in town; no sign of Odette or Jacques.

They returned to the Domino and found a table in the enclosed veranda overlooking the square. More coffee. Peter continued to scan the street and sidewalks, refusing to believe that Odette had been arrested. She was too smart.

But there was no one. This was the Marseille trip all over again. Only this time she had *soldiers* chasing her.

Peter's mouth went dry and he took a deep breath.

When he looked up, it was them! Odette and Jacques were coming toward the hotel, waving through the window as they entered. Peter smiled; Odette looked immaculate, polished shoes and all.

Before they could whisper what had happened, four Gestapo sat behind them. They spoke in German and Paul—who was from the Alsace region bordering Germany and Switzerland—listened intently. When the agents left, he repeated the gist of their conversation.

Cordons had been set up around the Bassillac airfield, one of them had said, at a radius of five kilometers. Before nightfall, the agent told his colleagues, he was quite certain they would capture the terrorists, or find them frozen to death.

PAUL AND JACQUES DECIDED to remain in Périgueux for two days, but Odette and Peter could not leave soon enough. By midmorning they were at the station, which was teeming with Germans and people who didn't look like travelers. Again they'd have to change trains in Toulouse and Marseille before arriving back in Cannes. The train arrived and they boarded, blending in.

At the Marseille station, the Gestapo were waiting.

When the train from Toulouse arrived, all passengers were removed and transported to headquarters for proof of identity and questioning, starting with their reason for the trip.

Peter and Odette were not on it.

Thinking that Marseille and Cannes might be hot, they disembarked at Toulouse and contacted Captain Maurice (code-named "Eugene") Pertschuk, head of the local circuit. A young Jew of only twenty-two, Eugene was so highly regarded among his Resistance colleagues that Peter thought he could have been a colonel. Eugene provided a safe house, and Peter and Odette awaited the arrival of a courier named Gisèle, who would know more about the situation in Marseille and Cannes.

The meeting could not have been more timely. Peter's flat at Quai St. Pierre had been raided by the Gestapo, Gisèle said when she arrived. How they had determined Peter's activity or acquired his address, no one knew. Police had also visited Antoine and again asked about Peter's whereabouts, but Gisèle had no further details. A Colonel Vautrin and his second in command at the Deuxième Bureau, she added, had fled across the Spanish frontier, and Peter's commando instructor in Antibes had been arrested, along with a number of agents in Marseille. Arnaud remained active, she said finally, but was in danger if he didn't change locations immediately. Prudence would have dictated that Peter and Odette remain at the safe house in Toulouse, but Arnaud—who was hiding out with a Corsican croupier named René Casale[18]—had to be warned, and the work had to continue, albeit in a new location.

---

18 Casale, who worked at the Cannes casino, hid numerous SOE agents during the war.

The following day Paul and Marsac arrived in Toulouse. Their headquarters in Marseille had been raided, they said, with more arrests. It was time, everyone agreed, to find a new base. Paul and Marsac suggested St. Jorioz, a small village five miles from the medieval town of Annecy in the Haute-Savoie, the French Alps district bordering Switzerland and Italy.

Peter said that he, Odette, and Arnaud would go if Arnaud's transmitting houses and living quarters were at least six miles from Paul's and Marsac's place, and if he and Odette were at least three miles away. Marsac said that Arnaud could set up in Faverges, ten miles from St. Jorioz, and that he and Lise could quarter in the Hôtel de la Poste; Marsac and his crew would rent a house nearby.

Peter thought the setup would work but insisted that no meetings should take place at the hotel; it simply brought too much risk. Paul and Marsac agreed. The task now was convincing Arnaud to leave Cannes. Peter sent word for the radioman to join them in Toulouse and in forty-eight hours, he was there.

Before Peter could explain the danger of remaining in Cannes, Arnaud beat him to the punch. The Gestapo had been to the Villa Diana, he said, asking for information about Monsieur Pierre Chauvet. "You should have caught that Lysander to England," he said. "If I'd been there, I'd have shot the bastards and made it."

Peter took Arnaud's bravado in stride and told him that they were moving to the Savoy Mountains.

"Good God! From the Maritime Alps to the Alps of Savoy. Always these bloody mountains! How I hate them!"

The complaint was reasonable, as Arnaud's job was difficult enough. To begin, he had to haul around a thirty-five-pound transceiver—transmitter and receiver in one—in a less than subtle suitcase. Added to that was Baker Street's B Mark II signal; it was so weak (less than twenty watts) that it needed seventy feet of aerial—a Gestapo lightning rod.

Peter assured they'd find a spot where Arnaud would have no issues. Besides, in Savoy Arnaud wouldn't have to worry about the German radio detector cars.

Arnaud begrudgingly consented, and Peter and Odette said good-bye to Eugene.

Sadly, they would never see him again. Eugene was later arrested and sent to the Buchenwald concentration camp, where he was executed on March 29, 1945.

RETURNING TO CANNES BY train was safe enough for Odette, but not for Peter, whose name was surely on every Gestapo list. They decided that Odette would return to Cannes and stay with Catherine, whose safe house had not been compromised, while Peter would entrain to Antibes and from there take a bus to la Bocca, a coastal village two miles west of Cannes. There he would stay with friends who owned a farm and Odette could bike back and forth twice a day, drawing little attention.

As always, Peter thought, Odette was indefatigable, optimistic, and elegant.

After ten days of wrapping up details, they left Cannes in mid-January and headed to the Alps. It was not without regret that Peter left the Côte d'Azur. They had been there for six months, but he had wanted to accomplish so much more; too many aborted landings, too much running around southern France, too little sabotage. Yet he counted his blessings: they began with Arnaud and ended with Lise. With them he could undertake anything. In short, he thought, the war had reduced itself to the deep-seated loyalty between a Frenchwoman, a Russo-Egyptian, and an Englishman. They were as one.

With the Gestapo searching for him, it seemed only a matter of time that lady luck would succumb and Peter would be arrested. Odette, once again, provided encouragement. As the train to Annecy rolled through the night, Peter glanced at her next to him. Her face was resolute and strong. There was no fear, no apprehension, no hesitation. Her expression was of a landlord traveling to collect rents. In a very real sense, Peter thought, he could feel her strength seeping into him. He closed his eyes and leaned into her.

Hours later he lifted his head from Odette's shoulder. *How long was I out?* Peter wondered. Odette simply smiled, thankful that he had rested peacefully. Peter looked at her and it dawned on him that she had remained awake, like a sentry protecting a wounded soldier.

She was indeed a rock.

WITH THE DAWN OF 1943, foreboding tremors rumbled along the Third Reich's fault line. On January 27 Americans launched the first Allied raid into Germany at Lower Saxony's Wilhelmshaven, the country's only deep-water port. Six days later German forces surrendered at Stalingrad, and days after that the Red Army recaptured Kursk.

Meanwhile, few places manifested peace more than Savoy. Annecy—"Pearl of the French Alps," as it is called—is indistinguishable from a Swiss village. Situated on the northwest border of Lake Annecy, an alpine loch with crystalline turquoise waters, it lies twenty-five miles south of Geneva and forty miles west of Western Europe's highest mountain, Mont Blanc. Through the middle of town meanders the Thiou River, its cafe-lined canals rivaled only by those of Venice and Amsterdam.

When Odette and Peter arrived they were welcomed by the snow-covered grandeur of Mont Veyrier, La Tournette, and the Dents de Lanfon. There was no war here, anyone could see; no, this was a place for bike rides and canal strolls, sailing and rowing—an alpine sanctuary to forget your troubles and disappear.

And so it was. For a time.

MARSAC'S WIFE, MICHELLE, MET Peter and Odette at the station and escorted them to the bus, which drove five miles south along the lake to St. Jorioz. It stopped directly in front of the Hôtel de la Poste, where Marsac joined them. The four had coffee and Marsac handed Peter and Odette new identity cards.

It was best to start under new names, he said, since Pierre Chauvet surely had quite a police file now.

Peter looked at his card and there, with his photo, was the name Pierre *Chambrun*. Odette would pose as his wife, they said, and they had a new identity for Arnaud as well: Monsieur Guy Lebouton—appropriate for the guy who turned the radio knobs, or buttons, as the word is understood in French.

Marsac ushered Peter and Odette into a private room and introduced them to the hotel owner, Jean Cottet. The proprietor seemed too young—late twenties or early thirties—to own a hotel, they thought, but Cottet's shrewd, watchful eyes revealed maturity beyond his years.

"These are my friends," Marsac said to Jean. "Although you might never think so, Monsieur Chambrun is a British Officer."

Peter glared at Marsac. In town less than thirty minutes and already his cover was exposed.

Jean asked how Marsac knew that he and the hotel were safe.

"Oh, we have ways and means of checking up on people's loyalties," Marsac replied, "and we know that you think as we do."

Jean introduced his wife, Simone, and the small group returned to the lounge, where Jacques Langlois and Jacques Latour had joined Michelle. Marsac pointed to a house through the window—the Tilleuls—and said that's where he and his wife were staying.

Peter asked who else was staying there and Marsac rattled off his group: Michelle and their son; his secretary, Suzanne; Roger Bardet; Jacques Riquet; the Lejeunes; and a French captain. Couriers, he added, including Jacques Latour, Jacques Langlois, and Louis le Belge, would be in and out. Paul Frager, he said, had also arrived and was staying with his wife in a house in Talloires across the lake.

The large group, coupled with Marsac's disclosure to Jean and Simone, meant that even the Hôtel de la Poste—seemingly a sanctuary in an alpine village of one hundred—no longer held airtight security. Odette's cover, which would ameliorate most inquiries, was that she had a medical condition which required her to reside at an altitude of at least twelve hundred feet. St. Jorioz, at fourteen hundred feet, was her prescription. If anyone questioned the veracity of the claim, she carried a forged medical certificate from a physician in Toulouse.

What none of the SPINDLE team knew, though, was that the influx of new residents was likely to draw the attention of the OVRA—Organizzazione per la Vigilanza e la Repressione dell'Antifascismo, the Italian Fascist secret police—which had a district office in Annecy. And since the Germans didn't trust the Italians, the Gestapo supplemented its staff with liaison officers.

Odette settled into the hotel and Peter and Riquet headed off on borrowed bikes to hunt for an alpine hideout where Arnaud could set up his radio. About twelve miles southeast of St. Jorioz they found their place: a forest ranger's house two thousand feet up the mountain near the village of Seythenex, just south of Faverges. It would provide Arnaud with an unobstructed line of communication and, equally important, unparalleled safety.

Riquet fetched Arnaud from his hideout in Montréjeau and within days Arnaud was in communication with London. When Peter caught up with him, the radioman said he was thrilled to be back with his team, and relieved that his new hideout would have no issues. London, however, was another matter.

While Peter and Odette were off finding a new headquarters, he said, he had assisted Eugene with transmissions since the Toulouse radio was inoperable. Not that it mattered, he grumbled, since London acted so slowly on his messages that many weren't worth sending.

"Another little trick they tried on me," he added, "was putting on a new pancake last Sunday who couldn't receive at more than twelve. Just imagine, Michel, twelve —— words a —— minute while I sit there sweating with the 'cars' closing in on me like hornets!"

Arnaud wasn't being melodramatic. The Germans had perfected radio direction finding and had mobile D/F units—*Funkpeilwagens*—which were disguised commercial vans with antennas mounted on the roof. If an SOE radio operator stayed on too long—perhaps as little as thirty minutes—or signaled too often from the same location, it was only a matter of time before the goons arrived. Almost all early operators were captured because of these D/F units, and of the 107 F Section wireless operators, 31 were executed or died in captivity.

Most operators in the field could process Morse and take down an incoming message at a rate of fifteen to seventeen words a minute. If the pancake in London could process only twelve—coupled with call sign recognition and repeats—an operator in the field might be on the wire for an hour; plenty long for the hornets to home in. If caught, the radioman was assured of death as the Vichy government had made it a capital crime to be found with a transmitter, but the Gestapo would utilize its various tortures to squeeze the lemon dry first.

Arnaud had little intention of being drawn and quartered because Baker Street was training a rookie. He handed Peter a message he was planning to send:

IF YOU PUT THAT ***** ON AGAIN NEXT SUNDAY I QUIT.

Peter chuckled and handed it back. "You can send that with my blessings, Arnaud."

Arnaud had good reason to make a stink, and everyone in Codes knew it. He was an outstanding radio operator, perhaps SOE's best, but when reception was bad, when D/F cars were closing in, every operator had to cut corners or cut bait.

WITH EVERYONE IN PLACE, the St. Jorioz group was soon running on all cylinders: Marsac was liaising with Paris, Riquet with Eugene in Toulouse, and Roger Bardet—Paul Frager's lieutenant and courier in the CARTE circuit—was busy with errands. Jacques Latour, Jacques Langlois, and other couriers, meanwhile, were traveling to Marseille, Lyon, Nice, Grenoble, Aix-en-Provence, Antibes, St. Raphaël, Clermont-Ferrand, and Cannes. During February 1943 alone, SPINDLE established forty new drop zones and, as shipments arrived, passed the weapons on to the French Resistance fighters known as the Maquis of Glières. With the newly acquired supplies, the Maquis sabotaged Nazi trains, railways, bridges, and barges, and raided German troops in hit-and-run guerilla warfare. SPINDLE and its net were finally wreaking havoc on the Germans.

About this time, Roger Bardet collected from Annecy station the bicycles Peter and Odette had sent from Cannes. The three met on a side street to conduct the transfer and Odette inspected him carefully: tall, thin, raven hair, and black hooded eyes that never came to rest. He was only about twenty-six, but had the facial lines of someone much older. He didn't smile, she noticed, and seemed to be worried, like a man hunted.

Perhaps for good reason. Bardet had been arrested on the Riviera in November, and again in Aix-en-Provence in January. On both occasions he escaped, he said, almost immediately.

"I don't like that man," Odette said to Peter after Roger left. "He's got shifty eyes."

"What d'you want me to do? Drop him in the lake?"

"Mark my words, Michel. That man's no good."

Paris

ONE DAY IN MID-MARCH Hugo Bleicher was shuffling through his files when he was summoned to the Hôtel Lutétia. Hugo thought it strange since he had met with Colonel Reile for two hours just that morning.

"I've got a complicated case here, Bleicher," the colonel said, "which you must take over." There was a Resistance leader coming to Paris the next day, Reile said, and the Abwehr had come up with a trap to arrest him. The Frenchman would be meeting a woman, he explained, who was an Abwehr confederate posing as an anti-Nazi activist. With limited information, Hugo thought the action was premature, possibly counterproductive. "We know next to nothing of this fellow and his organization, Herr Colonel! If we catch him, it is still uncertain that we can get him to talk. And if he does not talk, the arrest is a signal that will put all of his gang on their guard."

Reile stressed that they'd not get another shot at the big fish because he'd be in Paris only a few hours. Tracking the man in southern France, he said, was impossible since they didn't have the resources to do so.

Hugo conceded the point.

"Do everything necessary for the arrest," Reile said. The man would be arriving on the seven o'clock train from Marseille and would be meeting the woman at the Café Jacques off the Champs-Élysées the following afternoon at three.

The man's name was Marsac.

CHAPTER 8

GRAND DUKE

"Two umbrellas have been seen in Hyde Park."

"Red umbrellas or blue ones?"

"Two blue ones—with handles."

"Well, I hope they've rolled them up and taken a nice stroll down the Mall."

It had become almost routine for Maurice Buckmaster: eighteen-hour day, a few precious minutes with his wife, supper, bed, and then a call between midnight and dawn.

Two parachute drops had been made in the Jura mountains, the caller was saying, the precise spot where Peter, Odette, and Arnaud had just relocated. Buckmaster had asked if men or materials were dropped and the reply was two agents, with wireless sets and equipment.

THE SECOND WEEK OF March, Odette and Peter received disturbing news: the Germans were going after the CARTE circuit. The

Abwehr, it seemed, had finally decided to chase down the names it had found in Marsac's briefcase in November.[19]

They started at the top, arresting and imprisoning Carte's wife and two of his daughters. In Arles, seventeen agents were rounded up. Baker Street had no choice: it terminated the CARTE network and divided its work and agents between SPINDLE and a new circuit to be headed by Paul and headquartered in Auxerre.[20] Surprisingly, Baker Street gave Paul a territory so large—from Normandy to Nancy—that it was unmanageable.

Days later London contacted Arnaud. A Lysander was going to pick up Peter on March 14, they said, on a field in Tournus—some 125 miles from Annecy—for debriefing at headquarters. Another message stated that Baker Street would be sending a Lieutenant Francis Cammaerts, code-named "Roger," to take Peter's place during his absence.[21]

Peter read the messages and as he was burning them, Arnaud stewed.

"If they think they can send out raw recruits to give me orders, they've got another thing coming!"

"Don't be a chump, Arnaud."

"The —— cheek of sending somebody out to take your place! As though we needed somebody to teach us how to suck eggs! I refuse to send his messages, and that's flat! Besides, I know Lise feels just the same as I do."

Peter assured him that London would send only someone who

---

19 It was unclear why it took the Abwehr so long to take action on the materials found in the briefcase.

20 This circuit would be known as DONKEYMAN, although before official recognition by Baker Street, network members referred to it as the "JEAN MARIE" circuit.

21 Like Peter, the lieutenant was also a Cambridge graduate and had taught school before the war.

was qualified and fully briefed. It was tricky, to be sure: a green officer stepping into a labyrinth of intrigue with two headstrong subordinates under his command.

Peter made a decision. He told Arnaud that during his absence he was putting Odette in charge, and asked him to do what she said, and to watch out for her.

Arnaud agreed but grumbled that Peter wouldn't return.

Peter promised that he would and extended his hand. "Au revoir, *mon cher vieux*."

That evening Peter broke the news to Odette. He told her that she was in charge, that he would return, and that she must take care of herself and be vigilant until then.

It was somewhat inappropriate, she knew, Peter's putting her in charge. After all, she wasn't even a member of the army, much less an officer, and Arnaud was a lieutenant. But Peter trusted her, and that was enough.

The difficult part, she also knew, was not running SPINDLE; agents did their jobs with little instruction, and Arnaud could handle any sticky situation. The struggle now was the separation from Peter. Would London let him return or assign him elsewhere?

MARCH 14 CAME, BUT the Lysander didn't. Once again Peter was left in a field scratching his head. On the 23rd a courier brought a message from Arnaud stating that a plane would pick him up on a field ten miles from Compiègne.

Peter looked at the paper. Compiègne. The town on the other side of France, across the Control border, some fifty miles north of Paris. He spun into action and the following day a car arrived with Paul, Jacques Riquet, and Jacques Latour. They would have to figure it out on the fly.

ON THE 23RD, THE plane came with Cammaerts and another SOE agent, Georges Duboudin,[22] organizer of the SPRUCE circuit. Peter and Paul greeted the newcomers and exchanged places in the cockpit. At long last Peter was off for England.

Cammaerts's reception committee—Marsac, Riquet, Latour, and now four others—crammed into one car and drove straight to Paris. Not that it was conspicuous, eight men traveling in one car well after curfew. They did have a permit, sort of: a doctor's authorization for one of them to drive at any hour. If they were stopped, it would be precarious.

Fortunately, they encountered no checkpoints and Roger stayed with Marsac that evening and gave him two million francs and a pistol, compliments of Churchill's Secret Army. They had lunch the next day and then Marsac left, saying he had a meeting on the Champs-Élysées later that afternoon.

London

AT BAKER STREET, PETER and Paul updated Major Buckmaster on the reorganization of Carte's network. SPINDLE's work in St. Jorioz was going well, Peter said, and Odette was running everything in his absence. Paul added that his group was operating in Auxerre, with Roger Bardet liaising between St. Jorioz and Normandy, where Bardet's friend Jean Lucien Keiffer was based.

Buckmaster noted the personnel and locations, and Peter was called into the office of a young officer he didn't recognize.

"Can't you control your radio operator's language any better than this?" the man blurted, rustling a paper.

It was bound to happen, Peter knew: his prickly radio operator

---

22 Captured soon thereafter and sent to the concentration camp at Buchenwald, where he was executed.

was highly competent, but not quite the Cambridge or Oxford gentleman that many at Baker Street were accustomed to.

"I'm sorry about the language," Peter replied, "but I associate myself entirely with Arnaud in this matter and I challenge anyone to control him better."

The officer grumbled and Peter left without telling him that he had recommended the foul-mouthed operator for a promotion. Buckmaster agreed and the following day Arnaud received a wire:

FOR ARNAUD STOP CONGRATULATIONS ON YOUR CAP-
TAINCY

Paris

HUGO BLEICHER LISTENED INTENTLY as Colonel Reile and a man named Monsieur Gaston went over details of the Marsac investigation. Gaston himself was a mystery, Hugo thought. He spoke French like a Frenchman, German like a German, and English like an American. Not that it mattered; if Reile trusted him, so did Hugo, whoever he was.

Marsac's circuit originally had ten men in Paris, Gaston said, but almost all of them had been arrested in a recent raid. Marsac was coming to town, he explained, to replace these men and rebuild the operation. The key to the trap was a woman agent of Gaston's named Claire,[23] who would be coordinating the meeting. The rendezvous was set for 3 P.M., Gaston said, the time Claire was told to be at the cafe.

A FEW MINUTES BEFORE the hour they were ready: two agents at a table next to where Claire had taken a seat, two "lovers" at a table

---

23 Her real name was Helen James.

in the gallery, and Hugo and his assistant at a table behind the cafe's balustrade. A half hour later, the Russian came in with two companions: a tall thin man, about thirty—presumably Marsac—and a beautiful, elegant woman.

Bleicher's team watched discreetly as Claire and the Resistance trio discussed business. After about fifteen minutes, Claire retrieved a handkerchief to blow her nose.

Hugo pounced.

"Messieurs, mesdames!" he shouted as his team surrounded the table. "German police. You are arrested. Give us no trouble and come along without creating a disturbance."

Hugo deposited the captives in Fresnes Prison, and word was sent to headquarters. The beautiful woman with Marsac, it turned out, was his secretary, Lucienne Frommagot.

BACK AT MARSAC'S FLAT in the rue Vaugirard, Cammaerts was taking a nap, as he'd slept little the night before. Someone opened the blinds, and Roger flinched as he awoke. It was Lejeune.

"Sorry to startle you, Roger," he said. "I have the key to Marsac's apartment. I've some very bad news. Marsac has been arrested. Just a couple of hours ago."

Roger sat up and began lacing his shoes. "I'd better disappear."

Lejeune said he had a safe house at the Quai Voltaire where Roger could stay for the night, and then he'd better leave Paris. "Not one of us is safe here anymore if they make Marsac talk."

Roger spent the night at the Voltaire and then bolted for Annecy. He checked in at the Hôtel de la Plage and then went to St. Jorioz to meet with Odette and Arnaud, who introduced Roger Bardet. Like Odette, Cammaerts didn't trust the young man and determined to have nothing to do with him.

The situation was delicate. On the one hand, Baker Street had sent Cammaerts to run the circuit in Peter's absence. On the other, the lieutenant knew nothing about the local situation, the dangers that lurked, or whom he could trust. In addition, it seemed advisable to keep him away from Bardet.

When the shady courier left, Odette and Arnaud discussed the options and decided that since the area was hot and Cammaerts had barely gotten the lay of the land, he should lie low for the time being. They sent him to a safe house in Cannes, where he was to remain until the smoke cleared.

Only Odette and Arnaud knew the address.

Paris

THAT SAME EVENING, COLONEL Reile called his favorite spy-catcher. "Bleicher," he said, "we must get Marsac to talk quickly. Take over the whole Marsac affair and do it yourself under the code name 'Grand Duke.' You must show us now what you can do."

Over the next three days Bleicher spent countless hours in Marsac's cell, but the Frenchman refused to talk. Although he had not been trained as an interrogator, Hugo was a master. He changed tactics and patiently worked to win Marsac's confidence. The Nazis and the German people were wholly distinct, he told Marsac, and "the Hitler system" was "far from bringing happy conditions."

Hugo's distancing himself from Hitler was easy to follow. Nazis were a distinct minority in Germany—between 6 percent and 9 percent of the population—a fact noted in SOE training and one which Marsac likely would have known.

Marsac lowered his guard. "I cannot believe the Germans are happy under such a debased regime. That system will not appeal to you either, I imagine."

Hugo confirmed that it didn't and continued the pleasant dialogue over several conversations. With Colonel Reile breathing down his neck, however, Hugo had to turn up the heat. He told Marsac that while he had nothing to do with the notorious and hated Gestapo, he'd have no alternative other than to turn Marsac over to them if he and Marsac could not come to "an understanding."

Hugo let the threat—which was true—sink in for a day.

At their next meeting, Marsac broke. "Is it possible to settle my case between us," he asked, "without bringing in the Gestapo?"

"Yes, certainly," Hugo replied. "It depends on whether we come to some agreement. At the moment I am in sole charge of your case, and you will yourself have noticed that I do not get on well with the Gestapo."

Marsac swung for the fence, hoping for freedom. In room 13 of the Hôtel Bergerac, he told Bleicher, was a suitcase containing one million francs—half the money Marsac had just received from Cammaerts—and four crystals for transmitters. The crystals Hugo could toss in the Seine, he said, but the money was Bleicher's to keep. Hugo had the key amongst Marsac's belongings, he said, and need only tell the concierge that he had been sent by Monsieur Marsac to retrieve the case.

Hugo stifled his astonishment. This was too good to be true. He was at the hotel within a half hour and everything was just as Marsac had said. The suitcase—apparently belonging to Marsac's secretary—was full of lingerie, but underneath rested ten 100,000-franc notes and the crystals. Hugo gave the booty to Colonel Reile, who congratulated him and urged Hugo to obtain as much information as possible before Marsac's colleagues began to inquire about him.

The next morning Hugo returned to Fresnes, acknowledged having picked up the money, and asked Marsac what he wanted in return.

The chance to escape, he said.

"My dear Marsac, it is really not so simple as you imagine to escape from Fresnes." Hugo reminded him of the sentry who accompanied him to the cell, and of the ten locked doors that had to be passed before reaching the exit.

Surely they could leave the prison together, Marsac countered, on the pretext of an interrogation at Abwehr headquarters.

Hugo knew better. "If you get out of this prison," he said, "you will do a quick vanishing act, whereas I will be hanged by the Gestapo from the nearest gallows."

Bleicher was right, Marsac knew, but before he could offer a solution, Hugo made it himself: "The precondition for your escape is that I shall vanish with you—and to England. I would not be safe in France anymore."

Marsac acknowledged that he could get Bleicher to London, and for the next day or so Hugo continued to develop trust. On occasion, Marsac would mention something about his net, and one day Hugo heard the name Paul [Henri Frager's alias], whom he mistakenly believed to be the leader. Marsac disclosed in passing that Paul had been picked up from an airfield near Paris and was now in London. This meant that London controlled the circuit, Hugo surmised, and that it was being run by a British general.

Gradually, Hugo upped the ante. "Listen Monsieur Marsac, I must convince my Chief that I have won you over and that you are prepared to work for us."

Marsac agreed. "I will work for you for a few weeks, or seem to. Then you give me a job to do for you in the South of France and I don't come back."

"Yes, something of that sort."

Hugo pressed for a tangible asset to show his boss, like recovery of a wireless transmitter, but Marsac said they were all in southern France.

Colonel Reile was indeed pushing, and Hugo tried a new tack the next morning.

"Look, Marsac, with the best will in the world I cannot get you out of Fresnes just like that. You have no means of knowing how much I risk from the Gestapo. They have been watching every step I take for some time past. I have to operate cautiously."

There was only one way to pull it off, he said. "I must have one of your men in here to discuss the next move with us both. We can do that on the pretext of confronting you with a witness."

It was a bold move and Hugo knew that if it failed, his work would be in vain; Marsac's agents would soon go to ground and the Frenchman's usefulness would vanish.

Marsac asked for writing paper and a pen and wrote out two

short letters: one to his wife and one to the circuit lieutenant, Roger Bardet. He had been in Fresnes ten days, Marsac told them in the letters, but had become friends with the interrogating officer, who had agreed to help him escape. Bardet would need to visit him in Fresnes, he explained, to help orchestrate the plot.

Handing them to Hugo, he said, "You are to be 'Colonel Henri,' Monsieur Jean. It is the name of my friend in Düsseldorf who is now a colonel in the German air force. You must play his role. We must from the very start be ready to dispel any doubts that they may have in London about my intentions."

Bleicher was amused; promoted by his own prisoner.

Annecy

ODETTE TOOK HIM IN with a glance: fortyish, six feet or so, heavy-set, large brown eyes magnified by thick glasses. With a granite jaw and Gibraltar head, he looked incredibly strong. Were it not for the ill-fitting suit, the man was a dead ringer for a wrestling coach.

The Annecy-to-St.-Jorioz morning bus stopped, and Odette lingered to allow the man to get off first. There was something about him she didn't like. He lumbered out with a heavy gait and plodding, elephant-like steps. He looked around as visitors do and then stopped someone for directions. Going the same way, Odette walked close enough to hear the request: he was looking for a house called Les Tilleuls—the Limes.

She paid no further attention and continued on to the Hôtel de la Poste.

At lunchtime Odette headed downstairs to the dining room and was perusing the menu when Lejeune hurried over.

"Lise, there is a man here who wishes to speak to you."

Odette glared at him for breaking security. "You know Raoul's orders—that you should never come and speak to me here."

"Yes, I know. But this is urgent and—"

Odette cut him off and told him to leave. On his way out Lejeune stopped by the entrance and spoke with a patron who had just entered. It was the man from the bus, the plodder. He responded to the courier's remarks with a wintry smile, glanced hard at Odette, and found a seat and called the waiter. A moment later he was at Odette's table.

"Mademoiselle Lise?"

"I am she."

"May I be permitted to take my coffee with you, Mademoiselle? I would not intrude if I had not things of importance to say."

Flawless French, slight Belgian accent. A Frenchman living in Brussels, perhaps.

"You will forgive me, Monsieur. I do not know your name."

"My name is Henri and I am an officer of the German Army."

CHAPTER 9

LIFELESS

Odette read it quickly. It was indeed from Marsac—she recognized the handwriting—and stated that he was writing to Roger from Fresnes Prison, and that he had not been ill-treated. He stated that Colonel Henri was a friend who could be trusted, that they had prepared a plan for Marsac's escape, and that Roger was to provide Henri with a radio.

As she studied the letter, one of Marsac's lines struck her as forced: *"Je benerais le jour de mon arrestation si mes projets se realise."*— "I would bless the day of my arrest if my projects are realized."

When does anyone bless the day of their arrest? And "my projects"? What projects were those? The letter did explain how Colonel Henri found her: Roger Bardet. Henri apparently had met with him at the Limes before coming over for lunch.

Odette's stomach churned but she said nothing. She handed the letter back.

"It was I who arrested Marsac," Colonel Henri said, "in order to save him from arrest by the Gestapo and in order that I might make a certain proposal to this brave and patriotic Frenchman." That proposal was for Henri and Marsac to escape to England in a plane supplied by London, whereby Henri would offer to assist the British in ending the war. The colonel added that Marsac was on board, but that in prison he didn't have the ability to carry it out; they needed someone in the network who was at liberty.

Like Lise.

"Tell me, Mademoiselle, do you care for music?"

Odette said she did.

Hugo nodded and returned to business. "Germany is split," he said. "On the one side stands Adolf Hitler and his satellites, on the other stands the High Command of the German Army—and between the two is a vast and ever-widening gulf. It was not the High Command who made war, Mademoiselle, but Adolf Hitler. Germany's ultimate doom under Hitler is sure."

Odette mused the comments. They were valid, of course, but Colonel Henri hadn't traveled from Paris to discuss politics.

"What do you want of me, Monsieur?"

"I want you to give me a transmitting set and code whereby I can get into direct touch with the British War Office."

This explained why Marsac had told Roger to get a radio: either Colonel Henri was sincere in his suggestion of defection, or he was playing her to capture a bishop before arresting a rook.

She didn't have a set to give him, she said, but was prepared to communicate with London on his behalf, with certain conditions.

Hugo smirked. "Does it not strike you as a little odd that you, a British agent in France, should seek to impose conditions on a German officer—who has the powers of arrest?"

"Come, Monsieur, it is unworthy of the great issues at stake that you should remind me that I am at your mercy. We are both adults." She told him that she had no idea if Marsac penned his note under duress, and that his credibility could be confirmed only after Bardet spoke with Marsac at Fresnes.

"I suppose I couldn't induce you to come to Paris yourself to see Marsac. Next week they are giving Mozart's *Magic Flute*."

Odette declined, citing her medical condition and need to remain at high altitude. Hugo said he understood and agreed to discuss the matter further after Bardet's meeting.

Hugo left and Odette met with Arnaud the following day. She

told him about Colonel Henri, the Bardet letter, and the escape plan. The letter indicated that Henri was to receive a wireless set in Paris, she said, but that the operator would not be captured.

Arnaud smelled a rat.

THE FOLLOWING MORNING, APRIL 10, Odette met with Bardet and Riquet in Annecy and told them that it was unlikely that London would exfiltrate or communicate with Colonel Henri, and that they shouldn't go to Paris. Roger insisted, however, saying that they must spring Marsac. He was quite confident, he said, that he could do so with Henri's assistance. London notwithstanding, he would tell Henri that something was possible.

Livid, Odette met with Arnaud in St. Jorioz that afternoon and told him that Bardet was moving forward with Henri's rendezvous in Paris. Not only that, but it was Bardet who had told Henri where she was staying, and what she looked like. She had been right about Shifty Eyes all along.

Arnaud bristled. Marching outside, he jumped on his bike and tore off for Annecy.

Odette cycled after him, chasing the burning fuse. *Arnaud, no! Don't do it!*

Arnaud remained steadfast.

He was going to shoot the bloody traitor.

Fresnes Prison, Paris

THE CELL DOOR OPENED and Marsac beamed. He gave Hugo a hug and said, "Jean, my dear Jean. Now I know you are my friend. How can I ever thank you enough?"

Bleicher played along, saying nothing.

Turning to Bardet, Marsac said, "Colonel Henri is my good friend. Roger you must do exactly what he says, even if at times you do not understand why."

With their full confidence, "Colonel Henri" conjured up a phony escape plan. Roger would return to St. Jorioz, he said, and have Arnaud ask London for a plane. Meanwhile, Henri would sneak Marsac out of prison disguised as his agent. Marsac, for his part, would guarantee that Henri would not be mistreated in London.

Marsac and Roger agreed.

Sensing Marsac's weakness, Bleicher squeezed and asked for names. If Marsac would give him a list of agents in his organization, he said, he'd give it to a friend who would keep it as surety so that that nothing happened to Hugo in London. If Hugo was arrested, for example, Marsac's associates would in turn be arrested. If all went well in London, he said, he'd pass an agreed-upon code word through the BBC to his friend.

The suggestion was preposterous and called into question Hugo's sincerity. If he was arrested in London, his German colleagues would still have Roger Bardet, and a one-for-one surety should have been sufficient. Marsac objected, saying he'd rather die in a concentration camp than betray his associates.

"Do you really believe, Marsac, that your people can keep out of our clutches for long? If we have succeeded in getting you, it will be easy to catch the smaller fry, one by one." Most of them were already under observation by the SD, Hugo said, and some were already working both sides. "Is it not much better then if I keep control of this business?"

Hugo's counter was thin, almost laughable, but the Frenchman appeared moved. Hugo glanced at Roger, who seemed to consent. After a few moments, Marsac agreed and wrote out some twenty addresses of groups in Bordeaux, Marseille, Strasbourg, Nancy, and elsewhere.

Hugo was shocked—quarry marching into the cage.

St. Jorioz

BARDET RETURNED TO ST. JORIOZ the following day and told Odette that he had seen Marsac and that he was well. Roger assured her that

Henri was trustworthy, and said that they had come up with a plan: if London would provide a Hudson, Henri would release Marsac and his assistant and they, along with Lise, could return to England together. Henri would meet with Buckmaster and spearhead peace talks. If the British War Cabinet came to a firm resolution, Henri would even return to Germany to conduct the bidding.

Odette didn't buy it for a minute. Marsac was the tail-wagging puppy who'd nosed his way into the dogcatcher's net without the slightest discernment. And since when did colonels conduct business for their country? On top of that, she didn't trust Shifty Eyes, the rat who was lucky to be alive; for five miles she had badgered Arnaud not to kill Roger and not until they reached Annecy did he relent.

Yet the game was on and it was her move. She told Roger to go back to Paris and tell Henri that she was trying to arrange a bomber. The moon period ended April 18, she said, and she'd work toward that date. She'd let him know the chosen field later.

Roger left and Odette had Arnaud cable London about the cunning colonel.

London

BEFORE PETER LEFT THE War Office he was given devastating news: his brother, an RAF fighter pilot, had been dead for seven months, shot down the day Peter entered Cannes.

Peter visited his parents and did his best to comfort his heartbroken mother, who was almost unrecognizable. In addition to learning of one son's death, she had not heard from her third son—who had been fighting with the Italian Partisans—for a year.

Peter said good-bye, knowing it might be his last.

The fate of his two brothers, along with his mother's state, left Peter numb. There was a dullness, he noticed, a sadness which had transformed him into a sort of automaton. He was like a locust, he thought, flying with the swarm but whose insides had been eaten away; at any moment the shell would collapse and he'd drop from the sky without warning. Given the need for acute thinking and split-second judgments when he returned to France, he knew he'd have to snap out of it.

He returned to the office and Buckmaster informed him that Marsac had been arrested, and that Lise had just sent a telegram.

> FROM LISE STOP ABWEHR OFFICER BY NAME HENRI CONTACTED ME ST JORIOZ SUGGESTED IF YOU PRO-VIDED HUDSON HE WILL RELEASE MARSAC AND SU-ZANNE RETURNING WITH ME AND THEN DISCUSS MEANS OF ENDING WAR STOP

The major asked what Peter thought.

"I think it means Marsac gave Lise's address and that Henri is hoping to earn a Ritterkreuz[24] by capturing a bomber," he replied, "and that the whole thing is so dangerous it should not be touched with a barge pole. I think Lise should be told to buzz off to the other side of the lake and Arnaud to leave Faverges and stay up at Les Tissots beside his set."

Buckmaster agreed and told Peter that there was no need for him to return. Lise and Arnaud could be picked up by Lysander, he said, and they could start another circuit elsewhere, or Peter could have a home posting.

Peter would have none of it. "I want to go back," he said, "and now that the Glières men have been armed I should like to join them and end the war with a gun in my hands."

Buckmaster said he'd let Peter choose his lot and that he could have a plane drop him during the April moon.

St. Jorioz

THE NEXT EVENING ARNAUD gave Odette London's reply:

---

24 The Knight's Cross of the Iron Cross, Germany's highest military decoration.

HENRI HIGHLY DANGEROUS STOP YOU ARE TO HIDE
ACROSS LAKE AND CUT CONTACTS WITH ALL SAVE
ARNAUD WHO MUST QUIT FAVERGES AND LIVE BE-
SIDE HIS MOUNTAIN SET STOP FIX DROPPING GROUND
YOUR OWN CHOICE FOR MICHEL WHO WILL LAND
ANYWHERE SOONEST.

She pondered the priority: move across the lake first, or find
Peter's drop zone? Since London wanted to drop Peter as soon as
possible, and she figured Colonel Henri wouldn't return until April
18, she decided to find a new hotel first and then go with Arnaud
in search of the landing site; she could move, she assumed, after
Peter's arrival.

In the morning she went across the lake to Talloires and found
a small hotel, the Glaieulles, suitable for their next hideout. That
afternoon she and Arnaud looked on the map for a suitable drop
zone. Since security was now an issue, it was critical that the area
be remote. They found the perfect spot: Mont Semnoz. About three
miles southwest of St. Jorioz, the mountain rose some six thousand
feet, providing a splendid view of Lake Annecy. But did the apex
provide sufficient area for a night drop?

They rode their bikes to the mountain and then climbed—
sometimes through three feet of snow—until they reached the top.
The summit was shaped like a hog's back and was free of trees, they
saw, but the only flat area was extremely small.

"Well, will it do?" Odette asked.

Arnaud began pacing, counting his steps in each direction. The
flat portion was only one hundred yards by eighty. The buffer in
three directions was manageable, but if Peter drifted west, he'd
tumble down a sheer cliff.

It would do, Arnaud finally said, provided that the navigator
was dead on. "But it's a hell of a place to jump."

They gathered wood for a bonfire and set it in a nearby shed.
When they arrived back in town, Odette scribbled a message for
Arnaud to send to London with the landing coordinates and then

went to the Limes to see if Bardet was back. He was, and Roger asked if London had approved the bomber for Henri. Odette paused and then said, oh yes, she was trying to arrange it for the 18th. Roger asked if there was news about Peter and she told him that it was unlikely he'd return to France.

"Oh. One more thing, Lise. That British officer, Roger, who was in the Hôtel de la Plage, he's suddenly vanished."

Cammaerts. "I know. I sent him away."

Bardet's hooded eyes flickered. "Where's he gone to?"

"To an address of some friends. Why this sudden interest?"

"I only wondered where he had gone to, that's all."

London

THE MORNING OF APRIL 15 Buckmaster called Peter into his office. Arnaud had sent coordinates of the drop zone, he said. They retrieved a Michelin map and Peter paused when he saw where he would be landing: atop a mountain of more than 5,500 feet.

"Struth!" He rubbed a hand over his face. "They certainly took you at your word when you said I'd land anywhere."

A parachute drop was simpler than being tossed in a canoe eight hundred yards off the coast of Cannes, but this was different. His submarine insertion into France on New Year's Day was controllable; if he capsized he could always swim. Throwing yourself out of a plane at two hundred miles an hour into sheer darkness to hit the head of a pin—that was a mild form of suicide.

Buckmaster laughed, looking again at the summit. "An Alp all to yourself."

Peter would fly out that night, they decided, since the moon had only three days remaining.

During preflight Peter met with the Halifax navigator, Colonel Philippe Livry-Level. "This mountaintop," Level said, tapping the map, "there's nothing to it. I've dropped fifty-seven customers already, and if you go out when I give you the green light, I'll drop you on a six-penny bit."

Peter accepted the boast with a grain of salt. A night drop in the Jura—at altitude and with likely swirling winds—he'd be happy to hit the mountain.

The apex of Mont Semnoz, Peter's landing spot. ADRIEN BAUD (@ADRIENBAUDPHOTO)

At 7:15 P.M. Odette, Arnaud, and Jean Cottet huddled around three receivers, hoping to hear the coded message on the BBC broadcast. As the BBC news started, the Germans began their counterinterference, jamming the waves with ongoing notes: *aou . . . eou . . . aou . . . eou.* At half past seven Odette heard it: *"Le scarabée d'or fait sa toilette de printemps."*—"The golden beetle makes its spring toilet."

Peter was coming.

She bundled up and went to collect Arnaud. She found him, along with Jean and Simone, in the bar.

"Why aren't you ready?" she asked Arnaud.

"Ready for what?"

"He's coming! Hurry up!"

"What d'you mean, he's coming?"

"Didn't you hear the message?"

Arnaud and Jean looked at her blankly. If there was a message, Arnaud said, he'd have heard it.

Odette swore she'd heard it, twice. If they weren't going, she said, she'd go alone.

Arnaud relented, Jean offered to drive, and Simone said she

wanted to go, too. Jean fired up his charcoal-burning V-8 and at half past eight, bundled in boots and sweaters, they left. Before they reached the halfway point, the Ford petered out; the charcoal-gas conversion diminished power by 30 percent and the old car could proceed no farther. Odette and Arnaud would have to walk from there.

Jean and Simone decided to tag along, and Jean led them to a path he said would go to the top. At nine o'clock they began the steep climb, but there was a surprise: the moon was on the opposite side of the mountain and they lost sight of the snow-covered path. Worse, Jean admitted he didn't have a clue which way to go.

Odette looked around and spotted a telephone pole. "Look! I remember those poles go straight up the side of the mountain and end up on the top. Why there's even one by the very spot we chose for him to land on. Don't you remember, Arnaud?"

Arnaud said he remembered one at the top, but not the sequence going up. Odette promised she knew what she was doing and took the lead. Over and around cliffs and boulders they went, higher and higher, panting and struggling as they gained altitude. At half past one she saw the snowclad hog's back shimmering in the moonlight some nine hundred yards ahead.

"Look, Arnaud! Look!"

She checked her watch; Peter could arrive at any minute and without the bonfire, the plane would pass.

"Oh, God," she prayed, "let me get there before the plane!"

She encouraged everyone to step up the pace but remembered what Peter had told her some time before about cross-country treks on weary legs: "When you have ten paces to make and nine are done, only then can you say that you are halfway."

She urged the others on and they raced to the top, dashing back and forth to the shed to arrange the wood. As Arnaud doused it with petrol, Odette sank into the snow, exhausted. Arnaud set it ablaze and then turned toward the northern sky.

"Here it comes!"

All eyes turned heavenward and they watched as the Halifax cut diagonally across the drop zone. Nothing fell from the plane as it flew directly overhead and made a slow turn east.

"Oh, God!" Odette said. "I can't bear it. After all this sweat, they're taking him home again."

PETER GLANCED INTO THE nose of the Halifax and saw navigator Level prone, peering intently through the glass.

"Bonfire ahead," Level shouted. "Action stations!"

The plane banked for a direct run over the hog's back and the dispatcher patted Peter's shoulder and connected his tether to the static line. The warning light came on and Peter gazed into the hole: snow-capped mountains drifted by like mounds of fresh cotton. The plane decelerated as the flaps dropped and Peter felt the familiar butterflies raging in his stomach. Unlike all of his prior jumps, however, this one required split-second timing. If he paused after the go signal, he'd land on the wrong alp. Or tumble down a sheer cliff.

He gritted his teeth and waited.

The light finally turned green and he was out. A moment later his parachute opened and he watched as five more chutes—supply crates—opened behind him.

He enjoyed the majestic view of the Alps and Lake Annecy for several seconds and then cast his gaze below, squirming in his harness.

Bloody navigator.

I'll drop you on a six-penny bit . . .

Peter was dropping on a six-penny bit, all right—*directly into* the raging bonfire!

He yanked the forward set of cords, releasing air, and drifted backward. Below he could see two figures, the larger one—presumably Arnaud—running after a supply chute.

As he continued to drift, he saw that he was now descending directly over the second figure—apparently Odette—who was searching the sky. Just then a rising current caught his canopy and he was suddenly hovering only feet above her.

"Hallo, Lise. If you'll take a step backwards, I shan't land on your head."

Odette cried out and stepped back, opening her arms to catch him.

Peter floated into her embrace and Odette squeezed him tightly. "Pierre, Pierre," she whispered sweetly in his ear. It was in a tone that told Peter everything a man could ever wish to hear.

Arnaud came running, yelling, "Sacré Michel!" He hugged Peter as a long-lost brother and Peter beamed, an arm around each of his loved ones.

Jean and Simone arrived moments later, and Arnaud and Jean gathered up the five supply cases. Storing them in a nearby deserted hotel, they retrieved the parachutes and flung them into the fire. As they walked, Odette kept her arm in Peter's and recounted what he had missed over the last three weeks. She told him that the betrayal had come from Roger Bardet—the man she'd warned him about—and not Marsac. The fact that Bardet had now vanished was proof enough.

They returned to the abandoned inn and Arnaud tore into the crates like a child at Christmas: dynamite, a Sten gun camouflaged as a log, two Colt automatics, a Belgian pistol, clips, radio parts, crystals, batteries, two suits, a mackintosh, two pairs of shoes, and two pairs of sheepskin gloves. Someone had to stay with the supplies overnight, they decided, and Arnaud was happy to oblige.

It was now 4 A.M. and Peter, Odette, Jean, and Simone began their descent. Seeing the steep drops—sometimes vertical—Peter was amazed that they had made it up. In daylight, he reckoned, the descent would have been done with ropes.

They had Peter's flashlight.

Odette held Peter's hand and did her best to follow their path. Rock, ice, and darkness, though, made tracking footprints impossible. They pressed on, one boulder at a time.

Stepping gingerly, Odette made her way along a sheer cliff.

It happened without a sound.

Her foot hit a patch of ice and she fell toward the precipice, her weight ripping her hand from Peter's. He watched in horror as she dropped, her body bouncing off protruding rock like a rag doll.

There was a sickening thud thirty feet below.

Everyone scrambled down, sliding and skidding. Jean arrived first and was aghast; Odette's body was sprawled across a fallen tree, lifeless. He cradled her head and saw that she was unconscious. Peter rushed up seconds later and shined his light on her face. She was deathly grey. Grabbing a handful of snow, he rubbed it on her face and neck.

Nothing.

He slapped her cheeks. Nothing.

"Lise, Lise, for God's sake say something!"

He rubbed more snow on her forehead.

There was no response.

CHAPTER 10

THE BEAM

Peter feared the worst. It was a horrendous fall and it appeared that Odette had broken her back. She seemed to be breathing but was unresponsive.

Jean fished out his flask and began pouring drops into her mouth. Odette choked and opened her eyes. "What are we waiting for?"

At once she was on her feet and ready to move. Contrary to her demeanor, however, Odette was not well: she had a concussion and a shattered vertebra in the middle of her spine. She told no one of her pain, though, and the party moved out.

They arrived at the hotel at eight o'clock, and Odette washed and changed. A cup of coffee and she was out again to catch the bus to Annecy. There, she told a Maquis of Glières courier about the supply drop, and that Arnaud was watching everything until they arrived. When she returned to St. Jorioz, she and Peter had lunch and then rowed across the lake to inform Paul Frager's wife of the latest events, and to pay for the rooms at the Glaieulles. Peter suggested they move that evening, but Odette didn't think it was necessary. They had until the 18th, she said, before Colonel Henri would arrive.

"You should have gone before, Lise."

She tried to, she said, but there was a lot going on. Couriers kept coming in asking for money and assignments and she didn't think she could leave just yet.

"I still think you should have gone. My God, you're an obstinate woman."

"I know. But we're all set to go tomorrow. I've arranged for a boat to take us across the lake and I've even found a new hideout for Arnaud."

After lunch they cycled to Faverges to meet with Arnaud, who had messages for Peter, Odette, Tom Morel (leader of the local Maquis), and two others. It was late by the time they made it back to the hotel, and Odette told Peter more about the mysterious Colonel Henri over dinner. They'd move, they agreed, the next day. Going on forty-eight hours without sleep, they decided to turn in and shuffled up the stairs.

IN THE DISTANCE, A faint metallic echo.

Jean and Simone were in the hotel's office updating their books when about eleven o'clock a small man in a large hat rushed in. He was pale and agitated. His name was Louis le Belge, he said, and he came on behalf of Roger and Paul and had an urgent message for Lise.

Car doors.

The Cottets hustled up to Odette's room and informed her that le Belge was downstairs asking for her.

Odette put on her dressing gown and headed down.

Steps in general are dangerous for operatives because they are located at entrances and exits that can be watched, and because they provide no cover. Stairs are particularly bad because every corner is blind and one could stumble into an ambush.

Like the one at the turn to the lobby.

He was waiting at the foot of the steps.

Odette surveyed the reception party: the tall blue-eyed blond—

clearly Gestapo—who seemed a bit nervous and jumpy; the short one in the scarf with his hat pulled so low she couldn't see his face; and the Italian secret policemen milling behind them. She wondered if the one in the hat was le Belge.

Henri offered his hand but she didn't take it; it was clear this was an arrest.

"I think a lot of you," he said.

"I don't care what you think."

"You have done a very good job of work, and you almost won the game. It is not your fault that you lost," Henri said, explaining in vague references that her people were bad.

Odette thought for a moment and pieced it together.

Bardet.

She had met with Riquet and Shifty Eyes on the 12th and told them that Baker Street was unlikely to approve exfiltration. They had been mad, she remembered, and chastised the organization and the British government. They were going to tell Henri that something *was* possible, they had said, regardless.

He was the Judas.

"Don't try to warn Michel by shouting, Lise," Henri said. "If you do, he's sure to jump out of the window and I think I should tell you that the hotel is surrounded by Alpini troops who have orders to shoot. You've played the game well, Lise. But now it's over, so kindly lead us to Michel's room."

It was checkmate. If she screamed and Peter made a run on the roof, they'd shoot. No, she'd lead the pride to the prey and they'd be arrested together like professionals. Still. She remained where she was until she felt the thing jabbing her spine.

They marched up the stairs and someone opened Peter's door and turned on the light.

"There is the Gestapo," Odette announced as the group entered.

Henri, the tall blond, and an Italian secret police officer encircled Peter's bed.

"What's your name?" asked the Gestapo.

"Chambrun."

As the arrest team huddled around Peter, Odette slithered over to the foot of the bed where Peter's jacket was lying. In a flash she slipped her hand in and out of his pocket and into her sleeve.

"Chambrun!" the German snapped, "or perhaps Chauvet. They both mean Captain Peter Churchill, saboteur and filthy spy. Put up your hands!"

Before Peter could comply, two automatics were in his face. He was ordered to dress while two of the agents searched for contraband. Odette was sent to her room to change and she transferred Peter's chattel to inside her dress. When she returned to Peter's room, he was in handcuffs. Grabbing another of his coats, she draped it over the cuffs and smiled to him, silently conveying a hundred thoughts and prayers.

"Do you want to go with the Germans or Italians?" Henri asked him.

Rifle or gallows, what difference did it make? None, but the expected Gestapo torture beforehand made the choice easy. Italian, Peter said.

Outside it was as Henri described: the hotel was surrounded by soldiers. Two cars awaited and Odette and Peter were placed in the back of one with a chauffeur. They were separated by the Gestapo agent and the Italian secret police officer, sitting in front, turned around to face them, gun in hand. Thankfully, Henri—gentleman that he was—didn't handcuff Odette. As the car took off she figured this was as good a place as any. Pretending to adjust one of her garters, she slipped her hand inside her dress and, with a conjuror's sleight, retrieved Peter's wallet and wedged it under the seat. Neither Peter nor the German or Italian noticed.

Minutes later they arrived at the Alpini barrack in Annecy, and Odette and Peter stood together as Bleicher conversed with the Italian officer.

"Take good care of these two," Henri told him, "we can't afford to lose them."

Odette reached for Peter's hand, knowing this might be the last, and squeezed it tightly, pouring her strength into him.

Guards separated them and Odette was taken to an office with a camp bed.

Hell of a day. She was still without sleep, more than a day without food, and had a busted back. And yet there were a few bright spots. Colonel Henri had not captured Arnaud, after all, or Cammaerts, who was safe in Cannes. In addition, she and Peter had just distributed to the Maquis a Sten gun, pistols, ammunition, crystals, radio parts, batteries, two hundred blank identity cards, and a half million francs. More than a nuisance to the Germans.

She'd been lucky, really. The brothel in Marseille, Control on the return, the close call at Luberon, the German Shepherd—it had been quite a run. But now the beginning of the end; it was time to pay for her espionage sin. Nothing personal, she understood. Spies were denizens of darkness and every act of sabotage, every delivery of arms, every secret meeting meant that she was one step closer to capture. And what awaited.

She reclined on the bed but sleep, even now, was out of the question. Why had Colonel Henri come early? And how could she help Peter, who had trusted her in not leaving the hotel? She agonized over the fact that he, as head of SPINDLE, would be getting the worst.

She would find a way, she told herself—whatever the cost—to help him.

St. Jorioz

ARNAUD SWUNG BY THE Hôtel de la Poste the following morning to see if Peter or Odette had any messages and Jean and Simone informed him of the arrests. It had to be Bardet, Arnaud figured.

He should have killed the little charlatan when he had the chance.

But Bardet was only partially to blame. From the time he left Paris, Roger had telephoned Bleicher often to keep him informed of the progress of the plan, but he didn't know for certain that Buckmaster had rejected the proposal. The principal reason Bleicher had left early, it turned out, was an intercepted radio message.

On the evening of April 12 Colonel Reile had called Hugo in.

"Your plan to penetrate the St. Jorioz circuit," he said, "by promising Marsac to escape to England, was a first-class ruse. But will the Gestapo believe it? I have just heard from SS Sturmbann-Führer Kieffer[25] that they have intercepted signals[26] from an unidentified radio transmitter. Kieffer told me that some of these signals speak of a Luftwaffe officer trying to escape to England, together with his Resistance leader. So far, Kieffer had not connected you with this business. But at any moment, the Gestapo might discover the truth, and we shall all be in trouble."

It was time to end the charade, Reile said. He ordered Hugo to arrest Bardet and Marsac's wife, and then go to St. Jorioz and arrest anyone he could find.

Arnaud knew none of this, only that he was lucky to have been away when the posse arrived. And there was a minor victory, Jean told him. Before the arrest, he explained, Peter had given him a suitcase to hide in their back office. In it was a pistol, nearly a half million francs, and more than thirty cables exchanged with London; Bleicher and his men had completely missed it in the raid.

Arnaud accepted the booty and left. With two of the SPINDLE trio in custody, he knew they'd be coming for him next. Radio operators, after all, were the crown jewel of captives. If the Gestapo could torture an operator into giving his codes, they could "turn" a radio, contacting London as if the SOE operative were reporting in. This turning had caused the capture and execution of some fifty

---

25 Sturmbann-Führer (Major) Hans Josef Kieffer was chief of the Sicherheitsdienst (SD), the SS's counterintelligence branch, at its Parisian headquarters on Avenue Foch.

26 The second floor at 84 Avenue Foch was used by SD's Section IV (wireless unit).

SOE agents dropped into the Netherlands the prior year, all parachuting directly into German arms.

The success of Operation North Pole, as the Abwehr called it, encouraged the Gestapo to use whatever means necessary to extract codes. One radio operator caught in France earlier in the year suffered a typical interrogation. "Jacques" had been in the country only a few weeks when he was arrested near Moulins. He was tied up and beaten but refused to cooperate.

When kicks and punches failed to produce, the Gestapo moved on to a more persuasive approach. They set a flame in front of his right eye, very close, and continued to ask for the codes. Jacques held fast and so the torturer began to poke at his eye—through the flame—with a steel bar as the instrument conducted heat. Again and again the interrogator poked but Jacques remained silent. The Gestapo team then decided to break for lunch and handcuffed him to the chair. While they were gone, he escaped—still cuffed—through a window.

Sight in his right eye, though, was lost forever.

Others were not so lucky. An eighteen-year-old Yugoslav Partisan who had been caught with his wireless transmitter was given the full treatment. When he refused to identify his circuit leader he was taken to the cemetery—"no longer recognizable as a human being."

Arnaud had no intention of being a Gestapo guinea pig, or even being captured alive, but he couldn't go to ground just yet. He radioed London to tell them that Peter and Odette had been arrested the night before and that he'd send further details when he could.

The following day, April 18, he sent a lengthy—and therefore dangerous—message explaining that a German secret police officer, backed by Italian Carabinieri, had raided the hotel and taken Peter and Odette, he believed, to an Italian prison. Buckmaster responded by urging Arnaud to return immediately to England through the Pyrenees–Spain escape route.

Arnaud declined. If Cammaerts wasn't warned, Arnaud knew, he'd be captured within days. Only after Arnaud went to Cannes and warned the lieutenant personally would he return to London.

He cabled Buckmaster and told him he was going to ground and that he'd report in when he surfaced.

Alpini Barracks, Annecy

THE BEAM WAS THE answer.

Peter had noticed it on the way in. It was only seven feet off the ground and ran from the cell block to the security wall, behind which was the road to Geneva. But what about Odette? Would they take it out on her? Could he rally the Maquis to ambush the convoy that would transport her to the next destination?

The cell was suffocating and the smell of urine and excrement made sleep impossible, so he stretched out on the bed—a six-by-two-and-a-half-foot board without blankets—and recounted details of the arrest. Most upsetting was the loss of his wallet, which contained not only 70,000 francs, but names and radio codes for six operatives, including Arnaud. He knew it had been in his coat—which he now wore—when he had retired to bed. Had the Gestapo agent snatched it?

He shuddered at the thought. If he did, it was a death sentence for every name listed. He wrestled with the consequences and the fate of Odette all night.

At two and six in the morning the guards were changed. Someone brought him coffee at eight, and at noon he was allowed to eat lunch in the yard. He snuck glances at the beam.

Tomorrow.

THE SHUFFLING CAME PRECISELY at six; the new guard was in place.

Peter slipped the end of a cigarette stub through a hole in the door and asked for a light. Instead of lighting it, the guard came inside. Peter measured him quickly: young, steel helmet, rifle on shoulder.

Although an expert in William Fairbairn's silent kill, Peter decided not to use lethal action. Instead, he'd strike with an uppercut and knock him out.

The Italian smiled warmly and, opening his case, offered Peter a fresh cigarette. The friendly gesture touched Peter, throwing off his aggressive plan. Instead of thrusting the uppercut, he shoved him toward the back of the cell. Peter's assumption was that the young man would fall and Peter would lock him in and take off for the beam.

But the man didn't fall and there was a flash of metal and the bayonet went to work.

CHAPTER 11

THEY WILL
SEND FOR YOU

Peter parried the charge, taking the brunt of it with his left, and delivered a smashing right. The guard stumbled and Peter snatched the rifle and drilled the bayonet into the ground, snapping it. He then broke the muzzle.

Terrified, the young man shouted for help.

"Assistenza! Assistenza!"

Peter struck him in the solar plexus, ending the cries, and followed with a blow to the chin. The Italian was out cold.

Shouts and a rumble of boots echoed down the barrack as Peter scrambled outside and made for the beam. Just then a second guard burst through the door, rushing Peter headlong in another bayonet charge. Peter blocked it, a slight sting in his hand, and thrust a right cross. The man crumpled and Peter lunged for the beam, swinging his legs over. As he pulled himself up, a hand grabbed his coat and yanked him from the ledge. Peter crashed down, and suddenly nine bayonets were pinning him.

The sergeant of the guard pushed his way in and, without a word, hammered Peter with his own straight right. Peter dropped to his knees and the kicking began. After a few minutes the soldiers dragged him back to the cell and Peter took stock of his condition: hands bleeding from four bayonet cuts, possible broken ribs, a closed eye.

The officer on duty came by and began barking orders: "Double the guard. Put a padlock on the door as well as using the bolt. No food for two days. Keep his glasses and shoot at the slightest provocation. No medical attention and no one is allowed in."

So much for escape. Peter tended to his hands as best he could and thought of Odette. How was she making out?

An hour or so later he heard a discussion outside his cell.

"Let me have a look at this bastard."

"No one's allowed in."

"To hell with orders! Have you seen Angelo?"

The guard said no.

"Well, *I* have. He's in the hospital with his face bandaged up. You open that bloody door before I break it in!"

Keys jingled the lock and suddenly Peter saw Goliath. The behemoth was wielding a rifle with the bayonet turned back.

"By Christ, I'll kill you, you bastard English spy!"

Again and again he pummeled Peter with the rifle, cracking his skull, striking his body, crushing his hands. Raining down blow after blow, he didn't stop until Peter was no longer moving—unconscious or dead.

AT DAWN ODETTE'S DOOR opened and the Italian secret police chief came in.

"Your husband is a criminal Madame."

Odette paused, and then remembered that she had told the chief that she and Peter were married. "Why?" she asked.

"Well, he tried to escape last night and knocked a man down, and in consequence it has been pretty bad for him."

She gave no reply and the chief took her into another room,

where a noncommissioned officer joined them. The chief asked her about her work, but she refused to comment.

Her position was very bad, he said; she would be made to talk.

No, he was quite mistaken, Odette replied, she would not.

The chief waited a moment, and the NCO said nothing. "You are very strong," the chief finally said. He left without further comment.

WHEN PETER REGAINED CONSCIOUSNESS, he again took stock: pounding head, two ribs likely fractured, joints of two fingers crushed, good eye nearly closed.

It could have been worse. Executed as a spy. Tortured for attempting escape. He mulled the possibilities and longed to go out in a blaze of glory—with a Sten gun in his hands.

Perhaps in time.

After a day or so a secret police investigator came by. He sat next to Peter and opened a dossier.

"*Now* do you feel like answering some questions?"

"Go to hell!" Peter howled.

The agent closed the file and stood.

"I'll be back."

The man left and Peter thought about Arnaud. Surely Jean and Simone would have warned him immediately, and Arnaud would have informed London. By now, "Michel" and "Lise" would have been wiped off F Section's blackboard and replaced by others. One month you're delivering 168 containers to the Maquis of Glières, the next you're white dust clinging to an eraser.

Days went by and nothing happened. He thought of Odette and pictured the anguished expression she must have had. Maybe she was wearing the faraway look he'd seen when she yearned for her girls—girls she might never see again.

He wept.

EACH DAY ONE OF the friendly guards would bring Odette news of Peter and she had them send messages to him. Peter responded with romantic love notes, which the passionate Italians delivered with pleasure.

After a week Odette was summoned to leave and she boarded the lorry with equanimity; it had been ten days since her arrest and, without bath or hygiene, it was hard to sink lower. Her hair was matted and oily, her skin grimy, and the odor of her body clung to her like a shadow. She thought endlessly of her children and Peter's welfare. She'd heard about his escape attempt and beatings and knew the Geneva Convention provided no protection.

Where were they taking her? Where was Peter? And why the need for a dozen Carabinieri wielding Schmeissers?

Peter, meanwhile, was called from his cell and told that he'd be leaving with Odette. The Italians saw him off as one of their own; most came to shake his hand and wish him well, the first of whom was Angelo, the young man he had knocked out, now smiling ear to ear. Strange as it was—enemies treating one another as friends— the Italians had developed a deep respect and admiration for Peter. It's not every day, they must have thought, that one gets to see two bayonet charges dismantled by an unarmed opponent. Peter's combat skills, coupled with his passionate love notes, no doubt left the Italians envious.

No sooner than Odette had taken her seat, Peter was in the doorway, handcuffed. Amazingly, the Italians allowed them to sit together for the two-hour drive to their destination, Grenoble.

Odette grimaced at seeing Peter's condition: his face was a mess and his hands were mangled, one finger clearly broken. She wondered if he had been tortured. For Peter, the injuries no longer existed—he was with the woman he loved and all was well. The ride was like an oasis of happiness, he felt, and just sitting next to her bolstered him.

Odette filled Peter's pockets with cigarettes she had received from guards, as well as eggs she had saved. Addressing his wounds, she begged him not to do something rash and get himself killed.

It didn't matter, Peter said. He was certain he'd be executed on any number of counts.

Odette gazed into his eyes. "I know that you will survive all this. Promise me to face it with patience. I shall be thinking of you and praying for you all the time."

The words came as a shield and belt of salvation for Peter, and yet the encouragement was bittersweet; in the pit of his stomach, he felt sure that Odette didn't consider her chance of survival as great as his. Why?

He was the circuit leader. *He* was the dangerous animal. *He* was the filthy saboteur. The notion that she was going to do something crazy haunted him; he knew without question that she would do everything she could to protect him.

Then there were Arnaud and Roger Cammaerts. The Germans would move heaven and earth to find them, and Peter and Odette agreed that they'd do all they could to save them. When the interrogations came, they'd simply deny everything. With Roger it was business, but Arnaud was different. They loved him. Yes, he was impossible to get along with—Peter and Odette were the only ones who did—but he was the best wireless operator in France, was loyal to a fault, and was incredibly brave. When Peter wasn't around, Arnaud refused to work with anyone other than Odette. The trio made a perfect team and Odette was absolutely certain that each would lay down their life for one of the others.

THE TIME TOGETHER ON the bus was precious, but Peter and Odette didn't speak of the obvious: that they might never see each other again. They arrived in Grenoble all too soon and said their farewells. Odette was taken to a room in the barrack occupied by two other women. Peter's reputation preceded him and he was taken to a cell where his ankles were chained.

Sitting in solitude, he considered the impact Odette had on him. It was not until now that he fully realized the extent of his admiration and love for her. Surely, he thought, few people could ever experience such a boundless measure of love as he received by a woman weighed down by the knowledge that she might never again set eyes on her children.

On the second day a group of officers came to Peter's cell and one asked his name.

Peter wondered why they asked. Had the Gestapo not passed word?

Chambrun, he told them.

"We know all about that," the man said, "but what's your real name?"

Peter said that *was* his real name.

"No, it isn't. Your name's Churchill and you're related to Winston Churchill."

Perhaps the Gestapo *had* told them. Wait—the bit about relations with the prime minister? *That* didn't come from the Germans.

"What makes you say that?" Peter asked.

Never mind, the officer said. He just wanted Peter to sign a form—with his *real* name—and rank and number.

Peter complied. The crowd, he realized, had tagged along to catch a glimpse of the prime minister's kin.

TEN DAYS IN GRENOBLE and Odette and Peter were again loaded on a lorry, this time for a drive to the train station. On the way to Turin they were kept in separate compartments—each accompanied by seven guards. When the train arrived, they were locked in a waiting room with other prisoners while the guards waited for local transport.

Odette sidled up to Peter and said quietly, "It was I who told them your real name."

"Why did you do that, for goodness sake?"

"I told the Duty Officer at Grenoble that you were closely related to the Old Man, and that's a piece of information he'll never be able to keep to himself."

"Well, bang goes my cover story."

Odette brushed aside the cover. "They'll be so pleased with Henri for capturing you," she said, "that they'll probably give him the Ritterkreuz and keep you as a hostage."

"So that was the idea," Peter said. "Maybe you're right. We'll soon know. But I always thought it rather a dangerous name to travel under these days."

"Wrong psychology altogether. You'll see."

Odette was calm and quite confident, Peter noticed. She seemed to be one step ahead in the game.

"I told them something else, too," Odette said with a lopsided grin.

"What?"

"I said I was your wife, and that we'd been married since 1941."

Peter laughed. It was brilliant, actually. If the Churchill name would save Peter because the Germans thought that he was related to the prime minister, it would save Odette, too, if they thought the couple were married.

"Well, that certainly shows your confidence in this plan," he said. "I begin to like the idea, Lise. Yes, I like it very much. Sink or swim we shall be together."

Three Italian guards noticed that Peter and Odette were whispering and one came over, shaking his finger.

"*Niente politica*, eh!"

"As though reunited lovers would waste their precious moments in conspiracy and treason," Peter replied with a smirk. "Why, all we're doing is whispering sweet nothings to each other."

The guard seemed mollified and moved on.

"Naturally," Odette continued, "I need hardly add that this stunt is merely a war-time measure."

Peter held her eyes. Now was the time. "If I ever get the chance," he said, "I shall ask you if you'd care to make it a lifetime measure."

AFTER A NIGHT IN Turin they entrained for Nice. The Italians were quite pleasant, giving them oranges and singing most of the way. From the station, Peter and Odette were driven to a beautiful villa on a hill and put in separate rooms. There were no interrogations, and again the Italians treated them extremely well.

Nine or ten days later they boarded a big saloon, this one headed for Toulon. Peter was not handcuffed and they were again allowed to sit together. When the truck reached the coast, the driver turned west on rue d'Antibes, which runs through the center of Cannes.

Odette reached for Peter's hand. It was here, six months prior, that they had met. It was here, from their headquarters, that they had watched the Gulf of Napoule burning gold at sunset.

Life sometimes plays it back—mostly the beautiful—lest one forget the blessings, fleeting though they are.

The lorry lumbered along to Provence and they were teased again, this time with the warm scent of garrigue—an intoxicating mixture of sage, thyme, juniper, rosemary, and lavender—the scent of freedom. After a brief stop they carried on to Toulon, where they entrained for the twelve-hour trip to Paris. Once again, Peter and Odette were able to sit together.

The train chugged through the night and dawn broke as they entered the city on May 8. Odette squeezed Peter's hand and smiled.

"Bonjour, mon Pierre."

She retrieved something from her bag and held it out. It was a small crucifix. Peter took it, the encouragement as powerful as the symbolism vivid; they were about to embark upon their own trek down Via Dolorosa.

Colonel Henri greeted them at the Gare de Lyon station and, with apology, handed them over to two Gestapo, who drove them to Fresnes. Located seven miles south of the heart of Paris, Fresnes was Europe's largest prison. It was built at the turn of the century and offered some twelve hundred cells; cells which the Gestapo found adequate for three thousand prisoners.

Odette and Peter again said farewell and they were taken to holding cells for registration. Odette was strip-searched and then led down a flight of stairs to a ghostly, medieval underground passage. Colonel Henri appeared and carried Odette's luggage through the long corridor. Between chasms of darkness, they went through a series of doors, all of which had to be unlocked and relocked. Armed guards at all checkpoints.

The passage ended at the ground floor of the main center, above which were four catwalks. The place was clean and quiet and stale.

Like a morgue.

Henri took Odette into an open room and offered her a cigarette. She took it and they sat at a small table and smoked and talked as if a couple at a Champs-Élysées cafe. The German was extremely polite, she noticed.

"I don't like some of the things in the Nazi regime," Henri said. "One day I'll be put in prison for it. I was in prison in the last war. Could have escaped but didn't to save the life of a British officer." He shrugged. "I do my job as well as I can. I don't like it, though."

Odette smoked and listened.

"I don't like seeing you here," Henri went on, "and if I can I shall get you out." He paused a moment and then added, "Of course you don't love Peter, it cannot be."

Henri was probing, Odette knew, but why? He was smooth and charming and as dangerous as a domesticated tiger, so there had to be a motive. Technically, his job was over. The Gestapo was in charge of all prisons, so once Henri turned her and Peter over to them at the train station, he had no further need to see them.

Then it dawned on her: Henri was *recruiting*.

He didn't want to ask openly if she'd work for him; that would be clumsy and amateurish. But if he could get her to deny her love for Peter it would open the door, and Henri would then make his next move.

"You are making a big mistake," she said. "The arrest has nothing to do with it."

"Pity you're taking it like that. I could have done something for you."

Odette said nothing and Henri studied her. After a few moments his countenance suddenly changed, almost cheerful.

"Peter is a very lucky man," he said.

Odette smiled to herself. Henri got it. He realized that she knew his game, and that she'd just won the battle of wits.

After a while a guard came. Henri told Odette that if there was anything she needed, anything he could do for her, to let him know.

Odette was taken to an empty cell and locked in.

Cell 108. It was not unlike her prior quarters: plaster walls with fungus on the ceiling, rusted iron bed, chair with a broken back, lavatory with a brown enamel basin, shelf with a spoon and tin bowl. It was twelve by eight.

Fresnes Prison, Paris. *MUSÉE D'HISTOIRE DE LA JUSTICE*

She studied the walls and noticed scratches—a calendar ending February 17. And in another place, clearly visible: *"Quand j'etais petite, je gardais les vaches; maintenant ce sont elles qui me gardent."*—"When I was little, I kept the cows; Now it is they who keep me."

Cows . . . Somerset . . . Marianne, Lily, Francoise . . .

FOR SEVERAL DAYS ODETTE saw no one. She was in solitary confinement, she realized, and her coffee and starvation rations were inserted each day through the food hatch. One afternoon Henri stopped by.

He talked openly, almost like a probation officer. "Lise, I am truly sorry to see you in this place," he said. "Fresnes is not for . . . for people like you." Glancing about the room, he noticed that Odette had only two blouses, including the one she was wearing.

"You are not the sort of person who would wear dirty clothes," he said. "Do let me have one of your blouses and I will get it washed for you."

Henri's words seemed sincere but Odette remained cautious. No favors. She shook her head.

It was a gentle rebuff and Henri took it in stride. He was forced to arrest her, he said, to save her from the clutches of the Gestapo.

"I remember how you told me that you arrested Marsac for the same altruistic motive. The number of persons you claim to have 'saved' from the Gestapo would fill a landing at Fresnes. Abwehr or Gestapo, steel trap or foxhound, the end appears to be much the same."

Henri leaned forward. "Yes, but there is no need for you to stay here, Lise."

"No?"

"No, Lise. It is in my power to get you out of Fresnes, to restore to you a life of human dignity." He fingered a paper and brooded over it several moments.

"I see that you spent a week in jail at Annecy and were interrogated by the O.V.R.A., by the Italian Secret Police. You told them nothing. Then you were taken to Grenoble and to Turin where you spent a night in a cell with two prostitutes. After Turin came Nice for ten days, Marseille, Toulon and now Fresnes. It has not been a pretty grand tour, and it is time it came to an end."

Odette said nothing. This was like negotiating with a psychiatrist. If Henri really wanted to save her from the Gestapo, and now from the indignities of prison, he didn't have to arrest her. And if he did—simply to deceive the Gestapo watchdogs—he could have offered the release in Annecy that he was now offering in Paris. And what of Peter and Marsac? Was Henri's altruism reserved only for young, attractive women?

"Does the possibility of freedom amuse you?" he asked.

Odette frowned. Henri's every word was a shiny lure, flashed and flaunted, hooks tucked neatly under the cloak of liberty.

"I was wondering what bargain you were going to suggest," she said. "I am afraid that I can't offer either a radio set or a bomber pick-up from here."

"I have no bargain to offer. Here are some facts. Here in Fresnes you are under the name of 'Madame Chambrun.' It is not your real name. You told the Italians that you and Raoul were married and that your real name was Mrs. Peter Churchill. That is also untrue. I know a great deal about you, far more than you think. I know that you are the mother of three small daughters, that you are a member of the French Section of the War Office, that your headquarters are in Baker Street, London, and that your chief is Colonel Maurice Buckmaster, a tall, alert man, clean shaven, educated at Eton, speaking perfect French and good German."

Odette remained impassive, Henri's intel duly noted.

"You are a mother," he went on, "and your duty in this chaotic world is to your children. It is not to a collection of amateur spies and saboteurs from the French Section of the War Office. Do you really think for one moment that your friends Arnaud and Roger—

even your so-called husband Peter Churchill—would do as much for you as you seem to be ready to do for them?"

"Yes, I do. But the point is unimportant. I do not barter loyalty against loyalty. I am no shopkeeper, Monsieur, and I sell nothing by the pound. If these 'amateur spies and saboteurs,' as you call them, were indeed prepared to betray me—which I don't believe—that would not influence my decision in any way. I am only responsible to my own conscience."

Henri paused, and then said: "You told me in St. Jorioz at our first meeting that you cared for music. I heard, the night before last, Mozart's divertissements for string quartet and two horns. It was quite enchanting. It would give me great pleasure to introduce you to some of the almost unknown masterpieces of Mozart. At his best, he is exquisite, at his laziest, he is always lively and delicate and charming. There is a symphony concert in about a fortnight."

Odette knew that Henri wanted an answer so she didn't give one.

He collected his dossier and stood. "It still grieves me to see you here, Lise. I shall visit you again—very soon."

The guard returned Odette to her cell and she pondered what had just happened.

Symphony or isolation? Mozart or bastille?

Only in Paris.

In the morning a guard brought the Fresnes version of coffee—brown water—and later a bowl of thin soup and small piece of bread. It was insufficient for basic sustenance and as Odette caught glimpses of other prisoners, she noticed one thing in common: they were all starving.

TWO GUARDS, ONE GERMAN Shepherd. Thirty-foot wall.

It was possible, Peter thought, peering from the broken pane in his cell. Difficult, perhaps suicide, but possible.

Fresnes was indeed a fortress. One F Section agent had tried to escape and had come surprisingly close. Henri Peulevé, organizer of the AUTHOR circuit, had just returned from an interrogation at Avenue Foch and seized upon a rare opportunity. A group of visitors was leaving the prison just as he was entering and he managed to mix in with the crowd. When he came to the main gate, he handed the sentry a blank piece of paper instead of the visitor's pass and ran. The guard sounded the alarm and Peulevé was shot in the leg and recaptured. He was returned to his cell and left without medical attention.

He dug the bullet out with a spoon.

Just then Peter heard someone at his door and he stepped away from the window. The colonel came in and offered Peter a cigarette and sat on the bed.

"What would you say to the idea of being exchanged for Rudolf Hess?"

Peter laughed. "A wonderful idea, Henri."

"It seems reasonable to suppose that Winston Churchill would be glad to give up a person of so little real importance to get his nephew back."

Peter expressed doubt that the prime minister would go for it based on the distance of the relationship, to which Henri replied, "Don't forget that the closer your relationship with Winston Churchill, the further your distance from the firing squad."

Well, well, well. Odette's plan had worked after all.

Peter said it was all right by him if Henri could get it past the Gestapo.

"I'm sorry to see you in this plight, Pierre. Now that I've captured you I should like to do everything possible for your comfort. I was a prisoner in similar circumstances during the '14–'18 war and the British treated me very decently."

Henri's concern seemed sincere, and he may have been working behind the scenes to ease Peter's and Odette's discomfort. It was not uncommon at Fresnes for prisoners in solitary confinement to be manacled and chained by their feet in their cells. Thankfully, they were spared such treatment.

"You'll be interrogated fairly soon," Henri added in closing, "but in the meantime what can I do for you?"

"Arrange for me to meet Odette as often as you can."

"That will be a little difficult but I shall manage it somehow, and you shall see her next time I come." Henri tossed a pack of High Life cigarettes on the bed and stood.

After Henri left, Peter considered the meeting for several minutes. The German was being awfully nice.

THE FOLLOWING DAY A guard came by and escorted Odette again to the interrogation room. Charming Henri stood and again offered a cigarette. This time she took it and Henri lit it. Puffing once, she stubbed it out.

He asked why she did that and she said it was for a friend.

"But how do you give it to a friend if you are in solitary confinement?"

She slipped the cigarette into her pocket. "I have nothing to say."

Henri had hoped for a basic level of trust by this time but respected Lise's zipper-lipped approach to unnecessary disclosures. "I have been to see Peter Churchill," he said. "He is in cell number 220, in the Second Division."

"I know."

"How do you know? You have only been here for three days, and it is impossible for you to know."

Odette shrugged.

Henri told her that Peter was well and sent his love, and that Henri was working on negotiating a trade: Peter for someone in England. But the reason he came by, he said, was to once again urge her to leave with him. "If you choose to stay here in Fresnes," he said, "the Gestapo will send for you. They want to know the whereabouts of your wireless operator Arnaud and of the British officer called Roger . . . They know that you have this information and I frankly fear for you if you go to number 84 Avenue Foch. They are not excessively scrupulous in their methods, Lise."

84 Avenue Foch.

Some returned; some didn't. Of those who did, some retained a dram of dignity; others came back a shell of their former selves—physically, mentally, emotionally. Everyone has a breaking point and the Gestapo were professionals. The weak could be broken through hunger, hence the Fresnes starvation. Simpletons could be broken psychologically, repetition-to-attrition the favored technique.

We know you are a spy. Who is your contact?

Searing light, heat.

Your so-called friend betrayed you! Who is your contact?

Table slamming, barking.

No one can help you now, don't you understand? Who is your contact?

Good cop, bad cop.

Who is your contact?

With SOE operatives, however, this rarely worked due to extensive training and practice. Beatings were usually stage one for the difficult cases. *Sorry, but you brought this on yourself. Are you ready to talk now?* Stage two brought a variety of options: sodium thiopental, knife, cigarette, electrical shock, wet canvas. *"Whatever happens to amuse the Gestapo."*

Odette was unmoved. "Tell me, Henri, are you about to save me from the Gestapo again?"

He said he was.

"I am not sure which role I admire most—that of international airborne peacemaker or Teutonic St. George."[27]

Henri ignored the sarcasm. "If you have to go to the Gestapo, you will regret it. I can get you out of here, and I am prepared to do

---

27 Saint George of Lydda was a Greek-born soldier serving in Emperor Diocletian's royal guard. Sentenced to death and martyred for refusing to recant his Christian faith, George became a venerated saint in the Roman Catholic, Orthodox, Anglican, and Lutheran traditions.

so—without onerous conditions attached. I am a reasonable judge of character and I know that I would be wasting my time in asking you either to give away your friends or to work for me."

"Then why do you want to get me out?"

"I don't want you to have to go to the Gestapo, Lise."

CHAPTER 12

TICK, TICK

The silence hung.

"Why don't you want to leave this place?" Henri asked, frustration rising.

It wasn't that simple, Odette said. She wasn't comfortable leaving the prison under his protection and trying to keep her silence and self-respect, while others languished in their cells. She would stay.

"I impose no conditions, Lise."

"No, but I do—on myself. Do you think I could ever go back to England and look my friends in the face and say, 'I was captured but they let me out again and I had a fine war—under the benevolent wing of the Abwehr or the Gestapo'?" She stood. "You will forgive me if I ask that this interview now come to an end."

He asked if she was hungry and she said, yes.

"I could order you extra food."

Did other women receive extra?

"Some," Henri said. "Those who work for us do, the *Kahlfaktors*, the women who push the food trolley round and that sort of thing."

Odette said she would pass.

Henri asked if there was anything he could do for her and Odette said there were notices in German on her door; what did they say?

They walked back to her cell and Henri began reading: "That one means that you are 'grand secret'—most secret. Then these say 'no books,' 'no showers,' 'no parcels,' 'no exercise,' 'no favors' and that sort of thing." They also said that she was to have no contact with anyone, that her door was never to be left open, and that her food must be inserted through the trap door.

Henri left and Odette returned to her favorless secret life.

MEANWHILE, PETER LANGUISHED IN his cell. Boredom and the pangs of hunger were driving him mad. Things that he had always taken for granted—food, drink, cigarettes—were now precious luxuries. He measured his cell: fourteen by eight. He asked a guard when he could visit the exercise yard and the answer was sometimes once a week, sometimes once a month, depending on the mood of the guard on duty at the time.

That evening he conjured up thoughts of visiting Odette in her cell, projecting that he was there. For an hour he imagined conversation with her. He could see her face clearly and happily received the waves of strength she radiated. Her fortitude, he thought, was enough for two.

A FEW DAYS LATER Henri escorted Peter to the interrogation room for another visit. While they smoked, Henri warned that Peter's interrogation with the Gestapo was coming, and that they were putting their best man on him. It was a kind gesture and Peter knew he'd have to make his answers and rebuttals—and red herrings when possible—pick-proof. Henri also said that Berlin had forwarded the exchange proposal to London.

The conversation came to an end and Peter asked if he could see Odette. To arrange it would have been a direct violation of the Gestapo's orders and if they found out that Henri had done so, there would be significant repercussions. Nonetheless, he agreed, quietly telling a guard that he needed to interrogate Odette.

Moments later she was at the door, immaculate from head to foot, Peter thought. She was wearing her charcoal suit, a spotless blouse, silk stockings, and her square-toed shoes. Her thick brunette hair framed her slim neck and rested peacefully on her shoulders. She looked beautiful.

He jumped up to embrace her and for several moments they held each other. As they did, Henri was polite enough to move to the window to give them privacy.

Peter looked awful, Odette thought. Either he had been tortured or he was still suffering from his injuries at Annecy. Peter, in turn, was worried about Odette, telling her that she looked pale. Odette suggested that perhaps they should discuss other things.

Henri was gracious, giving them endless time to talk. After an hour or so he joined the conversation, almost as a friend, telling them again that he had been a POW in the first war and that the British had treated him very well. He was sorry, he said to Odette, that the Gestapo would allow her no books or exercise, and asked if he could do anything else for her.

From what Odette could tell, he was sincere. Henri was, for the moment, truly a Teutonic St. George. And yet she and Peter could never relax because Henri was cunning enough—as Marsac had learned—to play any part needed to extract information or gain advantage.

She said there was not, and Henri indicated that it was time for them to return to their cells. The "Churchills" parted with sweet sorrow, but the two-hour interlude was a precious milestone, Peter thought, that he could relive in the quiet solitude of the dark days to come.

IN HIS CELL PETER considered Henri's warning about the interrogator. It would all come down to one interview—a *tribunal*, the

Germans liked to call it. Whether he lived or died, was tortured, or would ever see Odette again, would hinge on that meeting. What the Italians had done to him after the escape attempt was nothing; those were beatings, somewhat deserved, by amateurs who would later shake his hand when he left. The Gestapo were intellectual and ruthless surgeons.

It was bad enough that he was up against their best, but they now had countless sources: reports from Henri, the Italians, Marsac, Roger Bardet, Carte's family, and others in or around the SPINDLE network. The interrogator would ask questions to which he already had answers, and he would bluff about facts he thought might be accurate but needed Peter's confirmation.

Torture was a distinct possibility, if not certainty. Worse, the Gestapo had the ultimate trump card: Odette. What would he do if they threatened to torture *her*? His rage would take over and two bullets later the unmarked van would take delivery through the back.

On the other hand, they could simply execute him as a spy. Peter had committed the crime and the punishment was established by international law. He was Dostoyevsky's Rodion Romanovitch: guilty as charged, clinging to a cross supplied by the woman he loved, and about to pass from one world to the next.

He tried to think of historical figures who had gone through similar ordeals. The Apostle Paul, he remembered vaguely, had undergone a multitude of trials but that provided little relief; Peter couldn't remember the details and wasn't a religious man anyway. Yet with death at the door, he welcomed any and all spiritual enlightenment.

It was time to invoke God's help. Up to this point he had always seen himself as a self-sufficient atheist. Cambridge man. Hockey star. Diplomat. Commando. The feeble could bolster themselves with prayers to the Almighty, but such weakness was not for him. Imprisonment and impending death, however, changed that. He had joined the ranks of frail and mortal humanity.

He gave thanks to the Lord for the lesson and tried to work through his helplessness and despondency. Though the thought of

God as a person was beyond him, he considered and admired the life of Jesus. Christ's voluntary sacrifice, his human temptations, his cry "Take away this cup from me" suddenly took on real meaning for the first time. Surely this was a man who had passed through it all and faced it well, Peter thought. Surely this was a hero one could worship with admiration, a Deity who would listen to one's prayers with understanding, for had he not passed that way himself?

Peter had never been a man of prayer, but this was as good a time as any to start. "God give me strength," he prayed, "courage, patience, and good judgment."

He recited the Lord's Prayer.

Give us this day our daily bread . . .

But deliver us from evil.

May 25, 1943

"TRIBUNAL!"

Odette jumped. It was six in the morning.

"TRIBUNAL!"

Peter stirred in his bed.

"TRIBUNAL!" THE GUARD SHOUTED again.

Odette began dressing and recalled the fate of inmates she had seen taken away for the dreaded interrogation. Most did not return.

She followed the trail of women being led to the underground passage and when they reached a holding area, she noticed that male prisoners were joining them.

Was . . . Yes, there was Peter! They held each other's eyes as the guards waited for everyone. When the group began trudging along, she and Peter moved toward each other.

"Bon courage, mon chéri," she said.

Peter echoed the sentiment and they shuffled together through the corridor.

Outside, they were separated and filed into two Black Marias—police vans.

They arrived at 84 Avenue Foch and Odette was taken upstairs to a small room and told to wait. Peter, meanwhile, was ushered to the fourth floor and seated before the Commissar—the chief interrogator.[28] A tall German about forty, he wore a dark suit and had an intelligent face with cold, indifferent eyes.

The man spoke flawless French and they covered the basics—name, date of birth, nationality, family members, father's profession, schools attended, degrees received, work history, and so on. Prewar history complete, the Commissar retrieved a stack of ten pages, single spaced—Peter's dossier.

"You see, Mr. Churchill, or Monsieur Chauvet, or Monsieur Chambrun, alias Raoul or what-have-you, we know absolutely everything about you. Three visits to France—one by submarine and two by parachute. You organized fishing-boat landings of men and material in the south of France, aircraft landings for the exchange of personnel, parachute drops all over the place for the railway sabotage plan, and you were responsible for the arming of the Maquis of the Plateau des Glières by twenty-five British bombers."

Peter feigned shock. "Who gave you all of that exaggerated information?"

He was responding straight out of the SOE playbook, which warned of the interrogation trick: "Reconstruction of offense exaggerating prisoner's share of it." The Commissar had everything right, of course, although the twenty-five bombers was a bit much. But what did the Germans actually *know*, and could prove, about him? It's a basic rule of interrogation to imply that you already have

---

28 In all probability, this was SS *Sonderführer* Ernst Vogt, Kieffer's interpreter and interrogator at Avenue Foch.

the information to extract it the fastest, and the Commissar was likely hoping for a quick meeting.

But Peter had been prepared well, and the SOE manual set the game's framework: "The Gestapo's reputation has been built up on ruthlessness and terrorism, *not* intelligence. They will always pretend to know more than they do and may even make a good guess, but remember that it *is* a guess; otherwise they would not be interrogating you."

The chess match continued and the Commissar made his next move.

"I don't think you quite understand our respective roles today. It is I who ask the questions and you who do the answering. Is it true that you were the Chief of the southeast zone?"

Per his training, Peter had two options: to answer each question quickly—which increased risk—or quite slowly, playing the village idiot. He chose the latter.

"There was no such thing as the Chief of a Zone," he said. "Each officer was in charge of the district to which he was sent."

The Commissar asked for names of British officers running neighboring districts and Peter said he never knew them; everyone worked in watertight compartments.

The German spread a handful of photographs on the table. "Ever seen any of these men before?"

Peter cast his eyes from side to side. He had met four of them, including Eugene, a radio operator he had winked at that very morning in the underground passage.

"Never."

"So you don't know any of these men, you never knew any of your neighbors and you weren't the Chief of the southeast zone?"

"No."

The Commissar ground his teeth and typed something. "This affair of the Maquis of Glières, are you going to deny that you arranged for their being armed by those twenty-five bombers?"

Peter said, yes, it was a de Gaulle operation.

"What do you take me for?" the Commissar shouted as he jumped from his seat, "a complete ninnyhammer?" He stomped around several paces and then turned back. "You realize what to expect from your stupid attitude in denying what is already known against you?"

"I am your prisoner, but I cannot accept the responsibility of all the things my enthusiastic betrayer has pinned on me."

The Commissar asked what Peter *would* accept.

"That I came over here to sabotage the German war effort, that I did my duty as a British officer, that I lived with forged papers in civilian clothes, was prepared to blow up anything and everything I was told to blow up, but that in fact I have never sabotaged anything, never carried arms and never killed a single German."

The Commissar cooled, still disbelieving Peter's answers but unable, at least for the moment, to disprove his lies. "What's the idea of trying to make out that you and Lise are married?" he asked. "Everyone knows that she joined you for the first time on November 2nd 1942 as your courier."

It was clear, Peter thought, why the Germans were pushing the marriage issue. If Peter was in fact related to Churchill, they'd use him as a bargaining chip, along with any supposed wife. But if they could prove that he and Odette were unmarried, they were free to execute her as any other spy.

"We are married," he said.

"When were you married?"

"On December 24th 1941," Peter said, using the date he had told Odette to remember.

More accusations, more denials, and the Commissar had heard enough. "I'm wasting my time with you. I'll see you another day when you've had a little more time to reflect on what you're letting yourself in for by this stupid attitude of non-cooperation."

Peter was floored. He had denied what the Germans clearly knew and had given them nothing new. Why had he not been tortured? Odette was looking smarter every day. *Don't touch this one, Herr Commissar—nephew of Winston Churchill himself. We may exchange him, so the goods can't be damaged. Get what you can.*

SOMEONE FINALLY CAME TO Odette's room and escorted her to a mess hall. They presented a hearty meal of meat, potatoes, and gravy, but figuring the food was designed to make her sleepy for the interrogation, she ate only half.

After lunch it was her turn to see the Commissar. He was polite and proper, she found, and smelled of eau de Cologne. Following some preliminary questions, he started in earnest by challenging Odette on her marriage to Peter, but she held fast to their story. Peter couldn't have been the brains behind the organization, the German asserted, as he was "the dumbest nincompoop I've ever met."

Odette almost stepped in it, but then saw the branches and leaves, carefully arranged.

She agreed, she said. Churchill really *was* a dolt. *She* was the brains of the operation. They carried on for another ninety minutes and Odette deflected, telling him next to nothing. The Commissar looked at the three lines of notes he had taken and ended the interview.

THE FOLLOWING MORNING, ODETTE heard it again.

"Tribunal!"

"But . . . but I went to the tribunal yesterday."

"You go again today. Tribunal. Tribunal."

Odette put on her skirt, her red blouse, and her only pair of silk stockings. When they arrived at Avenue Foch, she was taken immediately to the interrogation room on the fourth floor and put in a chair facing the Commissar, who was seated at a table.

"Lise, you wasted a great deal of my time yesterday," he began without pleasantries. "You will not be permitted to do this again."

Classic interrogation technique: alternate between geniality and hostility to get the prisoner to drop her guard. No buffet today.

The Commissar looked at her and seemed to be collecting his thoughts. He pointed to the window. "Have a look at those happy people outside."

Odette ignored the request and the Commissar asked, "Why are you doing this?"

"My father was killed for France in the first war and my family has suffered repeatedly. And I'm British now and love England even more than France."

"Are you doing this for money?" the Commissar asked, ignoring her patriotic motivation.

"No."

"A pity."

The Commissar then produced Odette's handbag, which had been confiscated during registration at the prison. Pouring the contents on the table, he asked if she'd like to keep anything.

Odette shook her head. "No. Except, perhaps, the Rosary."

The Commissar picked it up and extended his hand, but when Odette reached for it, he snatched it away.

Odette took it in stride, showing no emotion.

He returned it to the table and in a chilly tone said that he had three questions, all of which Odette would be made to answer. The first, he said, was the location of Arnaud.

Odette's stomach knotted. The Commissar knew she had the information and there was no avoiding the heat.

She said she had nothing to say.

"We will see. It is known to us that you sent the British officer, Roger, from St. Jorioz to an address in the South of France. I want to know the address to which you sent him."

Odette knew this as well, and she was the only one besides Arnaud who did. Cammaerts's life was in her hands.

"I have nothing to say," she repeated.

"Again, we will see. It is also known to us that you obtained from a French traitor a day or two before your arrest the layout of the docks at the Vieux Port of Marseille. I want to know the whereabouts of this document or the name of the person in whose possession it is."

"I have nothing to say."

"Lise, there is a parrot-like quality about your conversation that I find most irritating." He repeated the three questions and told Odette that she had one minute to answer.

He eyed the second hand of his watch.

Tick. Tick. Tick.

Odette's pulse raged. It was the most debilitating type of fear: fear of the unknown.

Thirty seconds. *Tick. Tick.*

Beatings were the norm, she knew. At least for stage one. No doubt they had torture devices, but those were typically reserved for men, as a woman's body offered numerous options for sadistic Nazis.

Ten seconds.

Betrayal or pain. Very simple.

Tick.

The Commissar looked up. "Well, Lise, I would now like the answers to my questions."

Odette sat there with her secrets.

"We have means of making you talk."

"I am aware of your methods."

Odette's arms were suddenly wrenched back—someone had snuck up behind her. The Commissar came over and began unbuttoning her blouse.

"I resent your hands on me or on my clothes," Odette snapped. "If you tell me what you want me to do and release one hand, I will do it."

"As you wish. Unbutton your blouse."

Whatever happens to amuse the Gestapo . . .

Odette unhooked the top two buttons and the man behind her yanked down her blouse, exposing her back. She never saw what was in his other hand.

She lurched forward in a visceral spasm as the red-hot fire iron scorched her skin.

"Where is Arnaud?"

It was for times like these that London had given her the L tablet. The cyanide was quite effective, Buckmaster had said, fast-acting and painless. But it wasn't Odette's style, and she didn't have it on her anyway.

She took a breath as the stench of burned flesh filled the air.

"I have nothing to say," she said again.

"You are more than foolish." The Commissar opened his cigarette case and offered her one. She declined and he began smoking. "Did they tell you that in your school for amateurs in the New Forest, to beware of poisoned cigarettes?"

Odette said nothing.

"You know the three questions. Are you now prepared to answer them—after the *hors d'oeuvre*—or do you want the full meal?"

"I have nothing to say."

The Commissar stepped closer, brooding over her, eau de Cologne unmistakable now.

"Perhaps you would prefer to take off your shoes and stockings yourself. If not, I can assure you that I am well experienced in the mechanics of feminine suspenders."

Odette slipped them off.

"My colleague here, Lise, is going to pull out your toenails one by one, starting at the little toe of your left foot. In between each evulsion—to use the correct medical term—I propose to repeat my questions. You can bring the ceremony to an end at any moment by answering these questions. There are those who faint after the third or fourth toenail, but I don't think you are of the fainting kind. If you do faint, we can always revive you with brandy and the ceremony will continue. Now, before we begin, where is Arnaud?"

The standard procedure with torture—with SOE and all organizations—is forty-eight hours. If the operative can hold out for two days, it gives others in the circuit time to hear of the arrest and go to ground. But Odette and Peter had been arrested on April 16, more than six weeks ago; Arnaud and Roger surely had long since disappeared and there was no reason for her to endure more torture. If she gave their addresses, it was likely the Gestapo would find nothing more than dirty dishes.

Still, Odette would maintain her silence. It was a matter of principle. Of never giving in. This was fortunate because—unbeknownst to her—Cammaerts was, in fact, still at the safe house in Cannes, and, perhaps foolishly, would continue living there another six weeks.

Odette wasn't tied to the chair so fighting was an option—eye strike to the man stooping, groin kick to eau de Cologne—but what good would it do? She was in the bowels of Gehenna,[29] the place crawling with guards. No, she would take the full ride.

She watched the man at her feet. He was French and young—maybe twenty-eight—and exceedingly handsome, with dark, thick hair, perfect teeth, smouldering brown eyes, and beautiful lashes.

He held Odette's foot and with the steel jaws of the pincers clamped down on the nail of her little toe.

29 Hell.

CHAPTER 13

THE BLACK
HOLLOW

With a slow even pull the man began to tear Odette's toenail from its bed.

A soundless scream. Odette clenched her fingers into tight fists and sat perfectly still as blood seeped around the cuticle. As the nail came forward, blood pooled behind it. A final jerk and it was clear, dangling from the pincers like a transfusion bag.

"*Now* would you care to tell me Arnaud's address?"

Odette tried to say "no" but her vocal cords had shut down. She shook her head.

The Commissar nodded to the torturer and the steel jaws clamped again. As he repeated the procedure, Odette squeezed her hands so tightly that her fingernails began to penetrate her palms. Blood collected on the floor and Odette's body trembled as nerves shot scalding flashes up her spine.

The toenail fell from the pincers and the Commissar repeated his question. Again Odette remained silent.

Third nail.

Extended torture is a journey through a long, dark tunnel. When the agony reaches its apex—the black hollow—the body's survival mechanism kicks in and the victim blacks out. The more skilled the torturer, the closer he brings his subject to unconsciousness without triggering the reaction. The Commissar was an expert.

Fourth toenail.

Question. Silence.

Fifth.

Blood now surrounded her foot but Odette had yet to call out or cry. Her palms carried eight puncture wounds and they still had the right foot to go. The Commissar asked about Arnaud again and Odette glared at him, sitting innocently as he directed the show. It was by design; the Nazis preferred to torture using locals so that no one could say they were mistreated by a German.

Odette said nothing and the Commissar nodded again. The pincers moved to the right foot.

Sixth toenail.

Seventh.

Odette was in the black hollow, her face drenched in sweat and her body quivering, fighting delirium. But she maintained consciousness. No answers.

Eighth.

Ninth.

After the last one cleared the young man stood. Blood was everywhere, the floor littered with skin and nails.

"Well, Lise," the Commissar said, "I think you will find it convenient to walk on your heels for some time."

He had tea brought in and Odette tried to sip while nosing in and out of nausea.

"You are a woman of surprising endurance."

She drank and tried to settle her nerves. She had taken the full ride through the long black tunnel and survived.

The Commissar asked how she felt and Odette said she had nothing to say.

"Conversationally we are becoming a bore to each other," he said. "I keep on asking the same questions and you keep on making the same replies. No doubt you see yourself as a heroine at this moment and me as a monster. I am not. I am a servant of my Führer, Adolf Hitler, and I have no regret for what I do. You should know that I shall stop at nothing to get the information I require. Last night, the charming R.A.F. dropped two thousand tons of bombs on Dortmund. I do not know how many good German women and children were killed or maimed or burned. If mass murder by the R.A.F. is considered to be a legitimate act of war, do you think I care for the sufferings of a single, obstinate, renegade French woman?"

Odette said she thought it interesting that he found it necessary to defend what he had just done.

"Nothing of the sort." The Commissar stood and again brooded over her. "Are you going to answer my questions?"

"No."

"Then I shall cause to be done to your finger-tips the same operation that has just been carried out on your feet."

Odette blanched. The metallic smell of blood was sickening and the thought of another round, numbing. Maybe she would pass out. And then what?

Brandy.

Twenty nails on the floor.

And what after that?

The fire iron. Perhaps to the face?

The Commissar waited for a response and Odette stared at him, her nerves stabbing as rivulets of blood continued to trickle and shock set in.

Suddenly the door swung open and the Commissar snapped to attention. A man in civilian clothes came to the table and observed the blood and nails. There was a brief conversation in German and the man left.

"The Major says that I am wasting my time," the Commissar said, "and that you will never talk. He has ordered that you be taken upstairs. You are a very fortunate woman, Lise. I have no doubt that we shall meet again. One more thing. If you speak about what happened to a living soul, you will be brought here again and worse things will happen to you."

TWO DAYS LATER A man came to Odette's cell. The uniform and medals indicated captain, and that he had served on the Eastern Front. About thirty-five, he was well built and had a fresh complexion. Behind the spectacles were soft, gentle eyes. Father Paul Steinert was his name, Fresnes chaplain.

"You will please forgive me, Father, if I fail to stand up."

"*Ma fille* . . . what have they done to you?"

Odette paused and then said, "You are a German officer, and you must know that it is not permitted to discuss what happens at Number 84 Avenue Foch."

"I am a priest."

Odette removed the bloody rags from her feet and Father Paul gasped in horror. He looked for other abuses.

"And your hands. What are those marks in your hands?"

She explained their origin and Father Paul was overcome with shame and compassion. He stood motionless, absorbing the injury and injustice. There were no words. With heartbreak in his eyes he kissed her forehead and left. He would return often.

Soon thereafter Colonel Henri visited again. He offered a cigarette and smoked while he contemplated his message.

"You've been to the Gestapo," he finally said.

"Yes."

"Lise, I know what they did to you. Believe me when I say how sorry and how utterly ashamed I am. It had nothing to do with me and . . . I couldn't stop it."

Odette said she believed him and Henri asked if there was anything he could do.

"Have you been to see Peter Churchill since I went to the Gestapo?"

Henri said he had not but was going to visit him as soon as he left her.

"Then there is something that you can do. You can keep silent about what they did to me." She explained the rifle butt treatment Peter had taken from the Italian in Annecy and said that if he found out what the Gestapo had done, he'd do something violent and foolish.

Henri agreed. "Lise, do you ever think of yourself?"

"Far too much. I am a very selfish woman."

Henri wrestled with his thoughts—what he had done in bringing Lise to Fresnes—and the consequences when duty and conscience collided like ships in the night. "I hate to see you here," he said at last, "in this place among these vile and sordid people."

Her warders weren't especially vile or sordid, she replied; prison simply revealed and accentuated character—the strong became stronger; the weak, weaker. She bid Henri good-bye.

"Give my love to Peter Churchill," she added. "And not a word about . . . anything else."

"Not a word. I will come again. Au revoir, Lise."

In the interrogation room for Peter's wing, Henri passed along Odette's sentiments and said he wanted to help them.

"Can't you understand now that I hate the Gestapo?" he asked.

Peter understood the rivalry between the Abwehr and Gestapo, and the mutual distrust and disdain wasn't altogether surprising; the British had their own version of it. As MI6 officer Malcolm Muggeridge recognized, "Though the SOE and MI6 were nominally on the same side in the war, they were, generally speaking, more abhorrent to one another than the Abwehr was to either of them."

Henri said he wasn't going to help the Gestapo or try to get anything out of Peter. "It's sufficient for me to have captured you, and now that you're here I can't bear to see you slowly starving to death in this lousy hole. I know all about the meager rations of Fresnes." He asked Peter for the name and address of a friend who could provide food parcels; Henri would arrange pickup and delivery.

Peter was incredulous. This was precisely how Henri had fooled Marsac into providing Roger Bardet. Besides, everyone knew that if Henri actually did this and was caught, he'd be shot.

"My dear Henri. If I were to give you anyone's name and address, you'd immediately suspect that they were implicated in Resistance activities and put them under arrest."

Henri's countenance fell. "You do me a grave injustice, Pierre. I have often been able to help people in this way, nor do I stoop to such low tricks in order to capture people."

Peter reminded him of the trick on Marsac.

"That was different. Marsac was a fool and played right into my hands. After all, you were a big fish and I certainly wouldn't have picked you up if the bomber had been sent for me."

Peter thought for a minute about Henri's ruse of leaving for London to help negotiate the end of the war on behalf of Germany.

"Do you really expect me to believe that, Henri?"

"I do. Marsac told the Gestapo about the bomber business and they began to smell a rat. If the bomber had come I should have vanished from the scene. As it didn't, I had to pick you up or I should have found myself inside your place."

Peter considered the story. It was plausible.

Henri gave his word that he would not arrest the person providing the parcels and Peter said he'd think about it. "Just give me a little time to digest the idea that you and the Gestapo don't work hand in glove," he said. "In the meantime, if you want to give me a treat, have Odette brought here."

Henri gave the order and a guard went to fetch her.

Odette fell into Peter's arms and he held her tightly, noticing that she was much thinner, but not catching that her steps were slow and soft. She asked Henri if she could return to her cell to get something, and he nodded to the guard. When they returned, Odette was carrying two half loaves and gingerbread.

"These are for you, Pierre. I know how hungry you must be."

Peter was speechless. She was starving but had saved for him a large portion of her minuscule rations. He tried to say something but was overcome.

She put the food in his hands. "You know I'm never very hungry."

Sweet Lise. Always sacrificing for someone else.

Henri stepped aside and allowed them several minutes to talk privately.

Back in his cell, Peter reconsidered what Henri had said about coordinating food parcels. At great risk to himself, Henri had just allowed Odette and him to see each other a second time. The spy-catcher, it appeared, had a soft spot.

Peter thought of who might be amenable to the task and Charles Fol—banker, broker, and gentleman farmer—came to mind. Peter had stayed with Charles and his wife two nights in March on his way to Compiègne, and he was confident they would help.

When Henri next visited, Peter gave him the Fol address, asking Henri to mention that Peter's "wife" was also at Fresnes.

It just might work.

IT WAS A SUNDAY when Peter awoke to a driving rainstorm, drops drumming his window like a cadence for the dead. He watched for several minutes as it matched his mood—he was starving and hadn't shaved for six days.

Behind him the door quietly opened. It was Father Paul. Peter turned and saw the light of goodness on him.

"I've just come from your wife's cell in the third division," the priest said. "She asked me to call on you and give you her love and to say that she was well. If I may be permitted to say so, she is a very fine woman. She hopes you are being patient in these difficult times."

Peter sighed. "Thank you, Father. You are the first German who has spoken to me as though I were a human being in seven weeks."

"My profession has no frontiers, Monsieur. We are all God's children and answerable only to him. If we have acted with loyalty to our friends or for a cause, there is no shame in that."

"Tell me, Father, how is my wife, really?"

"She is well and serene. She behaves with great dignity and has already earned the respect of many people, including myself."

Father Paul gave Peter a book on learning German—the only thing he had with him at the time—and said he'd visit again if Peter liked.

"Thank you very much, *mon Père*. Please give my love to my wife and tell her that I am well, that I think of her all day and especially at our meeting hour, and I pray for her every night. And *mon Père*, please come again."

It was still raining when Father Paul left but Peter noticed that his cell was no longer dark. Nor his spirit. It was that man, he thought. Since his first day of incarceration, Peter had suffered bouts of depression. The suffocating shoe box treatment—starved and degraded and deprived—had driven him to near madness. Father Paul changed that. There was something unique about the man—his goodness, his gentleness, his quiet calm. He had been on the Eastern Front, Peter remembered, so he'd seen the horrors: death, misery, frostbitten men who'd eaten their horses.

Without instruction, Peter realized, Father Paul was teaching and the first lesson was that the battle of faith required many scars before it was won.

A FEW DAYS LATER Father Paul returned. Odette was doing well, he said. He gave Peter another book: poems by Goethe. Peter was touched.

"How is it, *mon Père*, that you manage to leave something of yourself behind you in every cell you enter? There must be many cells and many difficult and painful encounters."

"Mine is a rather long day, Monsieur, but I have been blessed with faith that helps to conquer the fatigue of the body. My prayers for guidance are always answered and I sometimes find words are put into my mouth."

"Do you prefer this to the Eastern Front?"

"Man's needs are much the same everywhere," Father Paul said. "Whether I am sent back to the East or remain here is entirely the same to me. I am at God's disposal to be called wherever He may command."

Peter thanked him for the visit and book, and asked that he pass along his love to Odette. When Paul was gone, Peter continued to think about him. What a superb representative of God he was. He was more than a magnificent Catholic priest; he was a genuine saint.

Peter said a silent prayer, giving thanks for what this man was teaching him about what it truly meant to be selfless. When he finished, he opened Goethe and read the first verse of the first poem:

He who has not eaten his bread in tears,
He who has not sat up weeping upon his bed
    throughout the night of despair,
He knows you not, Oh Heavenly Father.

BY JULY 1943 ODETTE and Peter had adjusted to prison, and Odette was almost running the women's wing. One day four guards—two men and two women—came into her cell alleging that she had been talking out of the window; a forbidden practice. Odette denied it.

"Liar," one of the female guards hissed. "You have been talking. Get up."

Odette stood. "I have not been talking out of the window. You can see for yourself that the window is not only sealed but nailed."

Unmoved, the guard slapped Odette twice. "You will be reported," the woman crowed.

The following morning Odette asked to see the captain in charge and one of the guards fetched him. He looked fatherly, Odette thought—midfifties, grey, and rather small—maybe five foot six.

She informed him that she had been unfairly charged and struck twice the previous night by one of his subordinates. The captain apologized and said he didn't want her to think ill of all Germans. He asked if there was anything he could do to make up for the injustice. Odette didn't have anything on the tip of her tongue but mentioned Peter and the captain said he'd let Peter know that she was okay.

He added that he'd find a way to rectify the harm, a parcel perhaps. Just then he noticed the wounds on her feet and his countenance faded. "I am, of course, responsible for the actions of my prison subordinates. I am not responsible for . . . for what may happen outside the walls of the prison."

That night one of the guards delivered a small parcel. It contained twenty-three ginger biscuits—a king's ransom in the court of Fresnes. Even though Odette had been on starvation rations for three months, she removed only a few and closed the box.

The captain also sent something else: a protector. Trude was a forty-year-old SS guard—perhaps the most feared in Fresnes—who would call on Odette once a week and look after her. She was educated, Odette learned, and was impressed by the Churchill name. Trude immediately admired Odette and assumed the role of a servant, delivering the bulk of the ginger biscuits to Peter that evening.

Shortly thereafter, notwithstanding the Gestapo prohibition, the captain had Trude deliver books and more parcels to her.

At the end of the month Odette was again summoned to Avenue Foch. She was taken to the top floor and a well-dressed agent in his early forties offered her tea and began asking questions about a Miss Herbert and Madame Lechene. Odette said nothing and he left.

A few minutes later he returned with two men: the first was short and fit, with sandy hair and a limp. He was the man she knew as Emile, organizer of the CHANCELLOR circuit, which had been operating in Cannes. He was smoking and had some papers under his arm and Odette got the impression he worked there. The second man was a husky, highly decorated officer who resembled Hermann Goering.

Odette pretended not to notice Emile but it was shocking; she had not known that he had been arrested. The Germans asked if she knew him and she said she did not.

That was strange, they said, since he had returned in the same felucca.

"Yes, we have met before," Emile said. "I have been working with Raoul in Cannes. I came back a few months ago, and there you are, I am here!"

Emile told her not to worry and that the war would be over soon.

Odette processed. Emile was acting under duress.

"You must understand," she said to the Germans, "that I did not recognize this man because I met him only for a few minutes at two o'clock in the morning, and I was getting out of the felucca and I did not worry about the people getting in."

The Germans accepted it as a reasonable answer and Emile looked at her again.

"What about Fresnes, can you take it?"

"It is all right, I can take it."

Emile left and the Germans continued to probe, asking her what she knew about him.

Nothing, Odette replied. Peter had told her nothing of what he had done before, and she didn't ask.

Since Odette was French, the well-dressed German said, she in all probability had persuaded Peter to come to France. It didn't really matter.

They'd both be dead very shortly, he said.

CHAPTER 14

VIENNESE WALTZES

The German corrected himself. Peter had a chance of survival, but she did not.

She would be killed without question.

Odette asked why Peter had a chance and the man said that they were working on an exchange. Since he was an English officer and a Churchill, it might go through.

"Can you tell me anything about this exchange," Odette asked, "and for whom you are asking?"

"Hess."

ON AUGUST 19 HENRI visited Odette again. Like a nervous teen trying to ask the prettiest girl to prom, he fidgeted and mumbled.

"I went to a beautiful concert last night and thought of you," he said. "You would have loved it." He brought up Mozart and Shakespeare, rambling on as if mustering up courage to pop the question.

Odette didn't engage. Rebuff by silence.

Henri moved on to the topic of Odette's children, but still she said nothing. He was visibly anxious about something, almost distraught, and finally came out with it: "I would be very distressed, Lise, if you were to be sent to Germany."

Odette asked if that had been scheduled.

"No, no, there is no talk of it—yet. But against the Gestapo, one is helpless."

He retreated again to music, almost to take his mind off the Gestapo, and at length compared Haydn and Bach. Odette didn't engage, and after a few minutes, Henri circled back.

"Lise, I would very much like you to leave this prison with me— if only for a day. I have much to say to you, and it is impossible to speak inside these walls. I would take you out in the morning and give you lunch and that sort of thing."

Odette considered the proposal. Fresh air and real food—how desperately her body needed both. But it wasn't just about her.

A cardinal in danger sounds a distress call knowing that other birds will respond as cavalry. In unrelenting waves they will attack and harass the predator—cat, snake, or otherwise—risking their own lives. Though of different species they will share the terror.

The freedom Henri offered was enticing—lunch almost irresistible—but it would be unfair; no other women received these benefits, and she would not be singled out. No, she would suffer with her mates, even if it killed her.

Beyond that, accepting any favors from Henri posed a greater danger. If she accepted one—a lunch, extra food, even a shower— what would be next? Dinner and a movie? It would be a slippery slope and Odette feared that she would be unable to refuse later favors if she accepted the first one. And even if she could draw the line—accept this favor, reject that one—she sensed that Henri was making a romantic advance. She recalled that Henri had tried to convince her at their first meeting that she didn't really love Peter. Was Henri's luncheon a second attempt to woo her? Heaven forbid, he might even try to kiss her!

She would have none of it.

"You asked me that before," she said, "when I first came in. I told you then that there can be no compromise for the members of the French Section. That is still true. Being here has made no difference to me at all. Thank you for asking me, but I prefer to stay here."

NEAR THE END OF August a guard took Peter to the sergeant's office. There, beaming beside Colonel Henri, was Charles Fol. The elegant businessman was holding two large holdalls, one for Peter, one for Odette.

"Monsieur Fol has very kindly agreed to arrange for fortnightly parcels to reach you and Odette," Henri said. "They will come in small suitcases and when these are empty you will be able to place your dirty laundry inside them. This will be washed and returned to you with the subsequent parcel."

Peter didn't know which man to hug first, but there was more. Henri and Charles had also devised a plan to sneak Peter out later that week for a nice lunch at the Fol residence.

It seemed impossible but if anyone could pull it off, Henri could.

Days later Peter was called from his cell and taken downstairs, where Henri and a number of Germans—apparently Gestapo—awaited. Henri told the men he was taking Peter away for interrogation. The request was unusual as the secret police and Abwehr were out of the picture once a spy was taken to prison; Fresnes was the jurisdiction of the Gestapo.

That Henri slipped Peter out—uncuffed—was a testament to his credibility and persuasiveness. But one risk remained.

As the Citroën rolled through the gates, Henri said, "Now, Pierre, it would be a simple matter for you to bash me over the head whilst my hands are on this wheel, so I must ask you for your parole for the whole period of the outing. If you were to do the dirty on me, I should probably have to pay for it with my neck."

Peter gave his word.

The emancipation, even for a few hours, was surreal. The soft air, the parade of buildings, sunbeams trickling through tree-lined streets bustling with life—it was like bathing in champagne, Peter thought. Shopkeepers, pedestrians, cafes filled with patrons—this was life on the other side.

As they drove, Henri mentioned that Peter would soon have another interrogation. The Gestapo had gleaned nothing to send to Berlin from the first, he said, and wanted another go at him. Fortunately, the man doing the second interview was a dull spark and Peter should win the battle of wits.

They continued on and Peter noticed that Henri was not headed in the direction of the Fol residence, but down Avenue Foch. *Was the next interrogation so soon?*

Henri made a turn and parked on rue Pergolèse, two blocks from the SD office. They went up a flight of stairs and Henri unlocked apartment 56. The living room was large and decorated like something from a lifestyle magazine; forty cushions adorned seats lining the perimeter. Adjacent was a finely furnished drawing room—appropriate for discussing Proust and Flaubert and Saint-Exupéry.

This was Henri's flat. He had brought Peter here, he said, so that Peter could bathe and freshen up before lunch.

Henri introduced his French mistress, Suzanne, who would be joining them for the luncheon, and then showed Peter to the bathroom. Opening the tub tap, Henri set out his shaving kit.

Teutonic hospitality.

THEY ARRIVED AT 8 bis Chaussée de la Muette and Charles and Biche Fol—together with Biche's American mother—welcomed the Englishman, German, and Frenchwoman. Charles fetched a tie so Peter would not feel underdressed; never mind his laceless shoes.

The party conversed a few minutes and then made their way to the dining room. It was a marvelous group—conspirators, imprisoner, prisoner, traitor—all under the watchful eye of mother-in-law.

Eating and drinking, the party fellowshipped with the happy tension of a family reunion.

Coffee was served in the salon, where two grand Steinbachs proudly defied war and occupation. Knowing that Biche was a concert pianist, Peter asked her to play and the room came alive as she entertained with her favorite melodies. After several pieces she motioned to Peter.

"Now your turn, Pierre."

Peter surprised himself that he could still play. His fingers—even the broken ones—seemed to manage their way over the ivories as if he were still at Cambridge. On his second tune, he heard Biche join in on the other piano, harmonizing seamlessly. He swung his head to smile at her and gaped.

It was *Henri*, grinning like a schoolboy over the grand. He played magnificently, offering a descant to everything Peter played, in any key. Here they were, captor and captive, German and English, entertaining the French in their own salon.

Recognizing Henri's superior talent, Peter stopped and let the spy-catcher at it. Henri didn't disappoint. Little did the guests know, Hugo Bleicher's greatest ambition as a young man was to become a concert pianist. For years he had practiced in the family home at Tettnang, only to fall short. While his talent was immense, in a country which had produced Bach, Handel, Beethoven, and Brahms, Hugo's aspirations were a bar too far. With great disappointment, he abandoned his dream and commenced work as a banker's apprentice.

But here—in the company of friends, foes, and Fols—the passion he once savored had been stoked. For half an hour Henri performed, entertaining the awed guests with Viennese waltzes.

The gaiety was genuine but Peter remembered Henri's line to the Gestapo; they had left Fresnes under the auspices of an interrogation. It was now half past five so he suggested to Henri that Cinderella should be getting back to the castle soon.

Before they left, Suzanne gave Peter two large bunches of grapes—one for Odette—which Henri would have to sneak in.

Chaussée de la Muette, Paris. *CP ARAMA*

"I've got a transmitter tucked away somewhere," Henri said during the drive. "Why don't you come out with me one day and send a message to London asking for a Lysander to come and pick us up on any field you like? If you consent to do this, I can get you out on some pretext or another and we'll return to London together."

Peter replied that if he were responsible for the capture of a Lysander and pilot he couldn't live with his conscience. Besides, if Henri really wanted to get back to England, he could go with Peter to the Pyrenees and cross the frontier.

Fine idea, Henri said, but they couldn't get past the military Controls en route.

"A pity, Henri. Then I must simply sweat it out inside."

The Citroën passed through the gates.

Peter reclined on his bed that night but sleep wouldn't come. Who *was* this man who had arrested him, turned him over to the Gestapo, felt remorse over doing so, risked his skin to bring food, doubled the danger with the Fol outing, entertained with Viennese waltzes, and then asked for a Lysander?

A FEW DAYS AFTER the Fol luncheon, Henri returned to see Odette.

"I've decided," he said, "tomorrow I'm coming to fetch you very early in the morning, take you to Paris for the day, bring you back at night about ten o'clock. You can have a bath, you can have a good meal, you can wash your hair."

"*Are* you," she replied. "If you ever do a thing like that, I am going to scream so loudly that everybody will know that I'm taken out of this place by force. I will *not* go to Paris with you, not friends or anything. I will have no contact with anybody and you cannot take me away without people knowing that you are doing it through brute force. I will not go."

It wasn't that she thought Henri was going to trick her. She had heard about Peter's outing at the Fols' and that it went well and that Peter had come back with a parcel. It was a matter of discipline and integrity—she wasn't going to have any compromise with the Germans.

AS AUTUMN USHERED IN the winter chill and leaves began to fall, Odette's health followed suit. She acquired a cough and a gland on the side of her neck swelled. Going months on 175 grams of black bread and a thin bowl of cabbage soup a day—apparently the minimum to keep one alive—her body was eating away at the little muscle she carried.

On October 15 the captain of the guard moved her to a new cell—number 337—on the third floor. It would be warmer, he said, and she would have two fellow prisoners to keep her company. Before the transfer she was allowed a special treat: a shower.

It was the first she'd had since her capture in April.

Odette's cellmates were appalled at her condition. Simone Hérail testified after the war that when Odette came to live with her, "her health was seriously impaired by this inhuman procedure [solitary confinement] so dear to the Nazis; her weakness was extreme: she could no longer even eat the small amount of filthy and repugnant food which was given to us. On some days she had not the strength to leave her paillasse."[30]

Simone noticed something else, too: notwithstanding Odette's sickness, "at no moment did her courage or her determination to struggle to survive falter."

From Odette's standpoint, her cellmates offered a unique bene-fit: information. As they were taken to Avenue Foch for their own interrogations, they brought back comments about what they'd ob-served. Her other cellmate, Lucienne Delmas, thought it strange after one visit that an Englishman was there. Odette asked for a description and the woman described Emile.

He was a prisoner there, she said. The Germans were keeping him close at hand, Emile had told her, because he had a wireless set and they could get news from England before anyone else.

News.

They had turned his radio.

AS DAYS PASSED THE effect of slow starvation—going on five months now—exacerbated Odette's ill health. Her cough wors-ened, the gland on her neck swelled to the size of a grapefruit, and she developed pleurisy, a painful lung-related inflammation that re-stricts breathing. The prison captain requested that Odette be sent to a Paris hospital but the Gestapo refused. The only other thing he could think of was to allow her time in the prison sewing room. It would be warm, spacious, and permit greater freedom of move-ment. He presented the idea to her and she asked what they sewed.

They mended the uniforms of the prison staff, he said.

Odette voiced her disdain for patching the pants of Germans.

---

30 A thin mattress filled with sawdust or straw.

She would be delighted, however, to make dolls out of any odd material she could find.

"Frau Churchill, I must remind you that this is a prison, not a toy factory."

Odette was firm. Dolls or nothing.

The following morning she thought of her girls as she began crafting rag dolls out of unused scraps of cloth. After that, she created a unique gift for Peter. Worried that he might be cold, she made him a sleeping gown and embroidered his initials on the breast pocket.

Faithful Trude made the secret delivery.

Odette wanted to do something else, too—something for prisoners most in need of food. As she was working one day she noticed a fuse box, apparently the power center for the entire wing. It would be a long shot, but what the hell. She spoke with the other girls and collected names of prisoners dying of starvation.

The following morning she wandered over to the box and cut some wires and jammed scissors into fuse holes, blowing the circuits. Summoning guards, she gave them her list of starving prisoners; these were *electricians* who could restore power, she told them. When the inmates arrived, Odette slipped them food.

Other prisoners noticed Odette's altruism and were touched. But what could they do for her?

Near the end of the month, opportunity arose. One afternoon Odette heard shouting from other women in the block. They were shouting at *her*.

Odette! Odette! . . . Pierre!

She listened carefully . . . *Peter is in the exercise yard!*

She raced to the window—yes, it was him! She couldn't shout to Peter because, like her prior cell, her window didn't open. But a woman in another cell opened her window and shouted, *"Pierre, Pierre, votre Odette est ici!"*—"Peter, Peter, your Odette is here!"

Peter stopped and searched to find the woman shouting.

Odette pulled her chair to the window and grabbed a paper. Near the ceiling was a small, secondary window, partially open.

Maybe, just maybe. She jumped on the seat and began waving the paper, shouting to him.

"Can you see her waving the paper?" the woman hollered to Peter.

Odette continued to wave. Did he find her? *Yes!* But he couldn't hear a word she was saying.

"She sends you her love and says 'Courage,'" the woman yelled.

"Tell her to listen," Peter shouted back, "and I will sing her my reply."

Odette could vaguely hear him. He was singing—in French— Richard Tauber's "You Are My Heart's Delight":

> *You are my heart's delight,*
> *And where you are, I long to be*
> *You make my darkness bright,*
> *When like a star you shine on me*
> *Shine, then, my whole life through*
> *Your life divine bids me hope anew*
> *That dreams of mine may at last come true*
> *And I shall hear you whisper, "I love you."*

HUGO BLEICHER, MEANWHILE, TENDED to his work with a new assistant. Roger Bardet, the erstwhile CARTE operative, had thrown his lot with the Germans and become a full-fledged agent under Hugo's supervision. Working simultaneously for the Abwehr and SD, Bardet assisted in dismantling the INVENTOR circuit led by Sidney Jones.

Through Bardet, Hugo learned that Sidney's courier, Vera Leigh, lived in a flat on rue Marbeau—a block from his own on Pergolèse. Hugo watched her movements for a few weeks and on October 30 arrested her.

ON NOVEMBER 11, REMEMBRANCE Day, Odette was summoned again to Avenue Foch. The interrogator placed several photographs before her and asked if she recognized any of the men. She knew two of them—operatives from other circuits—but told him she didn't recognize any. He asked what she thought of Colonel Buckmaster and she gave no reply.

After an hour of questions and answers which ended in cul-de-sacs, Odette was put in an adjacent room and left until evening. At ten o'clock she was taken to a car parked in front of the building. Inside were two men in uniform and a third in civilian clothes— the Frenchman with the pretty face and Faustian scar on his soul.

"Since you are such a devotee of your country," he said, "I thought you'd like to go to the Arc de Triomphe on the event of November and see the German guards standing there."

Odette let it go.

They left and the car circled around and around the Arc, its eternal flame at the Tomb of the Unknown Soldier flickering in defiance of the occupation.

"Look well, Frau Churchill," the man said, "because I don't suppose you will ever see this again."

Odette sneered. "I shall see the Arc de Triomphe again, Monsieur, but without a German soldier. And when I see it, I shall be in uniform, in British uniform."

The man cursed at her and instructed the driver to return to the prison.

"You like what you are doing," she said to him, "the job you're doing. You're a sick man."

The Gestapo, meanwhile, had no interest in holidays or field trips. It was time to say au revoir to the grey eminence of SPIN-DLE. Odette Churchill had refused to provide information, even after torture, and proved to be more trouble than she was worth.

She was summoned to 84 Avenue Foch one more time and escorted upstairs to a large drawing room guarded by two SS. Inside she was seated at a small table without further instruction. Unlike the room of her interrogations, this one was quite elegant. Trickles of light danced from a cut-glass chandelier—a Quatorze or Quinze, she thought.

Ballroom party or Gestapo pedicure?

Large double doors opposite her suddenly were flung back and Odette looked up at a panel of uniformed officers staring at her. The SS guards flanked her and one of the officers barked out: "Frau Churchill."

At first it seemed like the beginning of another interrogation, but what of the formality? A smartly dressed man began addressing the panel in German and at once the purpose of the proceeding was evident.

This was a kangaroo court.

The man speaking—a senior Gestapo official—was the prosecutor; the officers, the judges. There would be no defense counsel and the proceedings would be conducted entirely in German.

Odette remained silent as the prosecutor read the charges and the judges deliberated. After some time the man in the middle—a colonel decorated with the Iron Cross—stood and began pontificating.

Odette interrupted to say that she did not understand German.

In French he said, "Madame Churchill, you are condemned to death on two counts. The first is because you are a British spy and the second because you are a Frenchwoman. *Heil Hitler!*"

The second charge, she assumed, meant that she was guilty of being a member of the French Resistance. Silently, she laughed. *For which country shall I die?*

So this was it. Here she was, alone, her brother in a camp and her lover in the clink and the free world clinging to the Old Man's "fight on the beaches" charge. She wouldn't live to see Hitler's demise, no, but at least she'd go to her Maker knowing that both Churchills were proud of her. Sadly, though, three little girls in London would learn the hard way for whom the bell tolled.

She flashed a patronizing smile. "Gentlemen, you must take your pick of the counts. I can only die once."

That night a sign was placed on her door.

A red cross.

CHAPTER 15

ALL MY LOVE

As Christmas neared the Red Cross brought parcels—including miniature Christmas trees—for prisoners in solitary confinement, and families and friends brought parcels for those who were not. Odette was a beneficiary of the generosity, receiving from others small items such as pots of jam. Peter, in turn, received a parcel from the Fols, which also contained a small tree. He set it below his crucifix and beside a poem that the Catholic Society had sent.

Christmas and sanctification all in one.

Meanwhile in the sewing room, Odette was busy. She crafted a small crib—complete with baby Jesus—to set beside the small tree someone had brought, and made two rag dolls for Father Paul's niece and nephew.

On Christmas Day, someone in the cell block began singing *"Il est né, le divin Enfant"*—"He was born, the Divine Child." As the words echoed down the hall, Odette fought back tears. She had sung this very carol to her girls many a Christmas night.

Joyeux Noël, Marianne. Joyeux Noël, Lily. Joyeux Noël, Francoise.

January 1944

THE NEW YEAR ROLLED in and little changed for team SPINDLE. Peter and Odette had minimal contact with the outside world and knew little about the status of the war. For them, each day brought the same sensations: hunger and thoughts of each other.

The Allies, in fact, were inching toward victory, one fallen soldier at a time. On the fourth the Red Army crossed the prewar Polish border, and later in the month the Americans would land at Anzio.

On January 14 Peter's door opened and there stood Trude—a collaborator's grin and something in her hands. Odette had not forgotten: it was Peter's birthday. He took the gift and beamed; it was a handkerchief that she had embroidered in the sewing room.

> *To Peter, with all my love.*
> Odette
> 14 Jan 1944

For two people in solitary confinement, Trude's messenger service was a gift all its own. Still, Peter and Odette longed to see each other. About three weeks later it appeared they might get the chance. Odette heard that she and a number of other prisoners were to be taken to rue de Saussaies, Gestapo headquarters, for fingerprinting. She called for the captain of the guard and asked if Peter also would be fingerprinted. He would, the captain said, but Peter was not on the list for tomorrow.

Since it shouldn't matter to the Germans in what order the prints were collected, Odette asked if she and Peter could go on the same day.

The captain looked at her. "Frau Churchill, is it your wish that I should be dismissed from my post?"

"Far from it, Monsieur. It is unlikely that your successor could be as just and as understanding as you are."

He grinned. "Eventually you will get me hanged, Frau Churchill. I will see what I can do—but it means approaching the Commandant."

THE FINGERPRINT LINE WAS a herded mass, but Peter spotted Odette and came alongside. No talking was allowed and a guard stood only feet away, facing him. Odette whispered something and a redhead nonchalantly slipped between Peter and the guard so the German couldn't see Peter's lips moving, but facing the soldier to give the couple privacy.

Peter asked who she was and Odette said under her breath, "Diana Rowden. One of us."[31]

Peter nodded and guards ushered the group up a flight of stairs to a landing where they waited for an hour. Odette explained how the captain allowed them to be fingerprinted together, and how Trude was so kind to deliver their messages and food. Odette mentioned the sewing room, and how she agreed to go there so long as she did no work for the Germans. She ended up doing some work, though—in a way. The room was working on the new Afrika Korps caps, she said, and she decided to help; on each piece of cardboard used for the peaks she wrote: "Made in England."

Peter smiled. This was the Odette who had confronted a German general on the train to Arles and forced him to fork over the Winter Relief tax. This was the gal who had persuaded three German officers to move a piano upstairs so the SPINDLE team could enjoy Christmas Eve in proper fashion. But it wasn't just pranks. Odette's morale was sky-high, he had noticed, and through her optimistic personality she had transferred a sense of joy to other

---

31 Rowden, an F Section courier for the ACROBAT and STOCKBROKER circuits, had been arrested at Lons-le-Saunier only days earlier.

prisoners and even guards. Peter realized now what Paul Steinert had meant by the regard in which Odette was held.

Odette asked Peter if he had been ill-treated during interrogations and he said he had not, although he had been called to Avenue Foch only twice. He asked if she had been mistreated.

"Never. But they've had me up fourteen times. They seem to think I know more than I do."

Peter asked why and Odette explained what the Commissar had said about him at her first interrogation—that he was a doorknob. She was just about to set him straight, she said, when it dawned on her that it was the dream defense.

"What do you mean?"

"Why, if I grudgingly admitted that you were a numb-skull I could make out that I was the grey eminence behind our movement."

Peter winced. "Oh God! You did that! No wonder they left me alone. Oh, Odette, you sweet, crazy fathead!"

Odette's bravery was highly dangerous, he knew, if not suicidal. What would the Gestapo do to her? Fourteen interrogations and they had not tortured her? One more visit, perhaps, and then the chopper?

She also told Peter how they could communicate in the future. She had been saving gifts of jam and she would have Trude deliver one to him every two weeks. Inside the cardboard top of the cover, she said, he would find her note written on cigarette paper. He would reply with a message coded in a book he would have Trude deliver. Starting on page fifty, she instructed, he would form words by placing a pinprick below each letter he wanted.

Peter was impressed; even the slide rules in Codes could not have come up with a better scheme. Faithful Trude began the courier service, and the SPINDLE team was back in business.

THE LOVE LETTERS, GIFTS, and meetings would end all too soon, however. On February 13 a guard told Peter to pack his things; he was off to Germany, the man said. Peter separated his items into two bags, one of which he packed for Odette. He gave the man cigarettes and asked him kindly to make the delivery.

As guards were inspecting Peter's bag downstairs, Trude came by and asked where he was going. Germany, he told her.

Trude gasped. "Frau Churchill won't like this thought. Am I to tell her this news?"

Yes, Peter said, and if Trude would please make sure the box he had just given to the guard was delivered to her.

Trude was on her way.

Peter signed for a small, mysterious parcel at the checkout desk and was whisked off to Gestapo headquarters downtown. While he waited in a detention room, he opened it. He couldn't believe his eyes. It was his *wallet*—the one Odette had hidden in the car when they were arrested some ten months ago.

He checked the compartments. Money? Gone. Arnaud's messages? Gone. He opened the flap to the special compartment. Yes! The small photos of his mother and Odette were still there. He kissed his mother and returned her to the wallet. As he looked at Odette, he wondered what the future held for her, for them.

The door opened and in traipsed the chief of the Paris Gestapo.

"I've got some good news for you," he said in German. "You are being sent back to England."

Peter said nothing.

"It's true, *nach Hause*." Home.

Peter smirked. "You're pulling my leg."

"Not at all. You and a British major are being exchanged for a German lieutenant now in British hands. We are offering two of you to get him back. Your colleague is already in Berlin where you will also be held until you go home via Switzerland or Sweden. Would you like your wife to travel with you?"

Surely it was a trap but Peter played along. "What do *you* think?"

The chief said he'd call Fresnes and make the arrangements.

When he had gone someone brought in a hot plate of meatballs, potatoes, and cabbage.

Peter looked at the food. *Could it be true?* He had been down this trail before. He sniffed at the scent, his mind pawing the possibility. If it was a hoax, why the hospitality? And would a man of this importance have time or inclination to conjure up such an elaborate scheme, complete with the underhanded enticement of someone's wife?

His spirits soared as he envisioned standing with Odette at the rail of a Swedish liner, the Aurora Borealis blessing their love.

Around eight o'clock guards escorted him to the second floor, where the chief was again waiting. Peter inquired about Odette.

Oh, right, the German said. Berlin reported that she would not be going after all. Sorry.

Peter stared at him. *Bastard.*

THE RIDE WAS SURPRISINGLY comfortable. There had been other passengers in the second-class compartment, but one of the Gestapo escorts flashed his identification and the squatters vanished. The secret policemen, it turned out, were quite friendly. One was an older gentleman—beyond the age for military service—and the other was a young man who was in the occupation reserve.

When dawn came they were well into Germany and Peter saw the handiwork of Allied bombers on factories, houses, and military yards. The RAF also seemed to have nailed a number of railways as they had to change trains twice before reaching Berlin's Anhalter Station.

It was eleven o'clock when the Gestapo car rolled into headquarters at the Albrechtstrasse, but even at night Peter could see the damage.

The agents checked Peter in, and the young one went home. The older man escorted him down a long corridor and then through a pair of massive oak doors. Before them was a panel of uniformed officers.

"Erik Hoffmeyer reporting with his prisoner from Paris."

The senior officer gave Hoffmeyer his leave and asked Peter to be seated.

Peter drank in the inner sanctum: six officers sipping tea, a raised dais with a battery of telephones, a radio set, a young girl taking shorthand, a large framed picture of the lord of the Gestapo, Heinrich Himmler, overseeing all.

It had all the trappings of a trial.

But not at half past eleven. So why the pomp? The setting was more formal than his Foch tribunals, but there was no way that official Gestapo business would be conducted at midnight. No, the routine was universal: *mornings* were for interrogations and trials; afternoons were for executions and tortures, and, after a full hard day, evenings were for drinking and dancing and putting the children down.

So what was *this*?

A major stood and picked up one of the phones. "Is that the chief receptionist of the Ritz?" A pause. "I want you to prepare your very best room with a private bath, of course, for a most important new guest."

Peter's pulse quickened. Could it be true? Perhaps there was a glimmer of hope.

The major set down the phone and burst into laughter. With a sneer, he instructed the guards to make a thorough search of Peter's belongings.

Ah, yes. Not every day you get to have a little fun with Winston Churchill's nephew.

Peter followed the guards out, then the familiar tramp along the cell block—*Yes, I have read the bloody regulations*—and the metallic clang of the lock.

No toilet, smaller than his cell at Fresnes, lovely rubber floor. The bed seemed nice—actual sheets and blankets—and a solid wood table and chair. There was also a high window with blackout cardboard over it. And the place was spotless.

The Ritz, indeed.

As he settled in, Peter noticed something else: on the back of his door were scratches. He examined them closely. *How?* He surveyed the room again. The window with the cardboard—the glass was missing. And the furniture was new; maybe the floor, too.

He had it now. Bomb blast.

His predecessor had been thrown by an explosion—a tossed salad of prisoner, glass, table, and chair—against the door. They had cleaned up the blood nicely.

Peter took it in stride.

He was a target.

Fresnes Prison

ODETTE WAS MAKING HER way to the sewing room when Trude motioned to her with a conspiratorial wave. They went into an open cell and Trude said, "Frau Churchill, I have something to tell you concerning your husband."

Odette sat to brace herself, nerves twitching. "Tell me."

"He has been taken away yesterday."

Taken away. Euphemism for horizontal exit. "Has he been shot? I want to know. I am strong enough to know the truth."

"No. He has been taken to Berlin, to Gestapo headquarters in the Prinz Albrechtstrasse, for interrogation."

Prinz Albrechtstrasse. It made 84 Avenue Foch look like Scarborough Fair. Everyone knew about their dungeons and tortures and confession killings. Dribble out the last betrayal and then the bucket to wash out the blood.

Odette absorbed it with composure. Today Peter was alive. Tomorrow he would be alive. And *after the war,* she told herself, he would be alive.

Berlin

PETER ADJUSTED TO LIFE in the Albrechtstrasse—no talking, no parcels, no visitors, no exercise. Nothing to read. Just silence. Deafening silence.

His was an open-air coffin in the Gestapo cemetery. *Here lies*

British saboteur Peter Churchill, nephew of Winston Churchill. Exterminated February 1944.

Strangely, though, he had yet to be called for questioning. No beatings or tortures. Prospects of an exchange lingered, teasing him each dawn as guards jingled keys and whistled through the halls. He was certain the Gestapo believed that he was Churchill's nephew, and in their minds the leverage was substantial. A trade for Hess seemed unlikely, but MI5 no doubt held any number of captured German spies, all of whom had appointments with the Tower of London.

He envisioned a Berlin cable being delivered to the German ambassador in Stockholm, the ambassador's visit with the British minister, and the ensuing call to the Security Service.

Who? Wait . . . Yes, we have him. Standartenführer Hans Wolfgang. Guilty of espionage, condemned to death . . . An exchange? We've had those proposals before. Sorry, old boy. 'Fraid the two chaps in Germany will have to take pot luck.

Once again, he would have to sweat it out. But this time, no dueling pianos, no love letters, no refreshment from Father Paul.

THE INACTIVITY AT THE Albrechtstrasse had a simple explanation: the Germans had their hands full with the onslaught of Allied bombers and fighters attacking their homeland. In January the Luftwaffe had lost 292 pilots—12 percent of its force—and February would be worse. With incredibly bad luck, Peter had arrived in Berlin just in time for a bull's-eye view of Big Week—one of the largest air offensives in history. Code-named Operation Argument, the raid was a six-day-and-night coordinated attack by RAF Bomber Command and the US Strategic Air Forces in Europe. Commencing February 20, more than 3,800 American and 2,351 British bombers dropped nearly twenty thousand tons of incendiaries on German fighter plane and other military factories in Berlin, Hamburg, and elsewhere.

The principal objective was to cripple German fighter production; the secondary aim was to thin the ranks of Luftwaffe fighter pilots. Both goals were achieved: the Luftwaffe lost 34 percent of its fighter aircraft in one week, and would lose 18 percent of its pilots during the month. After six days of pounding, the German air force was incapable of defending much of its airspace, which provided the Allies the tertiary goal: unchallenged attacks on Berlin.

From his cell Peter heard and relished the daily bombings. Payback for the Battle of Britain. But what he witnessed all week were attacks on targeted factories. Now, with a limping Luftwaffe, the Allies could hammer Nazi administration centers like the Reich Chancellery.

And the Albrechtstrasse.

The night of February 27, all hell rained down. For more than an hour Peter felt the concussions of incendiaries setting the city ablaze. It was Wagner's *Ride of the Valkyries*—antiaircraft batteries chasing bombers, bombers chasing targets, bombs chasing buildings, firemen chasing fires.

Bombs began exploding around the prison, tearing loose stone and plaster. The guards pretended not to notice—stiff upper lip and all that—but prayed as they paced.

"Let them all come," Peter said to himself, "and if some happen to drop on the prison, all the better. If the lights must go out for good I should never blame a British pilot. This is as good a way of going as any."

Call the Valkyries to carry him to Valhalla.

At that moment, high above the Albrechtstrasse, an Allied pilot dropped his load.

CHAPTER 16

LILY OF THE VALLEY

At midnight came the air-raid siren's song;
I thought of you in silence and for long—
how you are faring, how our lives once were,
and how I wish you home this coming year.
We wait till half past one, and hear at last
the signal that the danger now is past;
so danger—if the omen does not lie—
of every kind shall gently pass you by.

—Dietrich Bonhoeffer

Sirens wailed as shells pounded the prison.

Perfect, Peter thought. Surely some of these RAF offerings would be destroying prisoner files and the Gestapo would have a house full of strangers. As concussion after concussion rocked the Albrechtstrasse, guards began unlocking cells, keeping only the bolt. Peter jumped as a massive explosion came from the yard—every prisoner in the underground cells killed instantly.

The bombing finally stopped and a guard opened Peter's door and peered in.

"How goes it?"

"First class," Peter said.

He had survived the raid but many of his captors had not, which brought a new danger: vengeance. How many prisoners would be shot in reprisal? he wondered.

Days passed and nothing happened.

ON MARCH 2 A guard told Peter to gather his things as he was moving again. But why? He'd not been questioned once.

At the checkout desk, two Gestapo awaited, one sporting a grisly *Mensur*[32] scar. Scarface glared at Peter and opened his jacket. "If you try any funny business, you'll get this."

Peter shrugged at the Luger. "Good. Where are we going?"

To his new residence, the German said.

Scarface escorted Peter to an Opel, motor running. They headed north and the signs indicated the destination: Oranienburg.

---

32 *Mensur*, or "academic fencing" as it was sometimes called, was saber dueling. Thought to instill courage and mettle in young men, it had been practiced in German universities since the sixteenth century. Hitler encouraged the bouts, believing that they created fearless soldiers. Participants wore a small mask to protect the eyes and nose, neck armor, and a protective vest. The object of the duel—as evidenced by Peter's escort—was to disfigure an opponent's face. The matches were carefully regulated by a referee and timed. Seemingly to assure mutual destruction, the contests were scheduled for fifteen minutes, and no ducking, dodging, or flinching was allowed. A surgeon would be on hand to address any life-threatening cuts, but otherwise the mandated time was followed. Afterward, as Mark Twain observed after witnessing a bout in Heidelberg, the men would be "led away drenched with crimson from head to foot." The practice, it seemed, was appropriate for the Gestapo.

Home of the Sachsenhausen concentration camp.

As the Opel drew near, Peter could see the machine-gun towers and electrified walls. They stopped at the entrance gate and the ominous sign beckoned:

SCHUTZHAFTLAGER
PROTECTIVE CUSTODY CAMP.

Sachsenhausen Concentration Camp. O. ANG, BUNDESARCHIV

"PROTECTIVE CUSTODY" WAS THE Nazi regulation and procedure which allowed unbridled lawlessness. Its usefulness for terror came in three stages. First, after the Reichstag fire in 1933, individual fundamental rights were terminated by decree, and actions now taken by the Gestapo were not subject to review by courts. Second, in 1934, the Reich Criminal Code was amended to allow "preventive arrest" in the "interests of public security." Those who were considered risks to public security—and subject to unchallenged arrest—were "anti-social malefactors" such as career criminals, Communists, Jehovah's Witnesses, and prostitutes. The category was soon expanded to include Jews and anyone who challenged Nazi doctrine.

These two steps ushered in protective custody: incarceration in a concentration camp. Anyone charged with being a threat to public security was now automatically sent to a camp, and, as of 1939, such imprisonment was to last at least for the duration of the war. In addition, protective custody cleared the way for *Sonderbehandlung*: "special treatment" of prisoners.

In other words, execution or extermination through labor.

Peter had no idea what protective custody meant, but the meaning became implicitly clear when a line of pinstriped prisoners staggered by, all lugging sixty-six pounds of bricks on their backs. This was a concentration camp, he realized, the horrors of which he'd now experience firsthand. From what he could tell, Fresnes and the Albrechtstrasse were the country clubs; this was where real work was accomplished.

"Is this my new residence?" he asked.

Scarface shrugged. "What if it is? All you foreigners misrepresent these camps. Just look at those flowers over there. And every Sunday the loudspeakers relay the best music in the world. Why, they even hold football matches here."

Peter held his tongue. Flowers and Strauss and football. Sure.

Scarface turned Peter over to a guard and they walked along a path and through a wired gate. They came to two small wooden huts almost hidden beneath pine trees and the guard led him inside the first one and opened a door.

Peter's new home.

The makeshift cell had large windows and Peter stepped to them to drink in the marvelous sky. He thought of Odette and in what kind of hole she was now suffering. He replayed in his mind what had happened at Avenue Foch and grieved that she had accepted the punishment meant for him.

He replayed again and again his answers to the Commissar. Could he have been more clever during his interrogation? Could he have said anything to have improved Odette's lot? And what *was* her lot right now?

The huts, Peter soon learned, were for Allied POWs; the main camp on the other side of the wall was for Jews, Christians, Gypsies, malcontents, political prisoners—including Kurt von Schuschnigg, former chancellor of Austria—and anyone the Nazis wished to silence.

Created in 1936 to provide forced labor[33] for factories, Sachsenhausen would, with its sister camps Dachau and Buchenwald (created in 1933 and 1937, respectively), serve as Heinrich Himmler's model for concentration camps. Pitching the purpose of camps as "education" institutes, Himmler stated in a 1939 radio address: "The slogan that stands above these camps is: There is a path to freedom. Its milestones are: obedience, diligence, honesty, orderliness, cleanliness, sobriety, truthfulness, readiness to make sacrifices, and love of the fatherland."

What he didn't tell his compatriots was that the educational tools were hard labor, corporal punishment, starvation, terror, and execution. That, and the fact that common criminals and "dangerous" political enemies would never be released.

Selecting a special breed of sinister keepers for these camps, Himmler adorned their uniforms with a skull-and-bones badge and dubbed them Death's Head units. The moniker fit. At Sachsenhausen, SS guards would direct new prisoners to Himmler's slogan—"Work makes free"—painted on barracks in the roll call area. With a miscreant's grin, they'd then point to the crematorium and crack: "There is a path to freedom, but only through this chimney!"

The prisoners responded—among themselves—accordingly: "There is a path to the SS. Its milestones are: stupidity, impudence, mendacity, boasting, shirking, cruelty, injustice, hypocrisy, and love of booze."

Though not designated a death camp, Sachsenhausen became one. Through starvation, hard labor, and a myriad of tortures, some forty thousand would die here, including Stalin's son.

Peter learned soon enough. Occasionally at night he'd hear a

---

33 Sachsenhausen also used skilled prisoners for Operation Bernhard—the SD's devious scheme to flood Britain with counterfeit currency.

burst of machine-gun fire—a would-be escapee caught in the search lights. During the day it was the other—smoke and stench coming from the stack; another burned in the crematorium.

He thought of these men from time to time.

He thought of Odette constantly.

Fresnes Prison
May 1944

MEANWHILE IN PARIS, ODETTE was despondent. Peter was gone, she'd been sentenced to death, so what was left? A few more weeks of starvation and loneliness. More days without a bath or the ability to wash her hair or brush her teeth. And then what?

It was a torture all its own.

On May 12 a guard told her to pack her things; she was going to Germany. Odette asked to see Father Paul and minutes later the priest was at her door.

She gazed into the kind eyes—eyes that took you in and held you, comforted, and promised that everything he had was yours.

"I wanted to say good-bye to you, Father, because you have been more than a good friend to me. I am being sent to Germany."

Father Paul, quick to listen and slow to speak, said tenderly, "There is little I can say. You will yourself know that I am not very beloved by the Gestapo and I don't know if I will still be alive at the end of the war. I doubt it very much. But there is a thing I would hope to do for you. If you write a letter to your children now and give it to me, I will, if I live, see that they get it after the war. That I would like to do."

Odette wrote the letter and said good-bye to the saint.

Word spread that Frau Churchill was leaving, and one of her cellmates gave her a sleeping gown, another a bouquet of lilies of the valley. Trude brushed back tears as Odette made her way down the corridor for the last time. In the yard the captain of the guard stood by the waiting Black Maria and saluted her. In his other hand, more lilies of the valley.

"Frau Churchill, I have brought you some flowers," he said. "Please accept them."

She thanked him and again he saluted. The one prisoner Fresnes would never forget.

The captain wanted to say something more but couldn't find the words. Odette smiled, gave him her hand and the warmth of her eyes, and boarded the van.

THE BLACK MARIA TRANSPORTED Odette and six other prisoners to 84 Avenue Foch and the women were locked in a waiting room. As they looked at one another, it dawned on them—*they were all F Section agents*. They shared their code and real names, and what they did each network. Odette was amazed and impressed.

There was Vera Leigh ("Simone"), courier for the INVEN-TOR circuit; Diana Rowden ("Paulette"), courier for ACROBAT/ STOCKBROKER; Andrée Borrel ("Denise"), courier for PROS-PER; Yolande Beekman ("Yvonne"), radio operator for MUSICIAN; Madeleine Damerment ("Solange"), courier for BRICKLAYER; and Eliane Plewman ("Gaby"), courier for MONK.

The stories were different but, like Odette's, shared the same result. Vera Leigh, the forty-six-year-old dress designer, had been betrayed by none other than Roger Bardet and was arrested in Paris on 30 October 1943 when meeting another operative. Bardet might have had a hand in Diana Rowden's arrest as well.

When Rowden's circuit leader, John Renshaw Starr, was arrested in July 1943, Rowden and her wireless operator, John Young, went to ground. In November Young received a message from London indicating that they were to meet a newly arriving agent named Benoit, whose real name was André Maugenet. Rowden and Young met him in Paris at the Chez Mas cafe, in the Place des Ternes. Only it wasn't Maugenet—he had been arrested weeks earlier—but an SD imposter, apparently Bardet. That evening, Rowden and Young were arrested.

Vera Leigh
RECORDS OF SPECIAL
OPERATIONS EXECUTIVE

Diana Rowden
RECORDS OF WOMEN'S
AUXILIARY FORCE

Andrée Borrel
NATIONAL ARCHIVES/BNPS

Yolande Beekman
RECORDS OF WOMEN'S
AUXILIARY FORCE

Madeleine Damerment
RECORDS OF SPECIAL
OPERATIONS EXECUTIVE

Eliane Plewman
RECORDS OF SPECIAL
OPERATIONS EXECUTIVE

Andrée Borrel, the first female agent to parachute into France, was captured the night of 23 June 1943 with her wireless operator when their hideout was compromised. In many ways, Borrel was remarkably similar to Odette. As courier to F Section's leading network, PROSPER, Andrée was given tremendous responsibility and was viewed by her circuit leader as "the best of us all." And she, too, was a rock. After arrest, she refused to talk and maintained her silence with such firmness that several Germans said she treated them with fearless contempt.

Yolande Beekman, a thirty-two-year-old Swiss agent, was captured in St. Quentin when she committed a radio operator's unpardonable sin: routine. To avoid detection by the German direction-finding squads, wireless agents were safest if they transmitted sparingly, with brief messages, at irregular times, on multiple wavelengths, and from various hideouts. Beekman, perhaps with the approval of her circuit leader, did just the opposite: she radioed London at the same hour, the same three days of the week, from the same location. Although beaten after arrest, she refused to betray her colleagues.

Madeleine Damerment, a brave and gentle soul thought to be the best of available couriers in the spring of 1944, suffered an agent's worst nightmare: parachuting into enemy hands. It occurred the night of February 28–29, twenty miles east of Chartres, when she and her circuit leader and wireless operator sailed into a Gestapo reception committee.

Eliane Plewman parachuted into the Jura the night of August 13–14 and worked her way to Marseille to rendezvous with her MONK leader and wireless operator. They were betrayed by a local Frenchman and arrested at the end of March 1944, but not before putting *sixty* German trains out of action. Though beaten about the face after capture, Plewman told the Gestapo nothing.

The clock was ticking for these women.

After several hours the Gestapo commandant came in. He announced that the group would be departing for Germany on the six thirty from Gare de l'Est. Did they have any requests?

They had been cooped up for hours, Odette told him, and a cup of tea would be greatly appreciated. Not as it was made in France or in Germany, she said, but in the English manner, with milk and sugar.

The commandant gave a sidelong look and left. Minutes later tea arrived—English style—with seven Sèvres china cups.

At six o'clock a guard came with travel instructions. They would be handcuffed in pairs, he said, and departing momentarily. If anyone caused trouble or attempted escape, he added, his men would not hesitate to shoot.

Odette was handcuffed to Yolande Beekman and the party was led through a cordon of guards to the awaiting coach. The transfer to the train was conducted with typical German efficiency. The prisoners were herded into second class, two pairs per compartment; Odette and Yolande were seated across from Vera Leigh and Andrée Borrel. An SS man kept watch outside the door, an SS woman inside. Other guards patrolled the corridors.

The train whistle blew and the scorned seven were on their way.

When they reached the countryside, they passed through a station and marshaling yard; rubble was everywhere. "That is the work of the R.A.F.," a guard said to Odette. "They have also destroyed my mother's house in Dortmund. I only wish that an accident could happen to the train for, if it did, it would give me great pleasure to crush your skull under my heel and save the German hangman a job."

"You are a man under orders," she fired back, "and it is your duty to deliver all of us, alive and well, to Germany. If an accident were to happen, your first care should be to the safety of your prisoners."

He swore at her and Odette held his gaze as one with authority.

"You are neither clever—nor efficient." She held up her unshackled wrists. "For example, it has only taken me thirty minutes to slip my handcuffs."

The guard disappeared and returned with a key. He reapplied her handcuffs, snapping the steel so tight that it bruised the bone.

Dusk turned to darkness and Odette tried to sleep as the train rumbled through the night. The cuffs were cutting into her, though, and she could close her eyes only a few minutes at a time. At dawn they passed over the mighty Rhine—German bastion of superiority and power.

Odette stirred—gone was her beloved France; she was now in Hitlerland.

She turned to an SS man. "Where are we going?"

"You are going to Karlsruhe," he said, "where you will be killed."

CHAPTER 17

THE BUNKER

It was a suicide mission.

Peter was as moxie as they came, but this was pure madness. The twenty-odd hut prisoners were guarded by thirty-two soldiers—with dogs. The soil was sandy and too unstable for tunnels. The electric wire continued underground and if tampered with would set off a warning light in the guard commander's post.

They were going to do it anyway, these Brits: Johnny Dodge, Sydney Dowse, Jimmy James, and "Wings" Day. Dodge had been one of the seventy-six who in April had tunneled out of Stalag Luft III—the POW camp at Sagan—a breakout better known as "the Great Escape." The Germans quickly recaptured all but three and fifty were summarily shot. Luck be damned, Dodge wanted another go.

Peter wished them well. The tunnel would take three months to construct, but Dodge and the others were committed. Meanwhile, Peter was preoccupied with Odette.

Something told him that she was alive. His daily thoughts seemed to come into contact with hers and if anything dreadful had happened, he felt sure that he would have sensed it.[34] He was right: Odette *was* alive. And the longer his incarceration, the more he appreciated her.

He thought of her reason for joining the war: freedom. Freedom for her children, freedom for France, freedom for England. Her captivity, no doubt, was a price she was willing to pay to help that cause. She was a kind of Sainte Thérèse, it seemed—sacrificing her place in heaven to do good on earth, and prepared to face hell to accomplish it.

What Peter didn't know was that she was being sent there.

Karlsruhe, Germany
May 13, 1944

THE TRAIN CRAWLED INTO Karlsruhe and Odette and her six companions were locked in a platform office while the Gestapo ordered taxis. The women's request that their handcuffs be removed momentarily so that they could visit the bathroom privately was denied.

When they arrived at the Karlsruhe Criminal Prison, handcuffs were removed and Odette was searched and locked up. So that the SOE ladies wouldn't communicate, the Gestapo placed them in cells far apart. The isolation succeeded only partially: when one was in the exercise yard, the others yelled to her from their cells.

Days turned into weeks but there were no tribunals, firing squads, or hangings—just the soul-stealing drudgery of captivity without hope.

----

34 "Poetic knowledge," the ancients called it; truths that are grasped intuitively, such as another's love, or a mother's intuition that something awful had happened to a child far away.

MEANWHILE IN LONDON, BAKER Street started a Psy Ops campaign in preparation for D-Day. On the docks of Lisbon and garden parties in Madrid, rumors were circulated.

Did you hear that the Germans were putting dehydrated mules' brains in the sausage sent to their troops?

Can you believe that the German military hospitals will be using animal blood for transfusions in the event of an invasion?

They say the Germans have little ammunition in France because the High Command doesn't intend to put up much resistance.

When the invasion of occupied France was finally ordered, SOE went into overdrive. On the evening of June 5, the night before the landing, the BBC broadcast 306 messages. Buried within them were messages to Lieutenant Cammaerts, remnants of SPINDLE, agents whom Peter and Odette had helped in Marseille and other cities, and countless circuits throughout France:

"Vilma vous dit oui."—"Destroy all German rolling stock on the railway line Angoulême-Bordeaux."

"Madame dit non."—"Bring down all telegraph wires between Caen and Alençon, and Caen and Évreux."

After D-Day the Maquis were dispatched behind battle zones to disrupt German transport and communication. Telephone lines were sabotaged, cutting off Berlin from Wehrmacht officers at the front. The Germans responded by sending couriers to deliver messages and they were ambushed and shot. Bridges were blown, reinforcements were blocked.

Like Stalingrad, Normandy had become a German death trap.

AT THE BEGINNING OF July Odette was called to the Karlsruhe Prison office, where the commandant introduced a reporter from the *Völkischer Beobachter*, the daily newspaper of the Nazi Party. He was a small man with red shifty eyes and a notebook. Odette said nothing and the reporter jeered, "Well, Frau Churchill, you will be pleased to know that we already have three Churchills in our

German prisons. We look forward to the arrival of yet another—of Mister Winston Churchill."

"You will not have to wait long," she replied, "but when Winston Churchill comes to Berlin, it will not be as you think. He will drive through the rubble of your city in triumph."

Interview concluded. Odette returned to her cell.

ABOUT THIS TIME ODETTE had a disturbing premonition. For a week none of her colleagues appeared in the yard; strange, since at least one would be allowed exercise each day. Her intuition proved accurate: she would never see any of them again. Vera Leigh, Diana Rowden, and Andrée Borrel were executed July 6 at the Natzweiler-Struthof concentration camp. Injected with lethal doses of carbolic acid, the three were then fed into the furnace. Yolande Beekman, Madeleine Damerment, and Eliane Plewman would be executed two months later, on September 13, at Dachau.

Odette's fate seemed certain to follow. She was the only one of the seven, after all, who had been condemned to death. She accepted it stoically, without complaint or reservation.

Two weeks later, on July 18, she was told to pack; her sentence would soon be carried out. With her daily ration—one slice of bread—Odette returned to the station, where she entrained for her cemetery.

The train chugged along, apparently east, and she saw more RAF handiwork: pockmarked stations and yards, twisted metal, delays from destroyed lines. Word spread about the Normandy invasion and the sea of bombers heading deep into France. Allied troops would follow and soon they would be at the Rhine, rapping on Adolf's door.

In the next compartment, male prisoners began stirring.

"*Encore un peu de patience, comarade,*" came one cry, "Hitler's day is over."

British POWs began singing "It's a long way to Tipperary . . ."

The train steamed into Frankfurt around midnight and Odette noticed that the station roof was shattered; so, too, it appeared, dreams of the guards, who moved about somberly. She was taken to police headquarters and repeated the drill: questions, searching, incarceration. This time, however, there would be no cell.

She was locked in a cage.

Single iron mesh, it was five feet long by four feet wide by six feet high; Odette was now a circus sideshow. She had been given nothing to drink since departing Karlsruhe, and was given nothing now. The cage had no water and no sanitation facility. Within hours, two other women were thrown in, and for the next several days this was their home.

Odette was then shipped to Halle, 250 miles north, and shut in a windowless prison attic with some forty-odd Ukrainian women. Sanitation was nonexistent and many women had dysentery. July heat and the foul combustion of sweat, body odor, blood, urine, and excrement turned the room into a septic sauna. To compound matters, the Germans had scattered sand across the floor as a fire retardant against Allied bombing, and it swirled constantly.

One day a large man came to the attic and asked for Odette. He was either Gestapo or part of the local police; she wasn't sure. The man asked if she was English and when she confirmed that she was, he struck her twice across her still-swollen neck.

Yet the worst was to come.

On July 26, after four suffocating days in the septic sauna, Odette and the Ukrainians were loaded onto a train bound for the one place feared by every woman in Europe.

Ravensbrück.

Created by Heinrich Himmler himself, the notorious labor camp for women had been opened in May 1939 to house up to 4,000 political prisoners. Now it held more than 36,000, including criminals, prostitutes, Jehovah's Witnesses, and Resistance agents. Roughly 25 percent of the inmates were Poles, 20 percent were Germans, 15 percent Jews, and 15 percent Russians, with the remainder composed of French, Ukrainians, Belgians, Czechs, Yugoslavs, Dutch, Italians, Spanish, English, Norwegians, and others. By the end of the war, some 133,000 women would pass through its gates, as many as 40,000 of whom would perish.

Odette's train arrived at the Fürstenberg Station the following day, July 27, and a group of SS guards—men and women[35]—supervised the disembarking. The charming village on the banks of the Schwedtsee could not have been more different from the Ravensbrück community across the lake. Because the Havel River connected the Mecklenburg chain of lakes to the Schwedt, Fürstenberg was a popular boating destination and had become something of a resort area. Quaint cottages dotted the lengthy waterfront and quality homes built for camp employees attracted many SS officers and their families.

When the guards were ready, Odette and the Ukrainians left for the two-mile trek to the camp. It was impossible not to notice the town's many flowers, including white gardenias, which adorned Fürstenberg windowsills. Such was the visual delight that one prisoner later remarked, "Is there really a prettier village on earth?"

After they had marched a few minutes the lake appeared on the right, SS homes on the left, and then they could see it: Ravensbrück's fourteen-foot walls and gargoyle-like towers beckoned the damned and almost dead.

They continued alongside the tranquil Schwedtsee and were led through the massive iron gates and into the roll call area. The misery had been carefully planned, it seemed: the grounds were set into a man-made valley and there were no trees, bushes, or grass. The ground was cinder and, like the crop-wielding guards, hard and cold.

All around, Odette could see skull-and-crossbones warning that the triple barbed wires atop the concrete walls were electrified. In front of her was a sea of bullet-grey barracks—acres of them,

---

35 The female guards, or *Aufseherinnen*, technically were not members of the SS, which was an all-male organization, but of the SS Women's Auxiliary (*weibliche SS-Gefolge*).

perfectly aligned, perfectly dreary. To one side was what appeared to be a large canteen for the guards; to the other, an administrative office, another building, and the crematorium. More barbed wire, also electrified, separated the prisoner area from the canteen.

From what Odette could tell, it appeared that the camp was unprepared for their arrival, and the guards herded them down the main street to the washroom. The women showered and drank from the spigots and were told that they would be spending the night there—on the concrete floor. Odette was so tired it didn't matter; she was asleep in seconds.

RAVENSBRÜCK PRISONER INTAKE NORMALLY occurred in several stages. First, newcomers were taken to a desk to give up their personal belongings—jewelry, books, diaries, and purses—and then herded to another to give up their clothes. Stark naked, they would walk past a dozen leering SS men to the showers. After the icy cleansing, prisoners were inspected for lice—which infested the camp—and if any were found, the woman's head and pubic area were shaved. Traumatized by the experience, many cried; others committed suicide by throwing themselves on the electrified wire.

Still naked, the women then stood in line—often for hours—to receive a medical exam. The examination each group received, however, varied greatly. For some, a doctor simply inspected their throat and a dentist peered at their teeth; others received a gynecologic exam, the same instrument being used on every woman without disinfection.

Prisoners were then given a thin dress[36] and directed back to the SS men, who would roam their hands over every woman—front, back, and sides—in case she had pilfered a Luger or Schmeisser from a showerhead or the doctor's office.

---

36 Beginning in 1943, prison uniforms were not always issued, and by 1944, inmates were allowed to keep their own clothes.

Finally, inmates would receive a barrack assignment, but before exiting the building, female guards would search them again.

Perhaps because Odette was considered "on death row" and would not be mingling with others, she was spared the processing indignity. Around ten the next morning a Gestapo agent came to the washroom and called for her. He would be escorting her, he said, to see the commandant of the camp, *Sturmbann-Führer* (Major) Fritz Sühren.

Sühren was a prototype Nazi: Aryan as they came, fervent as ideologically possible. He had joined the Nazi Party in the early days, 1928, and volunteered for the SS three years later. While trained as a soldier, he was ushered into administration and in 1941 joined the staff at the Sachsenhausen concentration camp. The following year he was named deputy commandant and began to establish his reputation. In May he ordered Harry Naujoks—a Communist prisoner who was assisting as a camp *Lagerältester*[37]—to hang a fellow inmate. At the risk of his own hanging, Naujoks refused and Sühren made him stand by the prisoner and watch the execution up close and personal. To extend the suffering, a winch had been fitted on the gallows to raise the victim slowly.

In the summer of 1942 Sühren became commandant of Ravensbrück and his operating policy quickly became evident: exterminate prisoners by hard labor and starvation. And while he formally objected to the SS order to provide inmates to Dr. Karl Gebhardt[38] for gruesome medical experiments (fearing legal repercussions), he nevertheless complied when the SS overruled his complaint. These experiments were conducted on dozens—including seventy-four

---

37 An assistant for administrative or menial tasks, such as supervising labor.

38 Convicted of war crimes and crimes against humanity at the Nuremberg Medical Trial, Gebhardt was sentenced to death on August 20, 1947, and executed on June 2, 1948.

Poles—and more than one hundred Romani were sterilized by various methods, including exposure to X-rays.[39]

Ravensbrück Commandant Fritz Sühren. *CORRIERE DELLA SERRA*

This was the man who would be responsible for Odette's welfare.

He was strikingly young, Odette noticed—midthirties—with a baby face, fair hair, and blank blue eyes, almost without pigment. His lily-white skin shone bright against the green and silver SS Penal Section uniform, his elegant hands dangling like those of a mannequin.

"*Sprechen Sie Deutsch?*"

"*Non,* Monsieur."

Sühren frowned. "You are relation to Mr. Winston Churchill?"

---

39 The women were tricked into the procedure, either by statement that it was an examination or by the promise of release if they consented. Many women became ill from the X-rays, and some died.

"My husband is a distant connection of his."

In the camp she would be known as Frau Schurer, he said.

It was logical; the Churchill name would have been a distraction—half the guards wanting to know details about the British Bulldog, half wanting to beat Odette with vicarious blows.

He also told her that she would be put in the Bunker, the prison of the camp.

"Very well. As you wish."

Odette's mild response reflected ignorance about her new home. The Bunker was Ravensbrück's most severe punishment, reserved only for the most incorrigible prisoners. It was actually a building located near the camp entrance and was composed of seventy-eight cells—thirty-nine on each of two floors. Each cell was about the size of a closet—four and a half paces long by two and a half paces wide—and contained a plank bed, folding table, stool, and toilet.

To send an inmate to the Bunker, a guard was required to submit a written report to the Camp Leader for Protective Custody, and any sentence longer than three days required the commandant's approval. During winter, cells generally were unheated, though they had heating panels. Bunker inmates often went days without food, and most were beaten. One prisoner, a twenty-year-old pregnant woman, was found dead in her cell, frozen to the floor. She had been beaten.

As one condemned to death, Odette would receive special attention. Sühren spoke to the Gestapo agent, saying that Frau Schurer was to receive the normal ration of the punishment cells, no exercise, no books, and no bath.

The agent escorted her across the compound to the Bunker and turned her over to Margarete Mewes,[40] a beady-eyed guard with a beak nose engulfed by thick, black tussled hair—a bird chirping from her nest.

Odette drank in one last swallow of the peaceful blue sky and

---

40 Sentenced at the Ravensbrück war crimes trial in 1947 to ten years in prison.

followed Mewes into the compound and along a short passage. They came to a security gate for the inner Bunker, which Mewes unlocked, and went down a flight of stairs. Vestiges of daylight vanished, the corridor now illuminated by overhead lamps. Mewes unlocked a cell and Odette stepped in, the door slamming behind her.

It was pitch dark. Odette stretched out her hands—which she could not see—and gradually probed the confines of her compartment. She would live in utter darkness, unable to distinguish night from day.

As it was during her childhood blindness.

She closed her eyes.

SOMETHING MOVED.

The sound of a latch. Odette got up and shuffled across the cell. A sliver of light slipped through the food hatch and she retrieved a cup of weak coffee and slice of bread.

It must be morning.

The hatch closed and darkness returned.

Some four hours later—who could know for sure?—the hatch opened again and a bowl of turnip soup was inserted. A light in her cell was turned on for a few minutes, maybe five, and then extinguished. Hours after that, perhaps dinnertime, a second cup of coffee was presented.

Days went by and nothing changed. This was life in the Bunker—coffee, soup, and five minutes of artificial light a day. It was a black hole, this cell. Like the space-time phenomena, it absorbed everything—time, individuality, hope, sanity.

All except sound.

Odette's cell was next to the "punishment room," and she heard everything. Originally used for beatings about the head, the room adopted a formal procedure in 1942 when Heinrich Himmler ordered more brutal tactics—caning or whipping.

Sühren, who supervised the floggings, would instruct the prisoner to step up to a rack where her feet would be shackled in a wooden clamp. She would then be bent over the rack, strapped down, and her dress would be pulled over her head. Since she had been instructed to remove her underwear before leaving her barrack, her buttocks was bare. A blanket was then placed over her head to help muffle the screams. The prisoner would be instructed to count aloud the lashes—twenty-five being the norm—and if she could not, they would be counted for her. So that his hands would not be sullied, Sühren had an inmate—bribed with cigarettes or food—deliver the blows.

Ravensbrück whipping table.
NEW BULGARIAN UNIVERSITY

Every night at eight Odette would hear them. First the strokes—"*elf . . . zwolf . . . dreizehn . . .*"—and then the cries and pleas to make your skin crawl. Sometimes there was a pause when the prisoner fainted but—like the brandy trick at Avenue Foch—there would be a splash, and the beating would continue.

Unconsciously, Odette counted every stroke with them.

This was hell.[41]

In our darkest moments, Aristotle had said, we must focus to see the light. Odette did her best. To ward off madness, she began conjuring up images, vivid and colorful, and reliving memorable events. She had done this during her childhood blindness and that experience, she believed, prepared her for this life without light. She thought of her girls, dressing them and considering each outfit—accessories, color, cloth—and the outings in Somerset. In the meadows of her mind, she strolled with the girls and marveled at sunsets.

Reality, though—screams or otherwise—eventually would disrupt the pleasant thoughts and she would start anew every few hours.

Already thin from the meager rations at Fresnes, Odette's body began to take the shape of the skeletons who had died overnight and were put on the *charrette*—the wooden handcart which hauled bodies to the crematorium each morning. Without proper nutrients, sunlight, and fresh air, she became sick, her glands again swelling. A guard took her to the prison infirmary and on the way back, something spectacular happened.

She found a leaf.

There were no trees in the compound, so it had blown in. She scooped it up and carried it back to her cell. When the light came on for her five minutes she looked at it, a solitary but profound ex-

---

41 Corrie ten Boom, who could hear the cries from a punishment room near her Barrack 8, described it as such. These were "the sounds of hell itself," she wrote later. "They were not the sounds of anger, or of any human emotion, but of a cruelty altogether detached: blows landing at a regular rhythm, screams keeping pace. We would stand in our ten-deep ranks with our hands trembling at our sides, longing to jam them against our ears, to make the sounds stop."

ample of something—God, creation, life. In a small way, it gave her a glimmer of hope.

At the end of the month her light was suddenly switched on and the door opened. It was the commandant. He asked if everything was all right.

"Yes, thank you."

Did she wish anything?

"No, thank you."

Sühren saluted, shut the door, and turned off the light.

IN HER LIFE OF darkness Odette began to despair. She was sick, starving, lonely, and in a very real sense, dying. She prayed to God, saying that she had done all she could, now "you must take over." Almost immediately the food hatch was opened and a plate of food inserted.

It was the first plate Odette had seen in months.

Bunker life continued to take its toll, however, and scabs soon began to appear on her skin. Her glands festered.

A few weeks later, August now, Odette noticed that her cell was becoming unbearably hot; not summer heat, more like a Dutch oven. She felt for the central heating panels—they were on full blast. Pulling the blanket from her bed, she soaked it under the tap and wrapped it around her. This worked for the time being, but the heat from her body and the furnace eventually dried the blanket and she had to resoak it again and again.

No food came that day. Or the next. Or the next.

For six days and nights she was given no food and fought the inferno. Already deathly ill, she developed scurvy and dysentery. Her hair was falling out—she was almost completely bald—her teeth were loose, her skin was covered in scabs, and her gland was again the size of a grapefruit.

Her body gave up.

Everything went black.

CHAPTER 18

THE SLAUGHTER

The body was limp and still. Was she dead?

The guard called for help and Frau Schurer was carried to the infirmary.

She was alive, they found, but unconscious; she had slipped into a semicoma. A camp doctor gave her an injection and Odette was revived.

And returned to the Bunker.

Paris

MEANWHILE IN PARIS, THE Allies battled for control. The city was liberated on August 25 when Prussian general Dietrich von Choltitz, in defiance of Hitler's order, refused to level it and surrendered to the Free French forces.

Major Buckmaster flew in the following day to celebrate with F Section agents, and as he crossed the Champs-Élysées, a young boy—only five or six—marched up to him.

"Permit me," the boy said in perfect English, "to shake hands with a gentleman. We have not seen any gentlemen for four years."

Ravensbrück

ON THE LAST DAY of August Sühren stopped by to check on Odette.

"Have you any complaints?"

Odette maintained her composure. "Yes, I have. For no reason that I know, the central heating was turned on in my cell, and for a week I was left without food."

"There was a reason," Sühren said. "The British and the Americans landed in the South of France where you worked as a British spy. Because of this, you were punished by order of the Gestapo."

Indeed, the efforts by SPINDLE and Cammaerts's JOCKEY circuit had been highly effective; when the Allies landed at Provence and moved north, there was little resistance. "Peter Churchill and Odette had both been caught somewhat earlier," Major Buckmaster later explained, "but the organization in which they had been most concerned was still able to continue without them, so well had they done their work."

Odette held Sühren's eye. "You are aware that it is almost a year and a half ago since I was arrested?"

He said he was.

It was no use arguing; the commandant had his orders.

Sühren asked if she needed anything and she said no. She was likely to die at any moment anyway and they'd bring the *charrette* and she'd exit through the chimney. It was belligerent defiance, but she was determined to go down fighting.

Her condition continued to deteriorate and her glands began to swell again, so it was back to the infirmary. Strangely, all medical exams were conducted with the prisoners completely nude—a disincentive for unnecessary visits, to be sure, but perhaps also for intimidation.

A camp doctor took X-rays of Odette's throat and told her that she had tuberculosis, a common excuse for extermination. Odette asked to see the X-ray plates but was refused.

When Sühren next visited she demanded to see the plates and he relented. They showed that she did not, in fact, have tuberculosis. But what she overheard the doctor say to someone in passing was even more halting: if she continued living in the Bunker, he said, she'd be dead within a few weeks.

The commandant had a decision to make. If he followed Gestapo orders—keeping Odette in the Bunker—she'd soon be dead. But dark clouds were gathering over the Nazi dream and there were now other considerations. Paris had fallen and the Americans and British had just taken Bruges, Brussels, and Antwerp. It would not be long, he figured, before the Allies stormed the Rhine and he needed insurance.

Frau Churchill was his premium.

He sent Odette again to the infirmary and she was given injections for scurvy, something for her hair, and vitamins. He told her that she would be moved to a cell with light and fresh air once one became available.

Her gland was still the size of a grapefruit, however, and the SS doctor wanted to operate. Odette refused.

Soon thereafter Heinrich Himmler, SS *Reichsführer* and supervisor of concentration camps, visited. Prisoners who were sick, old,

Ravensbrück crematorium ovens. *GERMAN FEDERAL ARCHIVES*

or incapable of work, he told Sühren, were to be executed. Since Odette could hardly stand without assistance, the order placed her squarely in Himmler's crosshairs.

The slaughter began. And it wasn't just Ravensbrück. Himmler's orders extended to other camps and included executions of those perfectly capable of work. The first week of September, more than seven hundred prisoners were executed by firing squad at the SS concentration camp in Vught, Holland.

Surprisingly, Odette survived the September siege, but the fall brought a new hazard: Allied bombing. In November US bombers began nightly raids on the Siemens factory a mile away and Odette could hear the incendiaries landing dangerously close.

December came and Odette was finally moved to a new cell. She had been in the Bunker three months and eight days.

Her new cell, number 32, had light and a window for fresh air, but was located just six yards from the crematorium. Each day ashes and hair would float into her quarters, the last cries of the departed, along with the stench of burned souls. The sight of the cinders, which would cover every inch of her cell—together with the foul

Heinrich Himmler visiting Ravensbrück. *MAHN UND GEDENKSTATTE RAVENSBRÜCK*

smell—was nauseating. Each day, every day, remnants of fellow prisoners—women who only hours before had families and friends and hopes and dreams—were now meaningless specks of rubbish to be swept up and discarded in a trash bin like rotted fruit.

And while she had escaped the screams of the punishment room, she would soon hear something far worse.

To expedite executions, Himmler ordered the construction of a second oven, as well as a gas chamber; countless prisoners could be eliminated this way without the loss of bullets needed by the army.

And so the killings ushered in Christmas.

January 1945

ON JANUARY 12 THE Red Army launched a massive offensive, breaking through the Wehrmacht's Eastern Front and pushing into Prussia. Five days later the Russians took Warsaw. Knowing that the Communists would soon be pushing into Germany, Himmler ordered the evacuation of camps closest to the advance, and the execution of prisoners incapable of travel. At Auschwitz, thousands of inmates were rounded up and forced to evacuate on foot on the 17th. One in four would perish in what became known as the "death march," a procedure that occurred at most every camp.

With the closing of Auschwitz, Himmler ordered SS *Obersturmführer* Johann Schwarzhuber to transfer from there to Ravensbrück, where he became deputy commandant. Soon after arriving, Schwarzhuber was called into a meeting with Sühren and Dr. Richard Trommer, one of the camp physicians, to receive Himmler's latest: all women who were sick or incapable of marching were to be executed.

Almost every afternoon Schwarzhuber would confer with other camp officials and prepare a list for that day's executions in the gas chamber. The victims would be told that they were being transferred to "Mittwerda," a fictitious concentration camp, and that evening they were loaded onto a truck and driven to the killing building. They were told to undress for delousing and 150 were sent into the chamber at a time, the doors locked behind them. A male inmate would drop a canister of poison gas in from the roof, shut the hatch, and wait until the sounds ceased.

"I heard moaning and whimpering from inside," Schwarzhuber later testified.

FROM JANUARY ON, WITH the Red Army on their doorstep, SS camps began executing prisoners at a breakneck pace. On January 15, concentration camps had reached their maximum number of inmates: 714,211. By April 1, between executions and deaths from starvation and disease, that number had been reduced to 550,000.[42]

At Ravensbrück, Sühren estimated that 1,500 women were killed in the gas chamber alone, but his figure was highly conservative; the more likely number was between 4,500 and 6,000.[43]

With the passage of each week the carnage came closer and closer to Odette. From her cell one day she heard prisoners being herded into the crematorium.

Living prisoners.

"I could hear them screaming and struggling," she later testified, "and I could hear the doors being opened and shut."

As always, it was Nazi efficient: the line, the lock, and the screams. Endless screams.

Odette could only wonder when hers would be next.

---

42 In many cases, the SS simply shot the prisoners. On January 27 they mowed down 250 sick inmates at Fürstengrube (a subcamp of Auschwitz-Birkenau). At Palmnicken, 3,000 Stutthof concentration camp marchers were machine-gunned. On February 2, 1,300 infirm at Lieberose (a subcamp of Sachsenhausen) were slaughtered. At Dachau, they began burying the slain in mass graves because the incinerators could not keep up.

43 Some 3,600 girls and young women transferred from the neighboring Uckermark camp were taken directly to the gas chamber at Ravensbrück. The camp infirmary itself reported 3,858 deaths in the first quarter of 1945, also probably a conservative figure.

Auxerre, France

HUGO BLEICHER, MEANWHILE, HAD gone to ground. When Paris was on the verge of falling, he had requested that Colonel Reile post him to Auxerre. A number of Hugo's former agents had gone there and it was far enough from Paris to be safe, he thought. He requested ten agents from the Paris office and Reile sent them, but within days they all fled. It was now just him and his mistress, Suzanne.

Which made it almost too easy.

The men surrounding Hugo's house each night waited for their chance.

They would kill the traitor girlfriend, too.

WITHOUT AN EFFECTIVE FORCE, Hugo decided to join the main army for the time being. He had been staying in a private house but the Maquis were raiding homes and he decided to relocate to the local garrison. The four hundred troops in Auxerre, however, were pitiful—mostly elderly and Russians recruited from POW camps. When British forces were heard to be in Sens, only fifty miles away, the Auxerre troops disappeared. Worse still, the Maquis had blocked the line of retreat to Dijon.

Hugo was surrounded.

He decided to flee with Suzanne but soon discovered that his car had been stolen. Within hours he requisitioned a new Citroën and they set out to run the gauntlet. Fully aware that some of his French agents had joined the Maquis and would be looking for him, he brought along a machine pistol and several hand grenades. It would be the ultimate game of cat and mouse and he welcomed the challenge.

Along the main road leaving Auxerre, the Maquis were waiting. They had set up a road block and several surrounded the Citroën, guns pointed. Hugo spoke a few words of English and casually handed over his stolen identity papers.

Captain in the British Special Air Service.

The Maquis apologized and shook his hand. Hugo waved as he pulled away, gunning up. From Dijon, Hugo and Suzanne high-tailed it to Holland. There he was posted to Nijmegen, although he wasn't given any specific duties. As he waited for an assignment, one morning in March a sentry burst into his apartment.

"The town is encircled," he said. "The British paratroopers are here."

Hugo and Suzanne bolted for Utrecht, twenty miles south of Amsterdam, where German intelligence had set up underground operations. No sooner than they arrived, however, the Canadian army pushed in from the North Sea and took control. Once again, Hugo was cut off.

After three weeks Hugo's local captain called him in, saying that they had negotiated a capitulation to the Canadians and that everyone would go to a prisoner of war camp as one body.

Hugo refused.

"You are a soldier and must obey," the captain said.

"I can obey no order that obliges me to be taken prisoner."

Hugo pulled his hat down, walked out, and again went to ground.

He was now the ferret.

Germany

THE ALLIES, MEANWHILE, WERE racing through the German heartland. On February 26 the American Ninth Army had reached the Rhine near Düsseldorf and a week later, on March 7, the Third Army crossed it at Remagen. In the east, the Red Army entered Austria on the 30th, and also took Danzig in the north.

At Ravensbrück, help finally began to arrive. On April 4 a convoy of American and Canadian Red Cross trucks rolled into camp.

In high-level negotiations between Carl Burckhardt, president of the International Red Cross, and SD intelligence chief Walter Schellenberg, the parties agreed that 300 inmates would be evacuated to Switzerland, 299 of whom were French.

Odette was not one of them.

Three days later the Red Cross rescued all of the Danish and Norwegian prisoners. They left food parcels for the remaining prisoners, but between what was looted by the guards and given to the main camp barracks, Odette saw not one item.

WITH EACH PASSING DAY another stone fell from a Third Reich pillar. On April 9 the Germans lost Königsberg. On the 11th, the Americans and British reached the Elbe, while the Red Army closed from the east, taking Vienna on the 13th. Three days later, marshal Georgy Zhukov began his drive to Berlin.

Himmler recognized the immediate danger: witnesses. The Allies had already liberated two camps—Buchenwald and Dora—and would be at the gates of others within days. On April 15 he called a meeting of his camp administrators and ordered the complete evacuation of all remaining camps. The following day he sent Ravensbrück another order: *Execute every prisoner in the Bunker.* There could be no witnesses to the horrors of the hellhole.[44]

Although Odette was not in the Bunker at the moment, that formality was due only to her illness. As one under a death sentence, she was automatically a prisoner of the camp and part of the Bunker roster. Not only that, but having spent more than three months in the pit, she would certainly be called to testify in a war crimes tribunal.

She should be one of the first to go.

---

44 On the 18th he sent a similar message to Flossenbürg: "There is no question of handing over the camp. No prisoners [must] fall alive into enemy hands."

For days the stacks burned, their billows a palimpsest of lives snuffed short.

Odette waited.

THAT SAME WEEK, PETER was informed that he and his fellow prisoners—including the tunnel escapees, all of whom had been recaptured—would be relocated to Flossenbürg.

Peter knew nothing of this concentration camp but would learn soon enough. Upon arrival, the first thing he noticed was smoke rising from the crematorium; it rose all day and inmates he saw were but skeletons, shuffling through their labor until at last their bodies expired.

After quarters assignments, Peter and his fellow officers were allowed time in the yard and they used it to encourage other prisoners. "Keep your chin up!" they whispered through cell doors as they passed along the corridor. "The Allies will be here in a matter of days."

"It had better be soon," came one reply. "Only yesterday they took out four men and a woman and hanged them in the shed outside. I saw them pass through the slits in my door. All were naked."

Three of the naked were notable: Protestant pastor and theologian Dietrich Bonhoeffer, Abwehr chief Admiral Wilhelm Canaris, and Abwehr deputy chief General Hans Oster, all of whom were implicated in the July 20 attempt on Hitler's life.[45] Others would follow.

After five days at Flossenbürg, Peter and twenty other prisoners were crammed into a Black Maria designed for transporting nine.

---

45 Canaris and Oster were members of Berlin's St. Anne's Church, led by Lutheran pastor and anti-Nazi theologian Martin Niemöller. Dietrich Bonhoeffer and Niemöller were among the most prominent clergy to oppose Hitler and the nazification of the church.

Included among the group were Prince Philipp of Hesse,[46] Baron Wilhelm von Flügge, Lieutenant Fabian von Schlabrendorff[47]—adjutant to Brigadier General Henning von Tresckow—and Josef Müller, chief justice of Bavaria.

Three days later the lorry arrived at the Dachau concentration camp and Müller pulled Peter aside:

"I shall not be coming along with the rest of you," he said, "for they are taking me to a special cell. I just wanted to tell you that if this is the end for me, as I fear, I shall think to the last of the lovely singing that you and your friends performed as we entered this infamous camp. Good-bye, my friend."

As Peter clasped Müller's hand, he couldn't help thinking that he, too, could be singled out and executed in solitude. The possibility that he might never see Odette again was quite real, he knew, if she was even alive.

Within the hour Peter met Niemöller, as well as the chancellor of Austria, the mayor of Vienna, the German ambassador to Madrid, Bishop Neuhaüsler of Munich, and Bishop Gabriel Piguet of Clermond-Ferrand. Shortly thereafter he met the commander in chief of the Greek army, four of his generals, and General Garibaldi and Colonel Ferraro of the Italian Partisans.

The following morning Peter and this respectable group boarded two coaches bound for yet another camp: Innsbruck. As the lorries drove through Munich, Peter stared at the destruction—no houses, just rubble. Overhead, RAF bombers filled the sky. That night, he could see fires in every direction. Surely the Germans would surrender soon.

On the evening of April 21 they arrived at Innsbruck and mar-

---

46 Whose wife was killed by an Allied air raid on the Buchenwald concentration camp, where she was captive.

47 Schlabrendorff had tried to kill Hitler twice. On March 13, 1943, he placed a time bomb on Hitler's plane, but the detonator failed. On another attempt, the would-be assassin (who offered to plant the bomb) got cold feet at the last moment and failed to act.

veled at the snow-capped mountains shining majestically in the moonlight. Morning came and with it another delivery of dignitaries, including Dr. Miklós Kállay, prime minister of Hungary, and Dr. Hjalmar Schacht, president of the Reichsbank. Most important of the incoming group were two of Hitler's top military leaders who had fallen out of favor with the Führer: General Franz Halder, former chief of the German army High Command, and Colonel Bogislaw von Bonin, former chief of the operational branch of the army General Staff.

Not long after they had settled in, a woman approached Peter. Her name was Isa Vermehren, she said, a former inmate at Ravensbrück. Was Peter the husband of the woman named Churchill in that camp? she asked. Peter asked for a description and Isa described Odette. She said that Frau Churchill was called Frau Schurer in the camp, but some knew her real identity. Baron von Flügge, she said, had closer contact with Odette and would know more.

Peter raced to find von Flügge and explained to the baron that he had probably known Odette under a different name. He showed him the photo from his wallet.

"I'm sorry," the baron said. "This is not the woman I knew."

Seeing the dismay on Peter's face, von Flügge asked to see the photo again.

"Yes, yes. It might be she. People can change so much in prison. Forgive me, my dear Churchill."

Von Flügge handed the photo back and shuffled away, realizing that his words had devastated Peter.

Peter stood there, forlorn, until the room emptied. What had they done to her? Starvation . . . torture . . . sickness . . . disease . . . abuse so acute that Odette was no longer recognizable. The thought was more than he could bear.

BEHIND THE SCENES COUNT Folke Bernadotte, chairman of the Swedish Red Cross and nephew of the king, was negotiating with

Himmler for additional Ravensbrück prisoners, and on April 22 more trucks arrived. Two hundred French women were selected for immediate evacuation to Padborg, Denmark, and over the next few days, thousands more were rescued by caravans shuttling back and forth.

Odette was not one of them.

On April 26 Sühren released even more: four thousand women to be taken to Padborg by a sixty-car train. The day after, he began implementing Himmler's last order: march all women who could walk to Malchow, a Ravensbrück subcamp forty-five miles west. Strangely, Odette was not included. The remaining women in the camp—some three thousand—would be left to fend for themselves.

That night she sat in her cell, thinking. Of her fate. Of her children. Of Peter. Since she wasn't included with those who were evacuated or sent on the march, it seemed clear that she would be executed. She simply knew too much.

Tomorrow was her birthday. She would be thirty-three.

What would be her present? A bullet so she wouldn't be fed alive into the furnace?

It was midnight when her cell door opened.

CHAPTER 19

STILL WARM

It was Sühren. Alone.

He studied Odette several moments, perfectly still, a hunter before the pull. Raising one of his mannequin hands, he drew the nail of his forefinger across his throat.

"You will be leaving tomorrow morning at six o'clock."

He closed the door.

SHORTLY AFTER DAWN SÜHREN ordered the last batch of women to join the march to Malchow. But not Odette. She was summoned at eight and loaded with several others into a Black Maria for transport to who knew where. As the lorry and convoy of SS officers sped through the gate, a number of guards quietly slipped away, many wearing prisoner clothes.

The Allies, they knew, were closing on Berlin.

Later that day word came that Italian Partisans had executed Mussolini and his mistress. Sühren realized that many would be looking for the commandant of Ravensbrück, too, and he'd have to take three measures to survive: destroy records, eliminate witnesses, and go to ground with an assumed name.

They drove fourteen straight hours, arriving at Neustadt at nightfall. Odette and the others were locked up while the Germans waited for news. In the meantime, the killings continued. Though it seemed impossible, more were being executed at Neustadt than at Ravensbrück.

Meanwhile, the Russians were pounding Berlin and on April 30, with the Red Army just a half mile from his bunker in the Reich Chancellery, Hitler and his mistress, Eva Braun, committed suicide.

After a day or so, Odette and the others were returned to the Black Maria and driven to Münchof, twelve miles due northwest, to spend the night. Unfortunately for all, the camp had no food. The next morning, lorries arrived with a batch of male prisoners who, mad with thirst for liberty, rushed the gate.

They were slaughtered, mown down by SS machine guns.

Odette had seen enough. She demanded to see Sühren. The commandant came out of his office, tears streaming down his face.

"What do you want?"

"I want to know why you don't open the gates of the camp," she said. "The war is over. It is useless murder to keep people here."

"Adolf Hitler, Führer of Germany, is dead," Sühren said feebly. "He died as a hero in the forefront of the battle."

"Are you proposing to do the same thing, to die as a hero?"

"Go back to your hut. I have not finished with you yet."

Italy–Austria

PETER'S CONVOY HEADED FOR the Brenner Pass, the mountain path through the Alps at the Italy-Austria border. Near the top, the coaches pulled over to take cover from an air raid and Peter overheard a whispered conversation.

"If Hitler should be killed in the bombing of Berlin," a guard said to the driver, "I'll mow down these bastards like ninepins."

That risk, Peter knew, persisted regardless of the fate of the Führer.

The coaches got under way and continued south into Italy and then east toward Villabassa. It was en route that Peter heard the story about the other coach. One of the SS guards had become drunk, someone said, and a fast-fisted prisoner snatched his wallet. Inside was an order from Himmler's office:

Execute all British officers and other military personnel.

The revelation was enough to encourage action, but with what? The SS guards carried Schmeissers, but Peter and his colleagues had only weapons for rock-paper-scissors. Granted, Peter had been trained to kill with his hands, but he was the only one; the remaining men were civilians and officers equipped to fight with rifles and pistols.

They would need a miracle.

When they reached Villabassa, Colonel von Bonin snuck into the post office and made a phone call.

Western Germany
May 1, 1945

AT THREE IN THE afternoon a guard burst into Odette's hut.

"*Ist Frau Churchill hier?*"

"I am she."

"You are to come with me at once. It will not be necessary for you to bring your things."

She asked where they were going and the guard said she'd find out.

It will not be necessary for you to bring your things. Behind the hut, maybe? Perhaps they would drag her into the woods and do it there.

Her gut tightened.

She went with the guard outside and was told to wait beside other inmates. Most were the half-dead skeletons who normally roamed the camp, but there was a young girl—eighteen or nineteen—a few feet away. Her head was shaved but Odette knew that she had just arrived, as she was still "fresh."

Which made it all the more difficult. These things always seem to transpire in slow motion and this one was no different.

The shot came out of nowhere and the young girl dropped.

Odette flinched and jerked her head but saw no reason why the German had shot her. Before she could catch her breath, she watched in horror as the other women started in.

It was sickening. They were starving, yes. Mad, perhaps.

They went at the girl like dogs, biting and ripping and devouring her flesh. Odette was nauseous. The poor child was still warm.

A guard whisked Odette away and she was suddenly standing next to the camp gate, where three cars awaited. Two sedans were filled with SS officers and, in between, Sühren stood beside a sleek white Mercedes convertible. He took the wheel and told Odette to get in.

For two hours they drove in silence.

The convoy came to a wood and Sühren beeped the horn to notify the other cars to stop.

He turned to Odette.

"Get out."

Villabassa, Italy

DURING LUNCH PETER DINED with Fabian von Schlabrendorff. They were out of earshot of the guards and the lieutenant shared his story. His family had a long friendship with England, he said, and before the war the royal family had even invited him and his wife to Buckingham Palace. Like many Germans, he hated the Nazis and had been involved with the Kreisau Circle[48] in the thirties. In the spring of 1939, Abwehr chief Admiral Canaris had sent him

---

48 An anti-Nazi resistance group founded by Helmuth James Graf von Moltke (arrested by the Gestapo and executed on January 23, 1945). The dissidents met at von Moltke's Kreisau estate in Prussian Silesia, now Krzyzowa, Poland.

to England to warn Churchill of Germany's impending invasion of Poland, and to inform the prime minister of opposition working against Hitler.

He had worked under General von Tresckow, he went on, ringleader of the generals who participated in the attempt to assassinate Hitler on July 20, 1944. Their group had tried many times to kill the Führer, he said, but it was difficult because Hitler was rarely alone. The best plan, they felt, was to assassinate him on his plane while he was returning from a trip to the Eastern Front. Since von Schlabrendorff was the staff officer who attended Hitler's briefings, he was chosen to do the deed.

He created a bomb with plastic explosive concealed in a brandy flask. Setting a fuse for thirty minutes, he gave it to Hitler's aide just as the Führer was boarding the plane, telling the colonel to present it to a general in Berlin, compliments of von Tresckow. The fuse failed, however, and Fabian had to race to Berlin to swap it with the "one with the correct brandy" before delivery. His plot was never discovered.

The July 20 putsch was a different matter. When Colonel Claus von Stauffenberg's bomb failed to kill Hitler, he said, the gates of hell were unleashed. Five thousand German resisters, including twelve generals and two field marshals, either committed suicide or were executed. When news of the failed plot reached his boss, von Tresckow strode into the woods with a grenade and pulled the pin.

Though Fabian denied any connection to the plot, he told Peter, the Gestapo tortured him to unconsciousness on two occasions.[49] Now, after all that, Schlabrendorff was again at death's door.

---

49 He didn't give Peter details, perhaps because the experience was too gruesome to relive. Records reveal that when Fabian refused to confess any connection to the attempt on the Führer's life, he was tortured in four stages. First, his arms were bound behind his back. A device was then attached to his hands which enclosed each finger separately. On the inside of the mechanism were iron spines that pressed against the tips of his fingers. The spines were extended, gradually and slowly, by the torturer's turn of a screw. When the bloody procedure failed to draw a confession, the Gestapo moved on to stage two. Fabian was tied face down

"We are not out of the wood yet, Churchill," he said, "and I feel that tonight may be a danger spot."

Peter thanked him for his candor, and for the warning. The British would be on their toes.

That evening the male prisoners discussed sleeping arrangements. Since the guards apparently had been given no orders, Peter and the military officers decided that the men would sleep on straw in the town hall, and the women could have the few available rooms.

After dark a British officer named Jack Churchill—no relation to Peter or the prime minister—decided to take matters into his own hands and slipped away into the black night. Not long afterward, the SS lieutenant in charge of the guards came up to Peter.

"Where is your cousin?"

"I haven't a clue," Peter said. "Perhaps he's already upstairs and fast asleep."

"Well, we have a special room for you British officers."

Western Germany

ODETTE STEPPED OUT OF the car, accepting her fate with dignity. She had fought the good fight. Now, in a wood in the middle of nowhere, she would be fodder for wolves.

---

on what appeared to be a bed frame. A blanket was placed over his head, and iron pipes were affixed to his legs. Inside the pipes were nails, which, like the hand device, were extended into his thighs and calves by the turning of a screw. Fabian continued his claim of innocence, which brought on stage three. Once again he was tied to the bed with his head covered. This time, however, the contraption was pulled apart—slowly or joltingly—in an Inquisition-type of stretching and wrenching. When that failed, they moved to stage four. Fabian was manacled in a twisted fashion so that he could not bend in any direction. The Gestapo then beat him with clubs so that he fell forward. Since his hands were fastened behind him, his face would crash first onto the ground. He passed out and was carried to his cell. The next day he suffered a heart attack. When he could walk, the Gestapo repeated the four stages, and again he fell unconscious. Realizing that Fabian wouldn't break, the Gestapo gave up and he was sent to Flossenbürg, and then to Dachau.

Sühren went to the back of the Mercedes and began unloading papers by the armload: Ravensbrück records. Taking them to an opening in the field, he arranged them in a pile and struck the match.

Odette watched as the papers—evidence of thousands of unspeakable atrocities—went up in flames; smoke but no chimney this time. She waited for the Luger. Perhaps Sühren would drag her body over the fire so that it would be unrecognizable.

It will not be necessary for you to bring your things.

Good-bye girls. Good-bye Pierre.

Villabassa, Italy

WE HAVE A SPECIAL *room for you British officers.* Peter had no intention of being machine-gunned in a twelve-by-twelve-foot room. With confidence and a nonchalant answer, perhaps he could postpone the group execution. In a casual manner he told the guard in German that the British officers had already secured sleeping arrangements and wouldn't need a separate room.

The guard moved on without comment.

A moment later Dr. Kállay sidled up to Peter. "In God's name," he whispered, "don't go to any special room tonight. They're gunning for you. I feel it in my bones."

"Thanks, but don't worry," Peter told him. "We feel it too."

The British contingent went to the main sleeping area and Peter's pulse quickened. At the end of each row of beds, he saw, a guard sat with his Schmeisser across his lap.

Would the guards wait until the British were asleep and then begin firing?

What a way to go. He'd stay awake, Peter told himself. He assumed the other officers would, too, and if the firing began, perhaps they could wrest a Schmeisser from a guard's grip.

The hours ticked by as the Brits feigned sleep. Morning came and as the prisoners awaited their fate, Colonel von Bonin made his throw. He called the SS lieutenant aside and explained—

truthfully—his call when they had arrived. He had contacted Field Marshal Kesselring's Fourteenth Army headquarters in Italy, he said, and happened to know the staff officer who answered the phone. He told the officer that he and some others were being held by Himmler's SS guards in Villabassa and requested that a company of Kesselring's finest come to rescue them. The soldiers were promised to arrive at six o'clock the following evening.

Heute, junger Mann. In just a few hours.

If the guards were smart, von Bonin said, they'd disappear pronto.

The lieutenant had a choice. He could go with his orders and execute the prisoners as planned, or he and his men could vanish. If they killed what were now essentially hostages, a war crimes bureau would surely charge them with murder. If they didn't kill the prisoners but stayed, they would risk being shot by the Wehrmacht, which largely despised the Nazi private terror army.

The guards disappeared and, as promised, the Wehrmacht company arrived at six. After some discussion, von Bonin and the other leaders decided that the group should move up the mountain to the Pragser-Wildsee Hotel.

Peter admired the situation. Here, at five thousand feet—with snow surrounding the glimmering Lago di Braies and a view from every room—the concentration camp prisoners relaxed as tourists . . . under the *protection* of the German army. Von Bonin stationed Kesselring's men around the hotel in case any SS men— or deserting foreigners who had been conscripted into a German uniform and were now in need of a civilian suit—happened by.

Peter, Garibaldi, and Ferraro requisitioned a car and drove in the direction of the advancing US Army, perhaps anywhere from fifty to two hundred miles away. About ten miles into the trip, they found a tired American, Captain Attwood, with a group of exhausted men. Attwood had received a wireless message at 0215, he said, ordering his unit to rescue some Allied personnel at Wildsee. With only twenty minutes of sleep, he and his men set out on the seven-hour trek through the mountains. The main troops, he said, were days behind them.

Attwood and his men followed Peter and the others back to Wildsee but, perhaps because Kesselring's soldiers might be needed, Attwood didn't disarm them. At the hotel they heard over the wire that the Red Army had taken Berlin on May 2, and that Hitler had committed suicide two days earlier.

Peter now had just one thought: Was Odette alive?

Western Germany

SÜHREN WAITED UNTIL THE last of the evidence was gone. The starvation and forced labor, beatings and brutality, medical experiments and murders, all now memories. How many were there, the Poles, Jews, and Russians who perished under his charge? Fifty thousand? Of course, he was simply a man under orders; Ravensbrück was Himmler's responsibility.

Maybe the Allies would buy it.

They went back to the car and the commandant produced sandwiches and a bottle of Burgundy. Odette was terribly hungry but the occasion was intriguing, to say the least. Was this to be her last supper?

They ate without conversation and he told her to get back in the car. The convoy left and they drove all day. Odette could only wonder: Why had she been singled out? Where was he taking her? Why not just shoot her at Ravensbrück? The cut-throat gesture the night before and now the picnic in the park, complete with Burgundy and bonfire. None of it made sense.

As dusk approached Sühren finally spoke.

"Do you want to know where we are going?"

"No." She assumed it was to a deserted wood to be shot.

"I'm taking you to the Americans."

"You are? You must be mad!"

She assured him that the Americans would open fire on a convoy of armed SS soldiers. Sühren realized she was right. He stopped the cars and told the others that he'd take the lead and that they should follow at five hundred meters.

The party continued on and about ten o'clock that night, Odette and the commandant came to a small village and were stopped by American soldiers.

"This is Frau Churchill," Sühren told them, "she has been my prisoner. She is a relation to Winston Churchill, the Prime Minister of England."

Ah, there it was. Leverage. The cunning commandant assumed that if he was so kind as to protect and return unharmed a relative of the prime minister, all sins would be forgiven. No harm, no foul.

Zut to that.

"And this is Fritz Sühren," she retorted, "commandant of the Ravensbrück Concentration Camp. You make him your prisoner."

They stepped out of the Mercedes and one of the Americans took Sühren's sidearm, handed it to Odette, and escorted the German away. As she stood by the car, another soldier said he'd find her a room for the night.

"No, if you don't mind," she said, "I have not seen the sky for a very long time . . . and the stars . . . I would like to sit in this car until morning."

Odette did want to see the stars, but she also wanted to see—and take back to England—the documents in Sühren's briefcase and two albums of photographs, which he had left in the car.

She sat back in the Mercedes and gazed heavenward, the twinkling glitter absorbing her thoughts in the cool night. The Churchill name had saved her, no doubt. And where was Peter? Was he alive? Or did he do something foolish and get himself shot? And what about the F Section women she had traveled with: Diana, Yolande, and the others? Were they still alive? Such brave women.

And Marianne, Lily, and Francoise—to see their faces again!

Thoughts came and went as Odette drank deeply the precious air of freedom.

A clock chimed somewhere—it was midnight—and she reclined

to admire the moon, a luxury she hadn't experienced in years. The same moon that had guided the Lysander landings, the drops, and Peter's arrival on Mont Semnoz.

Footsteps.

Odette swung her head.

An SS officer from one of the other cars was looming over her.

CHAPTER 20

PIERRE

Wildsee, Austria

The main company of American soldiers arrived at Wildsee five days after Captain Attwood's escort. From the breakfast table Peter saw several jeeps and light tanks pulling in, Italian Partisans hanging from every toehold. Kesselring's soldiers turned over their weapons and Peter and the others greeted the Americans. Peter was given a fresh set of clothes—a GI uniform—and was told that an army general had promised the group transportation to Verona, Italy.

Meanwhile, the final Third Reich dominoes tumbled. On May 4 Wehrmacht armies in the Netherlands, Denmark, and northern Germany surrendered to British Field Marshal Bernard Montgomery in Lüneburg. The following day they surrendered in Norway, and on May 7 General Alfred Jodl signed Germany's unconditional surrender in Reims, France, which was ratified by Field Marshal Wilhelm Keitel the following day in Berlin.

The war in Europe was over.

THE NEXT MORNING PETER'S promised convoy arrived—more jeeps and tanks, personnel vehicles, even an ambulance—and they made it to Verona at one in the morning on May 9. The day after, Peter was flown to Naples, debriefing center for returning Allied POWs. Upon arrival, he sent a number of telegrams to England to report in and, more importantly, inquire about Odette.

Nothing back.

All afternoon and evening, he answered questions from Scotland Yard's Lieutenant Colonel Hedin. Peter was more than happy to provide details and names from Germany's finest camps, and Hedin asked him to summarize his comments in a report. Peter stayed up much of the night doing so, but it was important work, he understood. Hedin would have the information cabled to his counterparts in various Allied zones in the morning, and countless Germans—now in civilian clothes—would be receiving visitors by nightfall.

The following afternoon a general stopped by to thank Peter for his work, and to tell him that an air marshal was flying to Northolt the next day and had invited him along.

Peter's stomach churned the entire flight. London still had told him nothing and his mind raced through the possible reasons. Were they waiting to notify next of kin? If Odette was alive, why wouldn't they have said so? Would Buckmaster want to tell him personally? *I'm sorry, old boy. She fought like a Spartan but the Gestapo left none alive* . . . Fifteen months Peter had waited. Fifteen months of wondering if Odette had been shot, hanged, tortured, or had rotted away at Ravensbrück. The least they could do was call him or send something in the wire.

The aircraft swept over Cannes, and the memories flooded.

Yes, of course she could ride a bicycle . . .

While I talk my way through half a dozen Italian Control Posts, in the curfew, you're sleeping in my bed, mon cher . . .

I think that you, who are instrumental in bringing about the need for this fund, should pay for this ticket . . .

And you will come back, as you promised, won't you, Michel? . . .

Pierre, Pierre . . .

His altruistic angry gazelle. Where was she now?

The plane droned on, and the air marshal joined Peter and the other passengers for lunch. In the afternoon Peter finally saw it—the blazing green of England. They landed at Northolt but, strangely, no one from the War Office had come to receive them. Hugh Falconer, an SOE Spanish Section agent who was also on the flight, put in a call to his department but no one seemed to be in. Perhaps the office was closed on Saturday.

Finally, someone picked up. *Falconer? Sorry, I don't know that name. Can't clear you through Security.*

Hugh asked to be returned to the operator and asked if she would transfer the call to the French Section. She did, and Vera Atkins picked up.

"You won't know me, Miss Atkins," the operator said. "I'm the SOE telephone supervisor and I know people by their voices. A man called Hugh Falconer, whose voice I have known on and off for four years, is on the line from Northolt. He belongs to the Spanish Section but there's no one there who seems to know him well enough to clear him through Security. I can't bear the thought of someone returning from the Concentration Camps and being left hanging about in this way. Knowing your interest in these men I'm asking you, off the record, if you can do something?"

Vera told her to put him through, and Hugh handed the receiver to Peter.

"Hallo, there."

"Vera!"

"Peter! I didn't expect to hear your voice. Are you speaking from Northolt?"

Peter said he was and Vera said she was on her way. Peter had met this wonderful lady in '41 when she was Buckmaster's assistant and now she was F Section's intelligence officer.

Vera arrived with a driver and she, Peter, and Hugh sat in the back. Sitting in the middle, Vera conversed first with Hugh and then turned to Peter.

"Well, Peter, it's good to see you back."

"How is it at home?"

"I'm afraid your mother—"

"I know," Peter said. "Just tell me who's still here."

"Your father and—"

"Odette?"

He held his breath. All the world hung in the balance as he waited for Vera's reply.

"She's waiting for you in the office."

Peter's eyes teared. Vera continued talking but he heard nothing more. Nothing else mattered. *Odette was alive.*

The car arrived and Vera opened the door to let Peter burst through. There, sitting proudly in her uniform, was the woman he loved.

"Pierre!"

Peter was overwhelmed. Odette's eyes beamed with the love he'd longed to see.

BIT BY BIT, ODETTE filled Peter in—the torture, the cage, the Bunker, the heat—even the pleasant surprise when the SS officer had given her his coat that cold night in Sühren's car.

They went immediately to Queen Alexandra's Military Hospital in Millbank and Odette's condition was not surprising: her entire body had medical issues. X-rays revealed that her fifth vertebra had been shattered, but now—two years after the fall—had deteriorated to nothing. The starvation and scurvy, as well as the long periods without sunlight, had left her with severe anemia. She was given injections of calcium, vitamin D, and, according to her doctor, "intense general medicinal treatment." She also suffered from nervous tension and articular rheumatism, which had left her with a weakened heart muscle.

As the staff doctor continued to examine her, there was something else. He called in other doctors to have a look.

Odette was still missing a number of toenails, they noticed, and one of her toes had become terribly infected, causing sepsis—a life-threatening malady which arises when the body's response to long-term infection is to attack its own tissue. It was this very condition which had killed Reinhard Heydrich after his operation following the assassination attempt in Prague in '42.

The prognosis of the physicians was the same.

She would die.

CHAPTER 21

HUNTING THE HUNTER

Amsterdam

Throughout May and the beginning of June, the Allies scoured
Amsterdam searching for one Hugo Bleicher—aka Monsieur Jean,
Jean Verbeck, Jean Castel, Colonel Henri, Colonel Heinrich—the
German spy-catcher responsible for the arrests of more than one
hundred Allied agents.

Hugo, however, was well hidden. Not long after arriving in
Holland in March, he had been given the name of a German
businessman—Sams—who had lived in the country for twenty
years and knew Amsterdam well. Sams would be Hugo's interpreter and guide.

One day Sams mentioned that the SD had arrested a Dutch
friend of his, along with nine others, as part of a crackdown on an
Allied Resistance cell called "the Order Service." Hugo knew that
the SD was executing enemy operatives without procedure or fanfare and the chances of these men's survival were slim.

He contacted the SD, telling the local officer that he and Sams
needed the ten spies for a special operation. The SD consented to

the transfer and Hugo conducted a formal interrogation of each member. He then released them with instructions to go to ground until the Allies liberated the city.

When the Canadians approached Amsterdam, the tables turned; it was Hugo who now needed assistance, and the freed Dutchmen were happy to oblige. They provided Hugo and Sams with a hideout that was well-stocked with food. They also kept the German duo apprised of news as the city was liberated.

Once again, however, Hugo was trapped; he couldn't hide in this little room forever. He and Sams would need false papers to slip out of the city and the Order Service offered to help. If Hugo and Sams could produce photos, they said, the Order Service would do the rest. On May 31, he and Sams headed to a photographer's studio to have the photos taken; from there they would meet with the head of the Order Service to discuss an escape plan.

It was a beautiful day, a sunny Sunday, and their Resistance landlord decided to go with them. As they were crossing a canal bridge, Hugo noticed Dutch militia—carbines at the ready—coming directly toward them. He turned to look back—they were coming from both sides.

Betrayal! Hugo thought. Betrayal, the very method he had used with Lily Carré, Roger Bardet, Kiki, and others to arrest a hundred spies and Resistance agents.

The procedure itself was uneventful for Bleicher. He had orchestrated countless arrests himself and this was no doubt the reverse of the medallion, a poetic justice about which he couldn't complain.

FOR EIGHT DAYS HUGO waited in his cell. Finally, an interrogator came and the interviews began. When it became clear that Sergeant Bleicher had performed no effective work in Amsterdam, the Dutch lost interest. The Canadians and French, though—both of whom had files for "Monsieur Jean," "Colonel Henri," and "Sergeant Hugo Bleicher"—wanted immediate custody.

A French major claimed charge over Hugo and waited for a military truck to drive him to Paris. The Canadians, though, beat him to the punch. On July 15, while the Frenchman waited for transport, two Canadian military policemen took custody of Hugo and whisked him away. The following day he was flown to London and interned at Camp 020, interrogation center for high-ranking German officers.

Interrogations began after a week and Hugo did his best to be forthcoming. To his amazement, the British had run a highly effective intelligence war.

"The British Secret Service appeared to know everything—literally everything—about my activities as a member of the German Military Intelligence," he recalled. "I only had to confirm the facts as I was confronted with them. When I compared this to our hasty German interrogations, I was seized with professional envy."

Weeks later, Hugo learned that none other than SS General Walter Schellenberg, Hugo's chief when the Abwehr was folded into the SD in 1944, was in the camp, along with Schellenberg's boss, SD head and war criminal Ernst Kaltenbrunner, who was being held in solitary confinement.

AS TIME WENT ON, inmates in Camp 020 decreased and those who remained were given more freedom. "We had all sorts of pastimes," Hugo recalled, "and could sit out in the garden for hours. It was more like a holiday camp than a prison, and only the barbed wire and the discipline reminded us of captivity."

A rumor circulated in October that the camp would be closed and the inmates returned to Germany. On the 15th it seemed to be true: a guard summoned Hugo in from the garden and told him to change into his old clothes. They were leaving.

Hugo was handcuffed to a soldier and, with the escort of a staff officer, driven to the airport.

"Where is the plane for Paris?" the officer asked someone.

When they landed, a French agent appeared on the tarmac and the Englishman uncuffed Hugo and shook his hand. It was a pleasant parting from the British, the enemy who had treated him so well.

After the Briton left, the Frenchman locked eyes with Hugo.

"Do you know me, Monsieur Jean?"

Hugo said he didn't.

"But I know you."

CHAPTER 22

FANNING THE DAMNED

A number of specialists were called in to look after Odette, and one bright young physician, Dr. T. Markowicz, was chosen to serve as Odette's supervising doctor. Together the physicians decided that they might be able to save her life with several operations. Odette agreed, but good-byes were scheduled nevertheless.

Odette ran the medical gauntlet, however, just as she had the Fresnes–Ravensbrück–Neustadt trail—with dogged determination. Major Buckmaster's judgment back in 1940 had been accurate: this woman was *tenacious*. Odette's survival, of course, was due in no small part to the competence and swift action of Dr. Markowicz. By Peter's account, this young doctor saved Odette's life on more than three occasions.

Yet Odette's health would require specialized treatment long after the operations. A year later, Dr. Markowicz was still treating her for a nervous condition and anemia, and Odette was awarded a full disability pension.

ASIDE FROM MEDICAL CARE and rest, Odette had one remaining obligation: to assist in the prosecution of Ravensbrück war criminals. In 1945 someone had offered her $2,000[50] for Sühren's photographs but she declined, handing them over to the War Office. These photos, she knew, would be necessary to identify and capture camp officials, many of whom now went under aliases and had blended into the German landscape.

At the top of the list was the commandant himself.

He had escaped.

After turning himself over to the Americans, Sühren and several SS officers had been placed in the former concentration camp at Neuengamme, near Hamburg. Before the Ravensbrück trials began on December 5, 1945, however, Sühren and SS Sergeant Hans Pflaum disappeared. It was unthinkable, but true. Perhaps because of his experience as a camp commandant—and knowledge of security weaknesses—Sühren managed to slip out.

And he wasn't the only war criminal who had avoided justice. Holocaust architect Adolf Eichmann had fled to Austria,[51] while Gestapo chief Heinrich Müller had simply vanished.[52] With or without Sühren, however, Odette's testimony would be required.

Paris

HUGO BLEICHER STOOD ON the tarmac staring at the Frenchman. He really had no idea who he was.

---

51 And later, Argentina. He was captured by Israel's Mossad in 1960 and tried in Jerusalem for war crimes and crimes against humanity the following year. Eichmann was found guilty and hanged on June 1, 1962.

52 Some said he had died during the bombing of Berlin, but there was no body. Others said that Müller had been captured by the Russians or had fled to Argentina, but there were no trails to either.

"You arrested my best friend Pierre de Vomécourt," the man said, "alias Lucas of the French Resistance."

Hugo cringed. He remembered Lucas well. It was during the tail end of his dismantling of the INTERALLIÉ network in 1941–42 that he had arrested this courageous SOE operative.[53]

"Then Lucas will have told you that he owes his life to my intervention," Hugo said.

"Oh yes, we know that."

Hugo rested easy; so far, so good.

A special commissioner picked them up for the drive to town and seemed friendly enough. "Have you had a good flight, Monsieur Jean?" he asked. "Are you glad to be back in Paris?"

Hugo paused. Four years of living as Monsieur Jean in this enchanted city indeed brought back memories. "I suppose you are taking me to Fresnes Prison?"

"You are not a convict, Monsieur Jean. We asked for you from London because we require some information from you. You are the guest here of the Ministry of the Interior, and you will stay there. You must know the Ministry of the Interior in the rue des Saussaies."

The commissioner smiled. It was the painted smile of a clown.

Hugo nodded. Gestapo headquarters had been located at 11 rue des Saussaies, at the back of the French Ministry of the Interior.

---

53 Hugo had turned INTERALLIÉ's number two agent, Lily Carré, and Lucas—who had lost his wireless operator—had heard that Lily had a radio in Paris. Indeed she did, but it was Hugo who was now running it, contacting London as if he were the Allied circuit. Rather than arrest Lucas, though, Hugo had opted to give him line to see what bigger fish could be caught. In a labyrinthine operation, Hugo sent Lily to London with instructions to infiltrate British Intelligence. Lucas coordinated the submarine pickup and escorted her to England, all under the watchful eye of Bleicher and his Abwehr assistants. The Kriegsmarine (German navy) had been ordered to cancel patrols in that area, and local German soldiers were ordered to look the other way when they saw a man or two with a girl in a red hat.

When Lucas returned to Paris, his orders were to kill Monsieur Jean. Hugo was warned, however, and arrested Lucas before he could eliminate SOE's nemesis. But rather than have Lucas executed as a spy, Hugo had him interned in a POW camp.

They went into an office and Hugo was introduced to the ministry superintendent, who introduced his deputy. As they conversed, a parade of employees streamed by, all wanting to catch a glimpse of Monsieur Jean, famous German spy-catcher.

"I told you, Monsieur Jean, that you were our guest here," the commissioner said again. "You will have to live in the cellar. It will not be as comfortable as it was in England, but do not forget that it was the Gestapo who first put our people in this cellar."

It was only fair, Hugo knew. The cellar was a dungeon, but the commissioner assured that no harm would come to him; they only wanted Hugo's written testimony of his wartime activities. To Hugo's surprise, Suzanne was brought in. She had been convicted of collaborating with the enemy and espionage, he was told, and sentenced to death. The commissioner had spared her from the firing squad, however, when he learned that Hugo would be returning to Paris.

Hugo and Suzanne descended the stairs and at once the stench engulfed them—sweat and body odor. Suzanne was taken off to the women's section, and Hugo to the men's. He was shut in cell number 1 with fourteen prisoners. The foul odor, he realized, was because there was no fresh air coming underground. Air was sucked into the cellar by a huge hand-operated ventilator that required the strenuous effort of two prisoners, each pair taking half-hour shifts.

The next day Hugo began his written record and the interrogations began. He was confronted with a number of witnesses, many of whom he had arrested. "They were all truthful enough to make it plain that I had treated them decently during the war," he recalled. "Many shook me warmly by the hand. I was glad to be able to provide some explanations that cleared innocent people of the suspicion that they had denounced or betrayed Resistance men to the Germans."

One day another prisoner was brought in.

Marsac.

"*Mon Dieu*, Monsieur Jean, still alive?"

"My goodness, Marsac, you spent enough time a prisoner in German hands for the sake of France. How is it that you have been arrested by your own countrymen?"

He had been arrested on suspicion of betraying the Resistance to Germans, Marsac said. "Monsieur Jean, tell the Superintendent that I was not intending treason when I was in your hands. I really thought that in you I had won a friend for France. How was I to know that you were such a good actor?"

Hugo explained to the superintendent that Marsac was innocent; that he had fooled the Frenchman.

"The chief of an organization has no right to be outwitted in that way," the superintendent replied.

Hugo pressed the matter over several days and Marsac finally was released, mollifying Hugo's conscience.

Some days later Suzanne passed word that one of Hugo's turned agents was in the cellar: Roger Bardet. Roger desperately wanted to speak with him, she said, but as the evidence of his treason was strong, he was kept in solitary confinement.

Indeed, Bardet had been one of Bleicher's best. "Through him I had been in a position to protect the Wehrmacht from all sorts of dangerous sabotage," Hugo later wrote. "His collaboration meant much to me. It had saved the lives of countless German soldiers. His own personal welfare had become of lively concern to me."

Hugo told Suzanne that he and Roger could sign up to turn the ventilator and eventually they would be paired.

The day came and each grasped the heavy handles. Roger looked like hell, Hugo thought, haggard and spent—a man whose conscience had exacerbated the ill effects of prison. They began turning and the fan roared. Shouting at each other to be heard over the whirring, they discussed Paul—Major Henri Frager—who had been executed at Buchenwald.

Hugo had been almost tearful when he arrested him the prior August. While working under the assumption that Bleicher was sincere in his request to flee to England, Paul had given Hugo the name and address of his sister in Neuilly-sur-Seine. If "Colonel

Henri" had any trouble when the Allies arrived, Paul had said, the good colonel could take refuge with her. Trouble arrived first, however, for Paul.

Major Kieffer, frustrated at Bleicher's slack and often mysterious relationship with the enemy, summoned him to Avenue Foch.

"You should have arrested 'Paul' when you last met with him," the SD chief said. "Now we might never catch up with him again. Well, you're responsible for it. I give you one week. Then I shall send a report to RSHA. This means a People's Court trial for you, or worse."

Bleicher had no choice. He visited the sister and said that it was still too early for him to leave his "Luftwaffe post," but that he needed to see Paul. Her brother was out, she said, but would be arriving at five the next day at the Gare Montparnasse station.

At the appointed hour Bleicher and three Abwehr men, along with three supervising SD agents, were waiting when the train arrived. "I am sorry," Hugo told Paul, "I misled you. I am an Abwehr officer and I have come to arrest you."

Paul took it in stride. "I often suspected you might be a German counteragent," he said, "but one has to believe in one's fellow human beings. I believed you and I have only myself to blame."

It was the one thing that haunted Hugo. Paul was a wonderful man and respected by everyone, even Kieffer, who called him a true patriot. Frager's last words at Fresnes, Hugo told Roger, were: "Promise me, Monsieur Jean, that you will not harm Roger Bardet. I have always cared for him as my own brother."

Roger tugged the handle, sweat dripping from his brow. "Paul! Paul! Yes, he was the finest man I ever knew. It was his example that decided me to go into the Maquis with him. You must understand this, Monsieur Jean. I lost my head then. It was plain to everybody that Germany could not win the war. I saw myself with no foothold any more. The victors would march in and settle their scores with us. What could I do? I was young. Life still lay before me."

Hugo worked the handle, sweating and huffing. It made sense, really. If Roger could leave the Resistance so easily to work for Germany, it would have been just as easy to switch sides again once he realized that the Third Reich was doomed. Easy come, easy go.

Roger was likely to be convicted of treason, Hugo knew, and it became apparent that this was his last confession, ventilator substituting for booth.

"So I went into the Maquis to rehabilitate myself," Roger went on. "Who could have proved anything against me? Who knew of my past activities? The one witness who could give evidence against me was you, Monsieur Jean. So I came to the conclusion that I must kill you."

They continued to crank the handles, pulling and grunting as galley slaves, and Roger became agitated as he worked himself up, eyes bulging. "It was I who stole your car in Auxerre," he shouted. "I wanted to first immobilize you and make you helpless. I had ten desperate men ready for the job. We crept around your house, night after night. They were all determined to kill you and Suzanne at the first opportunity."

So there it was. Double cross, triple cross. *Et tu, Brute?*

"Today I am glad that the chance never came," Roger said, "and that I have not a murder on my conscience."

The joys of war. Betrayal, counterbetrayal, attempted murder, missed opportunity, confession.

The ventilator droned on and the men cranked, Hugo remembered, toiling "like two souls expiating our souls in an inferno of our own making, working the wheel, fanning the damned."

London

THE YEAR 1946 WOULD be busy and bittersweet for Odette. While her marriage with Roy had for all practical purposes ended years before, they were finally divorced. Strangely, the record is silent about Roy and the details of their broken relationship. One can only surmise that their relationship had cooled prior to the time Odette left for France.

That summer, another event disrupted family tranquility.

Odette had rented a cottage in Petersfield, a small town about sixty miles southwest of London, where she could disappear and relax with her girls for a few weeks. At seven o'clock in the evening on August 19, there was a knock on the door.

"Congratulations," the man said.

Odette gave a puzzled look and asked what he was talking about. As the man tried to explain, she cut him off: "You've got the wrong address. It's not my cottage, it's just rented."

"Oh, yes. No, I've got the right person."

Odette asked again what he was talking about.

"The George Cross."

"The George Cross. What's that?"

The reporter was incredulous. Everyone knew what the George Cross was—Britain's second-highest honor—and Odette would be the second SOE agent[54] and the first female[55] who had faced the enemy to receive it.

"I don't know what the George Cross is," she said again. "To do with me?"

"Yes. You'll read it in the *Gazette* tomorrow morning."

The following day, forty-two newspaper reporters showed up at the cottage; Odette had become famous overnight. She did her best to be hospitable but was still at a loss for what all the fuss was about, and what the journalists were saying.

One reporter asked what she would be doing in the future.

"I am going to stay home and do some knitting!" said the SPINDLE spy.

That evening, as Odette was putting the girls to bed, Marianne asked, "Mommy, is the George Cross the best you could do?"

---

54 Brigadier Arthur Frederick Crane Nicholls received the award posthumously on March 1, 1946, for gallantry and leadership during service in Albania.

55 Daphne Pearson, a corporal in the Women's Auxiliary Air Force, received in 1940 the predecessor to the George Cross, the Empire Gallantry Medal, for rescuing a pilot from a crashed bomber in Detling, Kent. King George VI replaced her EGM with a George Cross on December 31, 1941.

MORE HONORS WERE TO come. Odette was appointed a Member of the Order of the British Empire, and was awarded France's highest honor, the Chevalier de la Légion d'honneur, for her service to the French Resistance. Peter, in turn, was awarded a Distinguished Service Order and France's Croix de Guerre. In addition, Odette had been promoted to lieutenant; Peter, to major.

At Peter's suggestion, he and Odette would receive their British awards together at the investiture on November 17. That morning Odette received a couple injections to help her through the service, and they were off to Buckingham Palace. Not realizing that he could park in the palace courtyard, Peter parked on a side street and they walked to the main gates. As they approached, something peculiar happened.

The guards seemed to recognize Odette—perhaps from the news broadcast at Petersfield—and presented arms. Again and again, each set of guards followed suit. Peter could not have been more proud of the girl on his arm. He saluted each time, and they made their way to the reception area.

While waiting for seating instructions, Peter noticed something remarkable: of the 250 or so to be decorated, Odette was the only woman. He smiled.

They found seats in the back and a general recognized them and said a few words of greeting. No sooner had he left than the Lord Chamberlain appeared and stooped before Odette.

He whispered something.

Odette could not believe her ears.

CHAPTER 23

COMPLETING THE LOOP

"Madame, His Majesty has requested that you lead the investiture," the Lord Chamberlain had said.

Odette gasped. "Oh! I couldn't possibly do that."

"Oh yes, you can."

Odette was at a loss for words. Leading a procession of 250 soldiers and officers—all of whom were being decorated for valor—before King George VI?

The Lord Chamberlain smiled and said he understood that two of her daughters were in attendance. "If you will kindly point them out to me I will arrange that they are moved up close to the dais."

Odette did and the Lord Chamberlain ushered her to the front of the line. To her left were thirty senior officers lining the red carpet leading to the dais, and behind her five hundred guests. The king entered and took his place immediately across from her. As the orchestra played the national anthem, his eyes never left hers.

When everyone was seated Odette's citation was read:

Mrs. Sansom was infiltrated into enemy-occupied France and worked with great courage and distinction until April, 1943, when she was arrested with her Commanding Officer. Between Marseilles and Paris on the way to the prison at Fresnes, she succeeded in speaking to her Commanding Officer and for mutual protection they agreed to maintain that they were married. She adhered to this story and even succeeded in convincing her captors in spite of considerable contrary evidence and through at least fourteen interrogations. She also drew Gestapo attention from her Commanding Officer on to herself saying that he had only come to France on her insistence. She took full responsibility and agreed that it should be herself and not her Commanding Officer who should be shot. By this action she caused the Gestapo to cease paying attention to her Commanding Officer after only two interrogations.

In addition the Gestapo were most determined to discover the whereabouts of a wireless operator and of another British officer whose lives were of the greatest value to the Resistance Organization. Mrs. Sansom was the only person who knew of their whereabouts. The Gestapo tortured her most brutally to try to make her give away this information. They seared her back with a red-hot iron and, when that failed, they pulled out all her toenails. Mrs. Sansom, however, continually refused to speak, and by her bravery and determination she not only saved the lives of the two officers but also enabled them to carry on their most valuable work. During the period of over two years in which she was in enemy hands, she displayed courage, endurance and self-sacrifice of the highest possible order.

Odette was motioned forward and the king pinned on the George Cross and took her hand.

"I asked that you should lead the procession, Madame, as no woman has done so before [or] during my reign."

He continued to hold her hand as he offered gracious personal compliments.

Odette was speechless. She curtsied and gave way to the next recipient.

When Peter's turn came—some two hundred spots later—the king was just as gracious. He knew all about "Mr. and Mrs. Peter Churchill," the courageous SPINDLE spies, and Peter was touched by his remarks.

Odette with her George Cross.
CLANCY TUCKER/ATHENA PEARL

DECORATIONS, HOWEVER, THOUGH WORTHY and deserved, are worn proudly for a time and then forgotten by most. But the actions for which they were given are never forgotten by witnesses.

Odette's cellmate in Fresnes, Simone Hérail, would remember Odette long after their confinement. "Foreseeing that she would be sent to Germany," Simone wrote after the war, "she regretted only one thing: that she would not be able to go on serving freely what she called her two countries—Great Britain and France. Convinced that she would certainly be shot, she said that she had for a long time accepted the sacrifice of her life which she had wished to dedicate without reservation to the service of her country. An example of this order is unforgettable."

DECEMBER CAME AND IT was time for Odette to testify at the Ravensbrück war crimes trial in Hamburg. Fritz Sühren had been recaptured, they said, and Odette was a key witness for the prosecution. She made the trip to Germany to relive her nightmare one more time. On the eve of the trial, however, there was a slight catch: Commandant Sühren had escaped.

Again.

The official record is that he escaped under "mysterious" circumstances, but Peter Churchill saw no mystery: Sühren's guards were German.

The trial would go on, in any case, for Ravensbrück staff, officers, and medical personnel. When her turn on the stand came on December 16, 1946, Odette shocked the Allied military judges with her testimony. She had heard the screams of women being dragged to the crematorium, she told them. Doors were opened and closed, she heard more screams, and then silence.

Could Odette swear that the women were burned alive? Judge Advocate General C. L. Stirling asked. Odette said she could not. Only that she heard the screams as they were taken in, followed by silence. Others testified of similar atrocities.

With overwhelming evidence, the military tribunal convicted sixteen defendants of war crimes and crimes against humanity and all were sentenced to death.

Commandant Sühren, though, was still at large.

His time would come.

HUGO BLEICHER, MEANWHILE, WAS actively doing *his* time. The interrogations seemed to go on forever until every aspect of his war career had been plumbed. He had been scrutinized for misappropriation of property, lack of humanity, and countless other misdeeds. Through it all he went, though, unscathed.

The penetrating question—in regard to Bleicher and every other intelligence and counterintelligence agent of the war—was where to draw the line in zealous performance of duty. Hugo had lied so convincingly that Marsac and Roger Bardet readily handed over the citadel keys. He had then used the Frenchmen to trap Odette and Peter.

Maurice Buckmaster, for one, thought Hugo had crossed the line. "Bleicher's methods were insidious," he wrote after the war. "He subverted tough and loyal men, who would have withstood torture, by pretending that he was anti-Nazi and hated the thought of handing them over to the Gestapo; in this manner he managed to break them down with a sly and malevolent kindness, so bringing them to implicate their companions and introduce him, as a friend, to Resistance circles."

But Hugo's methods were less than novel; deceit has been an integral part of spycraft throughout history. And had not Odette and Peter and every other SOE agent used the lesser arts to accomplish their tasks, these saboteurs masquerading in mufti? That far, both sides could agree: there was an unwritten standard of acceptable skullduggery.

Perhaps the bottom line in determining whether Bleicher had gone too far was his conduct with captives: Had he mistreated prisoners? To his credit, Hugo could honestly say, no. Yes, he knew the Gestapo would, but that wasn't on his mantle. His job was to find and arrest spies, imprison them, and then entertain them with Viennese waltzes.

That was his story, at least, and he stuck to it with great success.

"It was generally conceded that I had done no more than my duty," Hugo wrote after the war, "and that my behavior had been humane." His wasn't the zeal of the Nazi convert, but the strident loyalty of a German soldier. "One after another," he pointed out, "the homes where I had been billeted during my service in France were painstakingly visited by the Sûreté, who ascertained that I had not been guilty of looting or depredations."

In what Hugo saw as proof of his professionalism, the Deuxième Bureau had delivered to him upon his release—neatly packed in a cardboard box—a suit and raincoat he had left behind in one of his apartments. The British, for their part, were wholly impressed by Hugo's work, and concluded that he had acted responsibly.

Ian Wilson, MI5's case officer for double agent Dusko Popov, Britain's top spy, had nothing but respect for his counterpart. "Bleicher has had an exceptionally successful career in penetration work in Paris and the North of France," he wrote in a 16 June 1945 report for Lieutenant Colonel Robin Stephens, Camp 020's supervisor. "Bleicher is believed to be an expert at his work," Ian concluded, "and a relatively humane man—he had no love for the Nazis."

And SOE's reports on Bleicher were no less complimentary. Among F Section agents interrogated by him, Hugo had a reputation as being "extremely nice and polite."

Even Buckmaster, who had a vested personal interest in tangling with this cunning character, had to admit that in the battle of wits, Hugo had his about him. "There is no doubt," Maurice concluded, "that he was a subtle and, on the whole, chivalrous opponent."

At the end of the espionage intrigue, the deft spy-catcher had once again proven his mastery of the game.

AFTER THE HAMBURG TRIALS Odette returned to London, the horrors and memories of Ravensbrück behind her. Physical scars remained, but her mind was at peace; she was alive, she was free, and she was happy. It was high time to knit and play with her girls and chase butterflies on the hills of Somerset.

And there was the other thing.

Two months later, on February 15, 1947, the SPINDLE spies completed the final loop. In a private ceremony at Kensington Registry, "Mr. and Mrs. Churchill" made it formal.

Peter and Odette were married.

Peter and Odette Churchill moments after tying the knot.

EPILOGUE

Fascinated by the Churchill name and her marriage to Peter, the press asked Odette often about how the famous name played a role in her survival.

"There is no other reason why I should have survived," she said in one interview, "because I was condemned to death, and, after all, I am the only one of all the girls who did the same job who was really condemned to death and they haven't come back; I came back. Furthermore, they had every right, if you like, to carry out the sentence. They should have done it."

Winston Churchill would later hear that his name had helped save the lives of Peter and Odette and he played along, never correcting the fictitious relation. Odette met him during a postwar ceremony and thanked him for protecting the secret.

"Madam," the prime minister said, "this is indeed an honor."

Trude, the Fresnes guard who took a particular liking to Odette, remained impressed with the Churchill name long after last seeing Odette and Peter. While serving a short prison sentence following the war, she sent Odette a letter. She had been a governess before the war, she explained, and asked if she could work for Odette in England as the governess of her children. Peter and Odette declined the offer but the gesture was touching. When Trude was released, she completed a journey of her own: she married the Fresnes guard captain who had given Odette the lily of the valley bouquet.

THE WORST PART OF her captivity, Odette would later share, was the separation from her children. "What happened to me in the field," she said in one interview, "didn't matter in a way, because I left England with a broken heart, so nothing after that could break it ever again. So the rest was physical. That [separation from her children] was the only thing that demanded courage, and I would never do it again."

Would she do it again if she had no children? "No, never," Odette said. "Because it is a game. I think it is not possible for that game to ever be completely a clean game. And I would not be involved in such a game ever again."

Notwithstanding her mistreatment and suffering, however, Odette harbored no bitterness toward the Germans. "They were in their situation," she told one interviewer, "I was in mine. I was their prisoner and they were the masters of the situation. If you accept to do that kind of job, call yourself an agent or something, you accept what goes with it. It's no good because you are caught to think 'they are wrong and you are right.'

"There was nothing to be bitter about," she added. "It is a duty one has to people who did the right thing, to one's comrades, to all the good and brave people. You have to remember them. There is no point in being bitter and wanting to create the same kind of feelings of hatred. It's pointless and harmful. And so I have been so terribly fortunate. I've got my wonderful family, I'm a very happy woman. People are most kind and generous to me, very much more than I deserve. It is extraordinary, and I'm touched every day by the generosity of people. And it has been fantastic. I'm only sad, extremely sad and always will be for the rest of my life, that my comrades did not come back."

When asked if the torture she suffered left her frightened of humans, she answered, "No. Why? Nothing has changed. There were always bad people. I've seen a lot of bad people, but because of those evil ones, I've seen the most noble people. So this is what I wish to remember of it. I consider that it has been an extraordinary experience."

The SPINDLE story was not quite finished, however. In September 1946 Hugo Bleicher was released by French authorities and returned to his hometown of Tettnang, where he opened a tobacco shop. In 1949 Louis le Belge and Roger Bardet, the snake who had shed his skin one too many times, were convicted of treason and sentenced to death. Their executions were stayed, though, and after serving a few years in prison, they were inexplicably released.

That same year saw the publication of *Odette: The Story of a British Agent*, an authorized biography of Odette's wartime activities by Jerrard Tickell, a former member of the Royal Army Service Corps and the War Office. While the book was a smashing success, some alleged that much of the story was fictitious. Neither the author nor Odette could counter the charges with proof, however, since all of the SOE files were classified under the Official Secrets Act. For now the story would have to be defended by Odette's George Cross.

Also in 1949, the slippery rat of Ravensbrück, Commandant Fritz Sühren, was located. After his escape from Neuengamme, the concentration camp where he had been interned while awaiting trial, Sühren had gone to ground, burrowing his way to the tiny village of Eppenschlag, some ten miles west of the Czech border. He took a job at a brewery under the alias Herbert Pakusch and laid low for months. He had been seen in Hamburg in November 1946, witnesses said, and again in February and September 1948, but eluded capture. The following month, a former Ravensbrück secretary saw him in Eppenschlag and notified authorities.

Fritz Sühren captured at last.
CORRIERE DELLA SERA

They were not fast enough.

Sensing danger, Sühren disappeared and not until 24 March 1949 was he recaptured by American troops in Deggendorf, a neighboring village on the banks of the Danube. That July he was turned over to the French to finally face the music.

ON MARCH 10, 1950, Fritz Sühren was tried for war crimes and crimes against humanity by a military court in Rastatt, Germany. He was convicted and sentenced to death. On June 12, at Sandweier, Baden-Baden, Sühren was hanged.

Perhaps most poignant of the postwar events, however, was the final news about Father Paul Steinert. Immediately after the war, Odette and Peter sought to get in touch with him but were told by three sources that he had died on the Eastern Front. It was crushing news, but Father Paul had expected it. The Gestapo were unhappy with the comfort he brought to enemy prisoners, and the Eastern Front was an honorable death.

Deeply saddened, Peter and Odette held a mass in his honor in London.

Three years later, while Odette and Peter were away on vacation, a stranger stopped by their London home. Odette's mother, who was staying in the house at the time, invited him in. He was tall and clearly German.

"Madame," he said, "I have no right to enter this home. My visit is a pilgrimage." He was Father Paul's cousin, he said, and he had brought a parcel on Father Paul's behalf for Captain Churchill.

Odette's mother began to weep. *Father Paul was alive?*

Indeed he was, the cousin said, and quite busy. He was shepherding a large parish in Karlstadt, Germany.

"In bringing Paul Steinert's sad greetings to Captain Churchill," he went on, "I beg to salute the mother of such a daughter."

Father Paul and the cousin were certain that Odette had perished at Ravensbrück.

Odette's mother explained that no, Odette had survived; she and Peter were away on vacation. Now it was the cousin's turn to be swept with emotion.

A German priest and a French-British spy, both lost, had been found.

When Odette and Peter returned from vacation they opened the parcel. In it were the two rag dolls Odette had made for Father Paul's niece and nephew while imprisoned at Fresnes in 1943.

He had saved them for Odette's children.

Odette with the rag dolls she had made for Father Paul's niece and nephew in 1943. *ALAMY*

IN 1950 ODETTE'S STORY was released to great fanfare in the British film *Odette*. Anna Neagle played the role of Odette, with Trevor Howard as Peter, Peter Ustinov as Arnaud, Marius Goring as Hugo Bleicher, and Maurice Buckmaster as himself. None other than the king and queen of England attended the world premiere at the Plaza Theatre in London's Piccadilly Circus.

To prepare for the role, Anna Neagle asked Odette to take her to the various sites and walk her through what had happened. Neagle absorbed the information, reliving the events before she portrayed them.

Odette ends with this title card:

> *It is with a sense of deep humility that I allow my personal story to be told. I am a very ordinary woman to whom a chance was given to see human beings at their best and at their worst. I knew kindness as well as cruelty, understanding as well as brutality. My comrades, who did far more than I and suffered far more profoundly, are not here to speak. It is to their memory that this film has been made and I would like it to be a window through which may be seen those very gallant women with whom I had the honour to serve.*

Odette Churchill

The film was a box office hit, Britain's fourth most popular of the year. Afterward, Neagle remained emotional, almost damaged by the story. "It took her one year after the end of that film to get back to normal," Odette said later. "She was more upset by doing that film than I was by living the experience. It really did things to her."

Three years later, in 1953, Peter and Odette decided to return to France and revisit some of the old sites, including Cannes and Arles. It was a bittersweet reunion. It was here they had met, had fallen in love, had shivered together on barren airfields, and had tested their mettle against Germany's best. And it was here that their love, their ruse of being married and being related to Winston Churchill, had saved them.

But the towns also reminded them of their running mate, Arnaud, for whom they would have given their lives. Arnaud had returned to Cannes to warn Cammaerts after their arrest, they had heard—saving him—but was later arrested just before D-Day. Since Arnaud was Jewish, they sent him to the Rawicz extermination camp in Poland, where he was gassed.

TOO OFTEN ALL GOOD things come to an end, and in 1956 the SPINDLE team unwound: Peter and Odette divorced, and she married Geoffrey Hallowes later that year. The record doesn't reflect how a marriage forged in such fiery conditions could cool, but after nine years, it did. But for the rest of his life, Peter always spoke highly of her, particularly when the issue of Odette's bravery arose.

They remained lifelong friends, until Peter's death in 1972 at the age of sixty-three.

ODETTE DIED IN 1995 at the age of eighty-two. On February 23, 2012, almost seventy years after she joined the SOE, the Royal Mail released a stamp in her honor as part of its Britons of Distinction series.

Of Maurice Buckmaster's 424 F Section agents operating in France, Odette was one of three[56] awarded the George Cross, and the only one to receive it in her lifetime. She was the most highly decorated spy (and woman) of World War II.[57]

Her grandfather would have been proud.

----

56 Violette Szabo and Noor Inayat Khan received the George Cross posthumously (December 17, 1946, and April 5, 1949, respectively).

57 Odette was awarded the George Cross, the Order of the British Empire (M.B.E.), the Chevalier de la Légion d'honneur, the 1939–1945 Star, the France and Germany Star, the War Medal 1939–1945, the Queen Elizabeth II Coronation Medal, and the Queen Elizabeth II Silver Jubilee Medal.

Odette's stamp in the Britons of Distinction series. *ROYAL MAIL*

APPENDIX

The SOE Official History Affair

Beginning in the 1950s a number of books were published which criticized the SOE, its effectiveness, and even its integrity. In particular, some alleged that Maurice Buckmaster had been incompetent in his handling of the German infiltration of the PROSPER circuit, and pointed out that the enemy turned no fewer than four F Section radios.

Others attacked the agents themselves. In 1950 six members of the French Resistance signed a letter protesting the accolades and awards given to Peter and Odette. Two of the signatories clearly had an ax to grind: André Girard, the CARTE circuit leader whom Peter had effectively fired; and Baron de Malval, who had been suspected of embezzling SPINDLE funds. In Odette's debriefing on May 12, 1945, she had stated: "There was some trouble with the Baron de Malval. He was left in charge of some money and when they asked for it, it could not be found. There was some argument and they rather suspected him."

The letter quietly died but in 1956 de Malval printed and circulated privately *Le Journal de la Villa Isabelle*, a recitation of Peter's alleged failures as circuit leader. In it the baron charged that Peter had botched the reception of men and arms in 1943, exhibited poor judgment, and disregarded standard security. As an example of a security failure, de Malval referenced the wireless signal found in Peter's wallet after his arrest, which the Germans used to arrest the baron:

ON LANDING IN FRANCE THE SEVEN PASSENGERS WILL PROCEED STRAIGHT TO BARON DE MALVAL'S VILLA ISABELLE ROUTE DE FREJUS CANNES.

Edward Spiro, writing after the war as E. H. Cookridge, wrote in *Inside S.O.E.* that he reviewed de Malval's documents, found the charges wanting, and surmised the root of the allegations. "The Baron and his wife were kept for many months at the prison of Fresnes," he wrote. "M de Malval lost the sight of an eye, following the torture he had suffered. It is, perhaps, understandable that he bore a grudge. There is, however, no evidence that these arrests can be blamed upon Peter Churchill's disregard of security."

Two years later, in 1958, the original complaint letter mysteriously resurfaced. It was published by the London and Paris press, prompting critical inquiries on both sides of the Channel. Regarding Odette, the challenges came in three scandalous assertions: (1) that her work with SPINDLE had been negligible because she had spent most of her time in bed with her commanding officer; (2) that she survived Ravensbrück because she had an ongoing affair with Commandant Fritz Sühren; and (3) that she had made up the stories of her torture and experience in the Bunker.

All of the charges are refuted by SOE files, but in 1958 those files were classified. It was Odette's word against theirs, and they went on the attack. Forgetting that Odette was a courier and Peter a circuit organizer, they asked for proof of at least one act of sabotage or act of military significance that Odette or Peter had performed.

Odette's response was reported in England's *Daily Telegraph* on November 24, 1958:

"She [Odette] pointed out that the six men who were making the attack had waited thirteen years before doing so. 'I know why,' she said. 'They are uneasy. And the three men concerned in this thing whose names I know all had a grudge against Peter Churchill. I was not a saboteur, so of course I did no sabotage. I did my job as a courier and it was for that that I got my M.B.E. The George Cross was for my time in captivity."

The bad publicity, however, had taken root in London; Dame Irene Ward launched a campaign to have Odette's George Cross rescinded, further stirring the French pot. Ironically, no one could explain how the protest letter was suddenly resurrected after eight years. One of the signatories, Captain Francis Basin, even told a reporter in Paris that he could not understand how it surfaced. "We signed the document in 1950," he said. "I am mystified that it should now come to light so late."

While Odette tried to stay above the fray, Peter attacked it head-on, explaining to the *Daily Mail* that his first assignment was to rescue Captain Basin himself, who was being transported by train in the company of three gendarmes. When Peter had his four French Resistance operatives in place for the snatch, he stated, Basin gave the signal that he didn't want to be liberated.[58] This was the courage of one of the men claiming that Peter and Odette were unworthy of their citations.

As for Odette, Peter was unequivocal in defending his now ex-wife: "I have never known such a brave woman," he told the *Daily Telegraph*. "She is an international heroine who faced every imaginable danger. She never shrank from any kind of danger." And to the notion that Odette's awards were undeserved, he stated, "It is the most amazing accusation ever made. We may be divorced, but

---

58 Basin replied to Peter's comment by stating that he called off the rescue because he was handcuffed to another prisoner. The excuse fails, however, since prisoners were always handcuffed; the rescues always occurred when the prisoner stated that he needed to use the restroom and was uncuffed for that purpose. When the prisoner was in the lavatory, the rescue team would confront the guards and, at gunpoint, force them off the train or escape with their man.

I can still say that but for Odette's courage under torture, hundreds of others would have been arrested by the Gestapo."

Peter's comment was backed up—though no one could see it—by a letter he had written to Colonel Perkins at the War Office on 25 May 1946 to assist in the award of Odette's disability pension. In it Peter detailed Odette's knowledge of locations for Arnaud and Lieutenant Colonel Francis Cammaerts, the Gestapo's torture of Odette to try to gain this information, and statements from Odette's doctors confirming her torture.

Even more valuable was an affidavit in the SOE files from Cammaerts himself. When Baker Street was investigating Odette's worthiness to receive her George Cross, Cammaerts had provided testimony on 20 November 1945 that she had saved his life, and the life of Arnaud as well:

> *I certify that on 17th April 1943, when Ensign Sansom was arrested: ——*
>
> *(a) The Germans knew of my existence and were most anxious to trace me.*
>
> *(b) Ensign Sansom was the only person who knew my whereabouts in France.*
>
> *(c) The Germans also knew that Ensign Sansom had this information.*
>
> *It is most certain that had she in any way told them where I was, I should have been arrested forthwith. As it was, I remained at the same address for three months, unsuspected and unmolested.*
>
> *Thanks to Ensign Sansom's courage and tenacity against determined attempts by the Gestapo, I was enabled to carry on my work without hindrance.*
>
> *I can also certify that Ensign Sansom knew of contact ad-*

dresses for Captain Rabinovitch and that none of those addresses were given to the Germans and that Captain Rabinovitch was able to leave France unmolested.

The document and Cammaerts's identity, however, would remain secret.

Colonel Buckmaster, though, would come to the defense of his famous agents, telling the *Daily Telegraph* that Odette's activities were unspectacular by design—she was a courier. If anything she had done before capture was bold or aggressive, he explained, she would not have been properly performing her job, which she did "impeccably." As for Peter, he added, "What Churchill did must still largely remain secret, but his work in the reconnoitering of means of landing secret agents in France was invaluable and made an entire difference to our operations. That alone would have justified all the decorations."

With Peter's and Buckmaster's rebuttals, the French controversy subsided. In London, however, the matter persisted. Dame Irene Ward continued her push for an SOE investigation, and the rescinding of Odette's George Cross and M.B.E. Working the political back channels, she sent correspondence to her colleagues in Parliament, including a letter to Prime Minister Harold Macmillan on May 6, 1959, urging action.

The response of the officials was cool. Robert Knox, British councilor and future mayor of Berwick-upon-Tweed, wrote to Cabinet Secretary Sir Norman Brook on May 8, pointing out that: (a) other than the press reports from November 1958 to March 1959, the validity of the award had not been challenged; (b) Major General Sir Colin Gubbins, head of SOE, had sponsored the original recommendation and retained the view that the award was valid; and (c) when a decoration for gallantry had been issued, only misconduct of a very particular nature—such as high treason—would warrant a recommendation for cancellation.

Considering the matter and relevant issues, Brook advised Timothy Bligh, principal private secretary to the prime minister, that any inquiry into the worthiness of Odette's decorations was unwise. In a letter on June 1, 1959, he stated:

"There seems to be no precedent for reviewing the grounds for a gallantry award. To reopen this case now on the basis suggested by Miss Ward would in effect call in question the wisdom of the Sovereign's original decision to make the award."

Brook advised that the prime minister should send a short response to Irene Ward politely dismissing her suggestion of inquiry.

Prime Minister Macmillan did just that. In a letter to Dame Irene on June 3, he wrote:

"I have studied the enclosed documents, which you sent to me with your letter of May 6. It would be a novel course to try to review, after an interval of 12 years, the grounds on which was made a recommendation to the Sovereign for a gallantry award. I do not think there is any precedent for such a review—or any procedure for carrying it out."

A week later, the impetus for Ward's bizarre preoccupation with Odette's decorations became clear. In a letter to Bligh on June 10, Secretary Brook wrote:

"In this further letter Dame Irene Ward comes out into the open and admits that what really bothers her is that the George Cross should have been awarded to a woman who had a lover. This confirms my view that her representations afford no ground for reviewing the award, even if it were practicable to do so."

The challenge to Odette's and Peter's decorations was officially over.

The attacks on their work and accomplishments, however, were just getting started.

PERHAPS TO RESOLVE ONCE and for all the myriad allegations and controversies surrounding SOE and many of its agents, the British government commissioned an official history of Baker Street's operations in France. Its choice for this monumental work was Oxford historian M. R. D. Foot, who began in the fall of 1960.

Strangely, in what some might call academic malpractice, the government prohibited Foot from interviewing the best primary sources: the SOE officers and agents themselves. Who would know better the procedures and decisions made than Colonel Buckmaster and his incomparable assistant, Vera Atkins? And how was Foot to write about events where little or nothing was recorded in SOE files? If the Oxford scholar was unable to speak with eyewitnesses, from what source or material would he establish a foundation?

As any historian knows, reports found in archive files are often inaccurate or conflicting; the only way to formulate what really happened is to review the files and compare them with the testimony of the participants themselves. Using established legal evidence rules such as "closer in time" and "customary recording procedures," the scholar can weigh, evaluate, and sometimes synthesize various accounts.

Buckmaster, for one, was repelled by the restriction. In a letter to Lieutenant Colonel Edwin Boxshall,[59] Maurice wrote: "I cannot think that the ban imposed upon the author against meeting me and discussing the more obscure questions can have served either the interests of the historian or of the readers, and I regard it as an unmerited discourtesy."

Foot compounded the problem by not allowing surviving agents who figured prominently in the book—including Odette and Peter—to review his completed manuscript before publication. He did, however, allow Maurice Buckmaster to review galley proofs, and the colonel challenged several inaccuracies.

Given that a number of SOE files had been lost or destroyed by fire at Baker Street after the war, the decision to not allow key

---

59 Boxshall had been an intelligence officer in World War I, was an SOE officer in World War II, and, after the war, had been employed by the Foreign Office to advise what should be made public about SOE activities.

agents a prepublication review was inexplicable. Foot also admitted that the files in Paris were "virtually unavailable" to him, that "good agents kept few papers when at work," and that "unpublished archives are often contradictory as well as confusing and confused."

Foot completed his original draft near the end of 1962 and offered it for review to several government officials and his publisher, Her Majesty's Stationery Office. Many, particularly those at the Treasury Solicitor's Office, were concerned that Foot's critical comments about some agents—including Odette and Peter—invited libel actions. During a discussion of the first galley proofs with Maurice Buckmaster on January 1, 1965, Foot apparently recorded a highly critical notation:

"Buckmaster affirmed to have been horrified when Odette was awarded the George Cross. He had recommended her only for the M.B.E. (which she got). He had no hand in drafting the citation for the George Cross. Odette was capable of disobeying orders. So was Churchill. Sex took the upper hand with the known dismal results. They should both have been court martialled."

The criticism was shocking on several fronts. First, the statements fly in the face of Buckmaster's own words in his 1958 memoir, *They Fought Alone*. Not only does Buckmaster fail to criticize the SPINDLE team, he goes out of his way to commend them. Regarding Peter, he wrote: "Peter Churchill was here, there and everywhere—testing methods of introducing our men into France, recruiting new units and encouraging existing ones—in short, doing the work of ten men."

And when evaluating the work of his best agents, Buckmaster named Peter first: "Men like Peter Churchill were tremendously valuable, and their dynamism and that of others like them held the organisation together. From the beginning of 1942 these men were the lynchpins."

Regarding Peter and Odette as a team, he stated: "Peter Churchill and Odette had both been caught somewhat earlier, but the organisation in which they had been most concerned was still able to continue without them, so well had they done their work."

Equally perplexing is that none of these allegations appears in SOE files recorded during the war. Indeed, Odette had made a grievous error in not leaving the Hôtel de la Poste immediately after receiving the cable from London, but her decision was partially mitigated by orders to find a landing spot for Peter, and her belief that she had several days before Hugo Bleicher would return.

The notion that Peter was capable of insubordination is also puzzling. Judging from Buckmaster's memoir, Peter seems to be Maurice's favorite agent, a conclusion supported by Leo Marks, SOE's chief cryptographer, who wrote: "Buckmaster was deeply involved with all his agents, but Peter was in a special category. He was not only Buckmaster's friend but a member of his headquarters staff with a detailed knowledge of his forward planning."

Finally, Peter's promotion to major seems to confirm the high regard in which he was held by his superiors.

Perhaps most troubling was the assertion that "Sex took the upper hand with the known dismal results." There is nothing in the SOE files to indicate or even intimate that Peter and Odette were having sex. Neither Buckmaster nor Peter in their works imply such activity.

And Foot appears to have assumed not only sex, but *regular* sex, based either on a comment from Buckmaster (which seems unlikely, given his lack of evidence) or perhaps from Hugo Bleicher's account of arresting them. If the latter, Foot seems to have misread Bleicher's statements, concluding that Hugo found Peter and Odette in bed together on the night of their arrest.

This is not the case. To the contrary, the German contends clearly that they occupied separate rooms. He writes: "Odette opened the door of her room . . . I ceased to watch Odette and looked *into the room next door*." (Emphasis added.) Bleicher's statement is in accord with Peter's *Duel of Wits*, wherein he states that they had separate rooms.

Nevertheless, having implied sex, Foot compounds the assertion by suggesting that sex was the *cause* of the arrest ("the known dismal results"). Worse, Foot, in his early draft, seemed to question the worthiness of Odette's George Cross by suggesting that there was no evidence of the Gestapo tearing out her toenails, and highlighting this charge by stating that Tickell's biography was "partly fictionalized" (without indicating *which* part).

As it turned out, some of the pages of Odette's debriefing on 12 May 1945 were inexplicably missing—one page ending with "They were to be," followed by a new section. To Foot's defense, the extant pages of the May 12 report do not mention the toenail torture. On page 13 the report notes that Odette claimed not to know the whereabouts of Arnaud and Roger Cammaerts, and that her captors held her hands behind her and burned her shoulder. It includes a detailed description of the Frenchman highlighted in the Tickell biography, and tracks the sequence of Odette refusing to give information and the Gestapo's frustration and concerted effort to extract more by torture. The page ends with: "the tall thin man said he would think of something else that might make her talk."

Foot should not have missed, however, the letter on 31 May 1946 from Odette's physician, Dr. Markowicz, wherein he declared: "Mrs. O. Sansom has been under my care since June 1945. At that time, *some nails on her toes were missing*; there was on her back a rounded scar of about half an inch diameter, the result of a burn deliberately inflicted." (Emphasis added.)

Further, Foot should have seen the War Office's 6 June 1946 recommendation to General Colin Gubbins for Odette to receive the George Cross: "I believe you expressed the opinion that we would have little chance of obtaining a George Cross for Sansom unless we were able to produce concrete evidence that she refused to speak under torture. I am afraid that such evidence is impossible to obtain for, as this torture was carried out in solitary confinement, the only witnesses would be the torturers themselves or the Gestapo interrogators. I hope and pray that these men have long since been shot.

"Circumstantial evidence is given in the statements by Mlle. Herail and Lt. Col. Cammaerts. Miss Sansom was definitely tortured as is evident from the medical certificate, and she did not disclose information regarding her contacts as can be seen from the statement by Lt. Col. Cammaerts and the continued freedom from arrest of those with whom she was working."

Others noticed these glaring issues, and Treasury Solicitor officials again voiced their fears of libel claims. On April 18, 1966, ten days before Foot's *SOE in France* was to be published, the Solicitor's Office put its objections in writing to Lieutenant Colonel Boxshall:

"I have been through Mr. Foot's three notebooks and can find no references in them to the Odette Sansom files. It is unfortunate that part of the interrogation of Odette Sansom dated 12th May 1945, and the shorter interrogation of the same date, are incomplete. There has clearly been removed from the main document at folio 326, certain pages at the end. I do not know why or where these pages are. It is of some importance because Foot says in his book that in her formal interrogation on her return she made no reference to this incident at all. I do not see how he can say this if he has not seen the whole of the interrogation. I feel that Counsel for Mrs. Hallowes could make considerable play with this document as it stands at the present."

Upon recommendation of its lawyers, the Treasury took out a substantial indemnity insurance policy to cover libel litigation.

They would need it.

The publication of *SOE in France* on 28 April 1966 was an unmitigated disaster. Neither Odette nor Peter had seen a page of text beforehand and both were fit to be tied. Other agents felt the same and, as expected, the Treasury began receiving letters from lawyers. Odette's counsel, Goodman, Derrick and Co., minced no words in her cause of action for libel in a letter five days later: "The British government have under their authority caused a book to be printed which leaves not a shadow of a doubt that its author and therefore by implication its sponsors regard Mrs. Hallowes (as she is now) as unworthy of the award."

The following day, May 4, Odette was compensated £646. But there was still the matter of addressing the text. The next month Treasury Solicitor officials met with Odette's attorneys—in the law firm's office—to address amendments and deletions. Foot agreed to make the changes.

But there was more. Given the damage to Odette's reputation, her lawyers demanded that Foot make a public apology, a request the Treasury thought was appropriate. Foot's apology appeared in the *Times* on 11 July 1966 in the form of a letter to the editor. Foot stated:

"There has been one major misunderstanding over my book on S.O.E. in France; it concerns awards of the George Cross to two women of exceptional gallantry, Mrs. Odette Hallowes and Mrs. Violette Szabo. I deeply regret that any references in the book have given rise to misunderstandings, and so caused keen distress to a very gallant officer. I never intended to cast any doubt whatever on the worthiness of the G.C. awarded to Mrs. Hallowes in 1946 [and] I shall take the opportunity, in any reprinting of the book, to make my views quite clear."

Peter, however, would not go away so easily. On August 10 his lawyers filed suit against Foot and Her Majesty's Stationery Office. Among the counts of libel they included this passage from *SOE in France*: "Luxury was as much a cause of SPINDLE's undoing as were the stresses in CARTE; Peter Churchill and his courier— Odette Sansom (Lise)—found that life could still be easy for people with plenty of money on the Riviera. The truth is that the military value of their mission was slight."

In addition, the complaint alleged that Foot and HMSO had suggested or insinuated that Peter had published false information about his missions to France in his three memoirs: *Of Their Own Choice*, *Duel of Wits*, and *Spirit in the Cage*.

In spite of the difficulty in prosecuting libel, Peter won: Her Majesty's Stationery Office was forced to recall thousands of copies of *SOE in France*, and Foot was ordered to remove offending passages from later editions.

Though slandered, defamed, and vexed, the SPINDLE spies survived.

As victors.

Again.

AUTHOR'S NOTE

Challenges in writing *Code Name: Lise* were everywhere, and many remain unresolved. How could Odette leave her children to work in France? I asked at the outset. Granted, her reasons (grandfather's admonition, mother's second loss of her home, patriotism) were compelling, but since her husband was also in the war, her children could have been orphaned. Further, once in France, why does she wish for the most dangerous assignments, preferring Marseille and Paris to Cannes and the Savoy?

Patriotism aside, did she have an itch to scratch?

And what of Hugo Bleicher? Was he a villain who escaped justice or simply a loyal German doing his job to the best of his ability? On the one hand, we see him using every trick in the book to capture Allied operatives, yet he became the consummate gentleman once he'd done so. We scowl as he arrests agents and turns them over to the Gestapo—knowing full well that some will be tortured or executed—but cheer as he helps Odette and Peter, often at great personal risk.

Bleicher walked that very thin line between duty and conscience, and at times was threatened with arrest himself. My impression was that he wanted to fulfill his job as a German soldier, while at the same time offer genuine respect and concern for Allied agents who were simply doing their jobs as well. Who takes a prisoner to his home, for example, so that the enemy can bathe and freshen up for a lunch with friends? Bleicher was in his element playing the piano with Peter, and I think Hugo genuinely saw Peter as a friend.

Hugo's relationship with Odette, however, was a bit more complicated. I think he was smitten by her from the outset and longed to court her. He knew from her dossier that it was unlikely she would talk or work for him, and that added to his admiration. He wanted nothing more than to take her to a concert playing Mozart or Beethoven, even as friends, hoping that a spark of romance might develop.

The principal players in the story—Odette, Peter, Arnaud, and Hugo—like Hemingway and Graham Greene, were adventurous, passionate, complex, inconsistent, and sometimes tormented. It's not a stretch to call the SPINDLE story a drama, each act moving and inspiring and frightening, and with many a tragedy. Odette was married, for example, when she and Peter fell in love, and Hugo was married when he harbored two mistresses (Suzanne and Lily Carré) and pursued a third. And two of the most dedicated agents—Arnaud and Paul—were executed by the Germans, while the treacherous Roger Bardet and "Kiki" Keiffer were condemned to death, but later released.

And so, in true Shakespearean fashion, the story ends bittersweet.

ACKNOWLEDGMENTS

I owe a debt of gratitude to many who assisted in this work.

As she did with *Into the Lion's Mouth*, Susannah Hurt provided ongoing encouragement and incomparable feedback throughout my writing. Once again, I was reminded that she is gifted to catch things that sound just a bit awkward, fail to connect dots, or could be written better. I say "gifted" because I'm not sure this skill can be taught or learned, but ruthless, objective, dispassionate criticism is an author's best friend.

To her, my endless thanks.

To Chakri Cuddapah, for his limitless passion for this book, and my work in general.

To those who graciously assisted in the launch of the book—Denise Carr, Jessica Smith, Donna Gotschall, Tracy King, Tameasa Provencher, Dallas Neeley, Robert Thomson, and Daniel Cavalier—so many thanks.

I am also thankful for those who encouraged along the way, including Barbara Damron (to whom this book is dedicated), Pam Sproles, Lona Youderian, Betsy Fadem, Ari Zach White, Mike and Naomi Wise, Pep Keely, Ryan Steck, Joshua Hood, Mark Sessums, Bill Keller, Don Carr, Tom and Ann Blastic, Charles Miller, Jim Crandall, Dony Jay, Steve Price, Gregg Page, Richard Skillman, Monica Taffinder, Lisa Thompson, Don Allison, Cristi Mansfield, Laura Yount, John Cook, Jose Arias, Wendy Henry, Connie Albers,

Sherri Seligson, Paul Zuccarini, Cindy Bertossa, Greg Bailey, and so many others.

And to my editor, Natasha Simons, for her belief and excitement not only in the story, but in my blending of nonfiction and thriller, and for her tireless effort in championing the book; to my publisher, Jen Bergstrom, for holding out on a title until we came up with a perfect one; to Lisa Litwack, for a cover that exceeded my wildest expectations; to Aimée Bell, Gallery editorial director, for her last-minute magic; to my publicists, Jean Anne Rose and Michelle Podberezniak, for their boundless energy and enthusiasm; to Kerry Fiallo, for her magnificent copy; to Hannah Brown and everyone "behind the scenes" at Gallery/Simon & Schuster; to everyone at Javelin for their commitment to excellence; and finally to my agent, Keith Urbahn, who is not only the best in the business, but a wonderful human being as well.

Finally, I'd like to thank Nicole Miller-Hard, one of Odette's granddaughters, for her comments to the first printing, her endless encouragement, and her passionate support of the book.

NOTES

v   *The world breaks everyone*: Ernest Hemingway, *A Farewell to Arms*, 216.

DRAMATIS PERSONAE

xiii–xiv See, generally, HS 9/648.4 and KV 2/164 (18a), UK National Archives; Maurice Buckmaster, *They Fought Alone*; Peter Churchill, *Of Their Own Choice, Duel of Wits, Spirit in the Cage*; E. H. Cookridge, *They Came from the Sky*; M. R. D. Foot, *SOE in France*.

PROLOGUE

xix   *"I simply don't"*: Churchill, *Duel of Wits*, 306.

xix   *"Keep an eye"* . . . *"There's someone"*: Ibid., 307.

xx   *"The plane ought"* . . . *"Listen!"*: Ibid., 308.

xx   *"Put out those lights"*: Ibid.; Jerrard Tickell, *Odette: The Story of a British Agent*, 160.

xx   *diving down . . . six feet*: Churchill, *Duel of Wits*, 309.

xxi   *"You make for the"*: Tickell, *Odette*, 161.

xxi   *German Shepherd*: Tickell, *Odette*, 161, identifies the dog only as a "police dog," but Churchill, *Duel of Wits*, 313, identifies the breed as Alsatian (German Shepherd).

xxi   *She plunged in*: Churchill, *Duel of Wits*, 313; Tickell, *Odette*, 162.

CHAPTER 1: DUTY

1   *Major Guthrie . . . photographs*: Tickell, *Odette*, 46–47; Imperial War
Museum (IWM), Oral History, interview with Odette Marie Céline
Sansom, produced October 31, 1986, catalogue number 9478, Reel
1. Website: www.iwm.org.uk/collections/item/object/80009265.

1   *Born April 28 . . . Gaston*: Tickell, *Odette*, 17; IWM, interview
with Odette Sansom, October 31, 1986, catalogue number 9478,
Reel 1.

2   *"In twenty or twenty-five"*: IWM, interview with Odette Sansom,
October 31, 1986, catalogue number 9478, Reel 1.

2   *polio . . . stole her sight . . . grandfather*: Tickell, *Odette,* 18–19; IWM,
interview with Odette Sansom, October 31, 1986, catalogue number
9478, Reel 1.

3   *rheumatic fever*: Tickell, *Odette*, 19.

3   *married . . . child*: Ibid., 21.

4   *Somerset*: IWM, interview with Odette Sansom, October 31, 1986,
catalogue number 9478, Reel 1; Tickell, *Odette*, 27–29.

4   *radio*: IWM, interview with Odette Sansom, October 31, 1986, catalogue number 9478, Reel 1; Tickell, *Odette*, 45.

5   *Mistakenly, however, she mailed*: IWM, interview with Odette Sansom, October 31, 1986, catalogue number 9478, Reel 1.

5   *Guthrie . . . return her photos*: Tickell, *Odette*, 46–47; IWM, interview
with Odette Sansom, October 31, 1986, catalogue number 9478,
Reel 1.

5   *"Has it occurred"*: Tickell, *Odette*, 47–48.

5   *"If I can be of"*: IWM, interview with Odette Sansom, October 31,
1986, catalogue number 9478, Reel 1.

6   *Red Cross*: Ibid.

6   *She struggled . . . tormented*: Ibid.

6   *June 28 . . . Selwyn Jepson*: Tickell, *Odette*, 49; Foot, *SOE in France*, 42.

6   *"set Europe ablaze"*: Hugh Dalton, *The Fateful Years*, 366.

7   *"We have got to organize"*: Foot, *SOE in France*, 9.

7   *Churchill . . . two directives*: Ibid., 14.

7   *MO 1 (SP) . . . NID* (Q): Ibid.

7   *role of Baker Street*: Colonel Maurice Buckmaster, head of SOE's
F Section, described their role this way: "Our role at Special Operations Headquarters was not that of spy-masters, but of active and

belligerent planners of operations to be carried out in advance of the Allied landing." *They Fought Alone*, 45.

8   *terrorists*: Foot, *S.O.E.*, 69; Philippe de Vomécourt, *An Army of Amateurs: The Story of the SOE Resistance Movement in France, by One of the Three Brothers Who Organized and Ran It*, 66.

8   *"Why did you have"*: IWM, interview with Odette Sansom, October 31, 1986, catalogue number 9478, Reel 1.

8   *"We train people"*: Ibid.

9   *Service du Travail Obligatoire*: Henri Michel, *The Shadow War: European Resistance 1939–1945*, 370, 372; Marcus Binney, *The Women Who Lived for Danger*, 1.

9   *"I hate them"*: Tickell, *Odette*, 50.

9   *"Yes, but they"* . . . *"You know that"* . . . *"The Nazis"*: Ibid., 50–52.

10   *"It's not possible"*: IWM, interview with Odette Sansom, October 31, 1986, catalogue number 9478, Reel 1.

10–11 *"This is where"* . . . *"the right sort of person"*: Tickell, *Odette*, 54–56; IWM, interview with Odette Sansom, October 31, 1986, catalogue number 9478, Reel 1.

11   *"Direct-minded and"*: Tickell, *Odette*, 57.

11   *"If everybody thinks"*: IWM, interview with Odette Sansom, October 31, 1986, catalogue number 9478, Reel 1.

12   *Buckmaster*: Buckmaster, *They Fought Alone*, 1–6; Marcel Ruby, *F Section SOE: The Story of the Buckmaster Network*, 12–13; Foot, *SOE in France*, 21, 49.

12   *March 17 . . . September*: Ruby, 13.

13   *"Good God, you"*: IWM, interview with Odette Sansom, October 31, 1986, catalogue number 9478, Reel 1.

13   *"In many ways"* . . . *"firing squad, the rope, the crematorium"*: Tickell, *Odette*, 75.

13   *As one agent*: George Millar, *Maquis: An Englishman in the French Resistance*, 14.

CHAPTER 2: JINXED

14   *"No. My mind is"*: Tickell, *Odette*, 75.

14   *"Would Céline do?"* . . . *"I'm going to"*: Ibid., 76.

15   *mirror*: Ibid., 77.

15   *July 18*: A memo in Odette's SOE personnel file states that she

began her training on July 18, 1942, and finished in October. HS 9/648.4.012, UK National Archives.

15   *Portman Square* . . . *"blushed"*: Tickell, *Odette*, 78.

16   *four stages*: HS 7/51 (history of SOE training), HS 7/52 (syllabus of the finishing schools), HS 7/55 (syllabus of Canada's Camp X lectures), HS 7/56 (lectures on tactics, demolitions, field craft; physical training syllabus), UK National Archives; Foot, *S.O.E.*, 79–90; Foot, *SOE in France*, 53–58, 95, 104; I. C. B. Dear and M. R. D. Foot, eds., *The Oxford Companion to World War II*, 1019–21; Pieter Dourlein, *Inside North Pole: A Secret Agent's Story*, 79–89; George Langelaan, *Knights of the Floating Silk*, 59–81; Churchill, *Of Their Own Choice*, 9–32; Denis Rigden, intro., *How to Be a Spy: The World War II SOE Training Manual*, 2–6.

16   *80 percent would be disqualified*: M. R. D. Foot, Britain's official SOE historian, concluded that as many as one-third failed the Arisaig training alone. *S.O.E.*, 84–85. Peter Churchill wrote that of the fourteen in his initial training group, only three qualified—a 79 percent failure rate. *Of Their Own Choice*, 32.

16   *Wanborough Manor*: Churchill, *Of Their Own Choice*, 9–19; Foot, *S.O.E.*, 79–90; Foot, *SOE in France*, 53–58, 95, 104; Dear and Foot, *Oxford Companion to World War II*, 1019–21; Rigden, *How to Be a Spy*, 2–4; HS 7/56, UK National Archives. Foot notes correctly that the stage one training was two to four weeks; Peter Churchill specified that his training at Wanborough lasted three weeks (19), while Pieter Dourlein recorded that his training with the Dutch section in Reading, England, was four weeks. *Inside North Pole*, 80.

16   *virtually every weapon*: For details on many of these weapons, see Pierre Lorain, *Clandestine Operations: The Arms and Techniques of the Resistance, 1941–1944*.

16   *"You will always"*: Rigden, *How to Be a Spy*, 379 (for the complete SOE weapons training instructions, see 376–413). George Millar, an SOE operative dropped into France in the summer of 1944, recalled the method and effectiveness after the war: "We were taught to use the forward-crouching stance and the quick, snap-shooting method. Some of us got so accurate with the pistols that we were like King George V knocking down driven grouse." Millar, *Maquis*, 17.

16   *"instinctive pointing"*: Rigden, *How to Be a Spy*, 379.

17   *Fairbairn-Sykes fighting knife, the pen pistol . . . ultrathin lapel knife*:
      See Lorain, *Clandestine Operations*, 157–61.

17   *Arisaig*: Foot, *S.O.E.*, 80–84; Foot, *SOE in France*, 53–55; Churchill,
      Of Their Own Choice, 19–27; Dourlein, *Inside North Pole*, 80–83;
      Langelaan, *Knights of the Floating Silk*, 59–77; Dear and Foot, *Ox-
      ford Companion to World War II*, 1019; Rigden, *How to Be a Spy*, 4–5,
      11–17; HS 7/55 (syllabus of Canada's Camp X lectures), UK National
      Archives. Note that Canada's Camp X was a duplication of Arisaig,
      primarily to train America's Office of Strategic Services (OSS), the
      forerunner of the Central Intelligence Agency (CIA). William Fair-
      bairn and Eric Anthony Sykes, the legendary instructors at Arisaig,
      were brought in for this purpose. Since the war, many SOE records
      were lost and there are no pages in Odette's personnel file indicating
      specifically that she participated in training at Wanborough, Arisaig,
      or Ringway. Her file does contain her final evaluation from Beaulieu
      (HS 9/648.4.083), however, and Tickell's authorized biography de-
      tails her training there and her accident at Ringway. Moreover, HS
      9/648.4.012 states that she began her training on July 18, 1942, and
      finished in October. Perhaps intentionally, records from these secret
      commando schools are scant. British double agent Dusko Popov,
      who completed three of the SOE training stages (operating osten-
      sibly as a German spy, he had no need for parachute training), has
      nothing in his voluminous MI5 files about his training, though he
      detailed in several interviews exactly what occurred at Wanborough,
      Arisaig, and Beaulieu, and specifically mentioned being trained in
      Scotland and learning the "art of the secret kill." See, for example,
      Larry Loftis, *Into the Lion's Mouth*, 160–63.

17n   *One radio operator*: Millar, *Maquis*, 17–18.

17n2 *rat charge*: For a detailed graphic illustrating the design and opera-
      tion, see David Stafford, *Secret Agent: The True Story of the Covert War
      Against Hitler*, p. 6 of photographs (unpaginated).

17n2–3 *time-pencil fuse . . . Gammon Grenade*: See Lorain, *Clandestine Op-
      erations*, 157–61.

18   *Vickers . . . MG 34 and 42*: Foot, *S.O.E.*, 81.

18   *William Fairbairn . . . Shanghai Buster*: Loftis, *Into the Lion's
      Mouth*, 161–65; Langelaan, *Knights of the Floating Silk*, 65–74; Dear
      and Foot, *Oxford Companion to World War II*, 1019; Rigden, *How to
      Be a Spy*, 15–17.

18   *silent killing*: Langelaan, *Knights of the Floating Silk*, 66–67; Loftis, *Into the Lion's Mouth*, 163; Dourlein, *Inside North Pole*, 81; Millar, *Maquis*, 22; Foot, *S.O.E.*, 84; Rigden, *How to Be a Spy*, 5, 15–16, 361, 367.

18   *Beaulieu*: Foot, *S.O.E.*, 79–90; Foot, *SOE in France*, 53–58, 95, 104; Dear and Foot, *Oxford Companion to World War II*, 1019; Dourlein, *Inside North Pole*, 79–89; Langelaan, *Knights of the Floating Silk*, 59–81; Churchill, *Of Their Own Choice*, 9–32; Rigden, *How to Be a Spy*, 5–8.

18   *clatter of activity . . . eight o'clock*: Tickell, *Odette*, 78.

19   *"Now we'll just" . . . "Céline!" . . . "Suppose"*: Ibid., 79.

20   *chance meeting with Christine Collard . . . "Fifi"*: HS 9/307.3, UK National Archives. Marie Christine Chilver was not the only agent provocateur, but apparently was the best.

20   *"What's this chap"*: Tickell, *Odette*, 80.

20n   *Kim Philby*: Kim Philby, *My Silent War*, 22–38.

21   *"What is the Morse sign"*: Ibid., 81.

21   *"All on"*: Ibid.

21   *men in German*: Imperial War Museum (IWM), Oral History, interview with Odette Marie Céline Sansom, produced October 31, 1986, catalogue number 9478, Reel 1; Buckmaster, *They Fought Alone*, 47.

21   *Recruits were stripped*: Buckmaster, *They Fought Alone*, 47.

21   *canoe, navigate by the stars, poach*: Tickell, *Odette*, 81.

22   *began to irritate*: Ibid.

22   *"She has enthusiasm"*: Finishing Report for candidate Samson [*sic*], HS 9/648.4.083, UK National Archives.

22   *"Well, Céline" . . . "I am very much"*: Tickell, *Odette*, 83.

23   *Ringway*: See, generally, Churchill, *Of Their Own Choice*, 27–28; Dourlein, *Inside North Pole*, 84–86; Foot, *S.O.E.*, 89–90; Foot, *SOE in France*, 55.

23   *"Now, ladies and" . . . "You will enjoy"*: Tickell, *Odette*, 84.

24   *"We'll have just" . . . "Be excused?"*: Ibid., 85–86.

24   *face crashed . . . medical clinic*: Ibid., 86.

24   *"Certainly, if you" . . . "That's like"*: Ibid., 86–87.

25   *"Good-bye, Francoise"*: Ibid., 88.

25   *Dropping her children off . . . heartbreaking*: IWM, interview with Odette Sansom, October 31, 1986, catalogue number 9478, Reel 1.

25   *"I therefore order"*: Binney, *Women Who Lived for Danger*, 9–10.

26   *"You happened to be"*: Tickell, *Odette*, 91.

27   *50,000 francs*: Ibid., 95.

27   *"Have your clothes" . . . "Do you" . . . "Now these"*: Ibid., 96.

28   *Whitley . . . Lysander . . . Catalina*: Ibid., 99–101.

29   *Cornwall . . . Whitley . . . rising and sinking*: Ibid., 102–3.

CHAPTER 3: MISSION TO MARSEILLE

30   *"Get out everyone"*: Tickell, *Odette*, 103.

31   *"You are going"*: Ibid., 104.

31   *In the middle of October*: The dates Odette left for Gibraltar and for France are nebulous. HS 9/648.4.005 and 9/648.4.007, UK National Archives, record that Odette "Left for the field" on October 30, 1942. Presumably this refers to the date she was to have left from Gibraltar for France. However, even this date does not allow sufficient time to travel by felucca to Cassis, where the party landed on November 2, a date firmly established. See, for example, HS 9/648.4.008, 9/648.4.012, 9/648.4.050, and 9/648.4.057, UK National Archives.

31   *"one of the most"*: Dear and Foot, *Oxford Companion to World War II*, 487.

31   *Jan Buchowski . . . Virtuti Militari*: Churchill, *Duel of Wits*, 153–54. Odette also describes Buchowski as "very brave." Imperial War Museum (IWM), Oral History, interview with Odette Marie Céline-Sansom, produced October 31, 1986, catalogue number 9478, Reel 1.

31   *feluccas on the Gibraltar*: See, generally, Foot, *S.O.E.*, 126, and *SOE in France*, 65–66.

31   *"too rough even"*: Ibid.

32   *"I am the commander"*: Tickell, *Odette*, 105–7. Odette confirmed that Buchowski initially refused to take a woman on his felucca in her interview with the Imperial War Museum in 1986. IWM, interview with Odette Sansom, October 31, 1986, catalogue number 9478, Reel 1.

32–33 *October 23 . . . Dewucca*: The time necessary for the felucca delivery is nebulous. Peter Churchill stated that it was a ten-day trip (*Duel of Wits*, 223), while official British historian M. R. D. Foot wrote that the felucca trip normally took twelve to fourteen days. *S.O.E.*, 126; *SOE in France*, 65–66. Thus, Jerrard Tickell's suggestion that the trip took eight days appears erroneous. *Odette*, 122.

33   *"Did they give you"*: Tickell, *Odette*, 107.

33n *Including Major George Starr*: In her debriefing on May 12, 1945, Odette stated that those on board (with her and Buchowski) were "Captain Young, Urbain [code name for Marcus Bloom], Madame Lechene [Marie-Thérèse Le Chene], Miss [Mary] Herbert, and [Major George] Starr," confirming Peter's passenger count. HS 9/648.4.079, UK National Archives. See also Buckmaster, *They Fought Alone*, 284 (Bloom), 286 (Le Chene), 290 (Herbert), 297 (Sansom), and 298 (Starr); Ruby, *F Section SOE*, 127.

34   *November 2 . . . Cassis . . . Marsac*: HS 9/648.4.008, 9/648.4.010, 9/648.4.012, 9/648.4.050, 9/648.4.057, and 9/648.4.079, UK National Archives; Churchill, *Duel of Wits*, 223–24. In *They Fought Alone*, Colonel Buckmaster cites the felucca's arrival date as November 4. See each agent's arrival date at 284 (Bloom), 286 (Le Chene), 290 (Herbert), 297 (Sansom), and 298 (Starr).

34   *Odette stood . . . calm . . . mimosa and thyme*: Tickell, *Odette*, 108–9.

34   *Villa Augusta*: HS 9/648.4.057 and 9/648.4.079, UK National Archives.

34   *Marie-Lou Blanc . . . "Suzanne"*: Foot, *SOE in France*, 187.

34   *languages . . . one of the finest*: Leo Marks, *Between Silk and Cyanide: The Story of S.O.E.'s Code War*, 17; Cookridge, *Inside S.O.E.*, 156.

35   *Dropped by submarine*: Churchill, *Of Their Own Choice*, 70–71.

35   *French destroyer*: Churchill, *Duel of Wits*, 164–65.

36   *"here, there and everywhere"*: Buckmaster, *They Fought Alone*, 76.

36   *Villa Isabelle . . . Baron Henri ("Antoine") de Malval*: HS 9/648.4.057 and 9/648.4.079, UK National Archives. See also Cookridge, *Inside S.O.E.*, 151–53.

36   *But what captured*: Churchill, *Duel of Wits*, 225.

37   *Auxerre . . . demarcation line*: HS 9/648.4.057 and HS 9/648.4.079, UK National Archives.

37   *a passeur*: Philippe de Vomécourt, *Army of Amateurs*, 55.

37   *"I don't need any"*: Churchill, *Duel of Wits*, 226.

37   *Adolphe Rabinovitch*: KV2/164 (18a) and HS 9/648.4.080, UK National Archives; Churchill, *Duel of Wits*, 317; Foot, *SOE in France*, 187; Cookridge, *Inside S.O.E.*, 165–66.

37   *temperament of a wolverine*: HS 9/648.4.080, UK National Archives. (Odette: "He had a terrible temper.") Peter dedicated *Duel of Wits*

to Arnaud, whom he described as "a violent, difficult, devoted, and heroic radio operator."

37   *could and did swear in four*: Marks, *Between Silk and Cyanide*, 74.

37–38 *Hercules . . . panther . . . bet*: Churchill, *Duel of Wits*, 201–3.

37   *"Rabinovitch swung his giant"*: Marks, *Between Silk and Cyanide*, 75.

38   *"Very tired"*: Tickell, *Odette*, 124.

39   *André ("Carte") Girard*: KV2/164 (18a), HS 9/648.4.057, UK National Archives.

39   *asked for something to do*: HS 9/648.4.057 and 9/648.4.079, UK National Archives.

39   *"I want you to go"*: Churchill, *Duel of Wits*, 227.

39   *Riquet . . . twenty-five . . . sergeant*: Cookridge, *Inside S.O.E.*, 170.

39   *"What was that" . . . "Very restless"*: Churchill, *Duel of Wits*, 228.

40   *"I seem to remember" . . . "Enchantè"*: Ibid., 229.

40   *November 6 . . . Marseille*: HS 9/648.4.057 and 9/648.4.079, UK National Archives.

40–41 *"I want you to take" . . . "Having got rid"*: Churchill, *Duel of Wits*, 230–31.

41   *General Charles Delestraint*: Foot, *SOE in France*, 204. He would later be captured by the Gestapo and was executed at Dachau on April 19, 1945.

41   *"Je vous apporte des"*: Tickell, *Odette*, 132.

41   *If Vidal was in . . . "When you've got"*: Churchill, *Duel of Wits*, 232.

42   *Marseille*: Tickell, *Odette*, 128–30. Tickell's account of the Marseille trip, while confirming Peter Churchill's account on the whole, includes a few discrepancies. Churchill, for example, specified that the amount given to Odette was 50,000 francs; Tickell, however, writes that it was 200,000. More glaring is Tickell's misstatement that Odette retrieved Peter's briefcase from the petrol dealer, Gontrand, who was not on the felucca pickup and could not have had Peter's briefcase. Tickell also seems to have inverted the order of Odette's route, citing that she visited Gontrand's garage before going to Vidal's hotel.

42   *Marseille . . . unruly population . . . underworld*: Foot, *SOE in France*, 194.

42   *three agents*: The agents were Ted Coppin (sabotage instructor), H. M. R. Despaigne (wireless operator), and Sidney Jones (to establish the INVENTOR sabotage circuit). Ibid., 194–95.

42 *It is forbidden*: Penny Starns, *Odette: World War Two's Darling Spy*, 64–65; Imperial War Museum, picture archive, album 854.

43 *"Monsieur Vidal?"*: Tickell, *Odette*, 132–34.

44 *"Here I leave you"*: Ibid., 135.

44 *raiding the waiting rooms*: Corrie ten Boom, *The Hiding Place*, 86.

44 *deporting millions*: Cookridge, *Inside S.O.E.*, 172.

44 *safest of safe houses*: Philippe de Vomécourt, *Army of Amateurs*, 78.

44n1 *brothel . . . "open to civilian gentlemen"*: Benjamin Cowburn, *No Cloak, No Dagger: Allied Spycraft in Occupied France*, 38.

44n2 *the razzia*: ten Boom, *Hiding Place*, 86.

45 *"Que désirez-vous, Madame?"*: Tickell, *Odette*, 136.

45 *curtains . . . cigarette . . . hairpins*: Ibid., 137.

45 *three in the morning . . . military police*: Ibid., 139.

CHAPTER 4: THE BRIEFCASE

46 *"Where's Lise?"*: Churchill, *Duel of Wits*, 244–45.

47 *Remember when you*: Ibid., 245–46.

47 *three hundred thousand guerillas*: Foot, *SOE in France*, 184. See also KV 2/164 (18a), UK National Archives.

48 *His mouth went dry . . . "Oh, God"*: Churchill, *Duel of Wits*, 247–48.

48 *Chez Robert*: Ibid., 249; Tickell, *Odette*, 143.

48 *smallpox*: Tickell, *Odette*, 139. In Churchill, *Duel of Wits*, 250, the madam had said that the niece was suffering from scarlet fever.

48 *He congratulated her*: Churchill, *Duel of Wits*, 250.

48 *"Cannes has nothing"*: Tickell, *Odette*, 140–41.

49 *"It's easy and silky" . . . "No very ordinary"*: Ibid., 141.

49 *"Lise, this Auxerre business" . . . "How much?"*: Churchill, *Duel of Wits*, 250–51.

50 *SEND LISE*: Ibid., 251.

50 *Hugo Bleicher . . . Geheime Feldpolizei*: See, generally, Hugo Bleicher, *Colonel Henri's Story*; KV 2/164 and 2/2127, UK National Archives; Tickell, *Odette*, 178–81.

50 *somewhat of a celebrity*: KV 2/164 (10B), UK National Archives. MI5 would later characterize Hugo's ascent as a "meteoric climb to fame." KV 2/2127.1 (24a).

50 *INTERALLIÉ*: See, generally, Roman Garby-Czerniawski, *The Big*

Network; Mathilde-Lily Carré, *I Was "the Cat": The Truth About the Most Remarkable Woman Spy Since Mata Hari—by Herself*; Bleicher, *Colonel Henri's Story*, 37–39; KV 2/164 (20z, 10B) and all of KV 2/72 and 2/73, UK National Archives.

51   *"There had been nothing"*: Bleicher, *Colonel Henri's Story*, 22.

51   *August 11 . . . wife, Lucie . . . son*: Among Hugo's possessions when he was transferred to British custody was a gold wedding ring with the inscription "Lucie 11.8.29." KV 2/164 (4c), UK National Archives. In his wallet at the time was a photo of his child (KV 2/164 (7c)), whom his personnel file states was age five. KV 2/2127.

52   *Was he a soldier*: Bleicher, *Colonel Henri's Story*, 24.

52   *Geheime Feldpolizei and stationed in Caen*: Ibid., 28. For a history of Bleicher's training and original duties with the GFP, see KV 2/164 (4B), UK National Archives.

52   *Keiffer . . . "Kiki"*: Bleicher, *Colonel Henri's Story*, 37–38, 62–63, 117–18; Garby-Czerniawski, *Big Network*, 209, 231–32; Carré, *I Was "the Cat"*, 90, 117–18, 129, 135; KV 2/164 (18a), KV 2/72.3 Supp. 4, UK National Archives. Czerniawski recorded on his network chart (209) that Keiffer's first name was "Raoul" (apparently an alias) and that he also went by the code name "Desiré." Depending on the source, his name is variously spelled "Keiffer" or "Kieffer."

52   *INTERALLIÉ*: Garby-Czerniawski, *Big Network*; Bleicher, *Colonel Henri's Story*, 37–38; Carré, *I Was "the Cat"*. See also KV 2/72.3 Supp. 4, KV 2/2127 (unpaginated, but p. 3 of Bleicher's personnel file), UK National Archives.

52   *"Every spy who is"*: J. C. Masterman, *The Double-Cross System in the War of 1939 to 1945*, 1.

53   *"there are others"*: Ibid.

53   *Colonel Oscar Reile . . . former chief . . . forty-six*: KV 2/164 (8a), UK National Archives. Bleicher refers to Reile as "Major Relling" in *Colonel Henri's Story* (42), and editor Ian Colvin incorrectly identifies him as "Colonel Rudolf" (43n1). Bleicher properly identifies Reile during interrogation at Camp 020 on June 20, 1945. KV 2/164 (8a).

53   *"We are fighting"*: Bleicher, *Colonel Henri's Story*, 42.

54   *perfect French . . . English or Spanish*: KV 2/2127.1 (unpaginated, but appearing at the beginning of P.F. 600, 861), UK National Archives.

54   *"Monsieur Jean"*: Ibid., 19, 46. Bleicher also would use aliases of:

Jean Castel, Jean Verbeck, Colonel Henri, Colonel Heinrich, and Gottschalk. KV 2/164 (12a), KV 2/2127 (throughout), UK National Archives.

55 *November 11 . . . 1940 armistice*: For a detailed chronology of the war, see Dear and Foot, *Oxford Companion to World War II*.

55 *1,800 calories*: Philippe de Vomécourt, *Army of Amateurs*, 26–27. See also Cowburn, *No Cloak, No Dagger*, 17 ("A little simple arithmetic soon showed that in practice a human being could not subsist on the quantities awarded by the monthly ration cards."), 38 ("half of the nation were going hungry and concentrating their thoughts and energies on occasionally achieving a tasty meal.").

55 *briefcase . . . list of network agents*: KV 2/164 (18a), UK National Archives.

CHAPTER 5: CONTROL

56 *two hundred letters long*: Marks, *Between Silk and Cyanide*, 10.

56 *Shakespeare, Keats, Tennyson*: Ibid., 11. Marks emphasized to agents that the Germans knew their Shakespeare, too, and could look up Keats, Tennyson, Poe, or any other famous poet in reference books. The safer poem codes, he told them, were obscure poems or ones they had written themselves. Since Leo took a liking to Peter, he offered him this gem:

> The boy stood on the burning deck
> His feet were full of blisters
> He hadn't got them from the fire
> But from screwing both his sisters.

Peter opted to keep it as a backup. Marks, *Between Silk and Cyanide*, 190.

57 *20 percent . . . "indecipherables"*: Ibid., 9.

57 *Norgeby House . . . "having it off"*: Ibid., 136–38.

57 *"You've been kept"*: Ibid., 139–40.

58 *culprit was Peter Churchill*: Marks, *Between Silk and Cyanide*, 126.

58 *I danced two waltzes*: Ibid., 66.

58n *"direction-finding" vehicles*: Michel, *Shadow War*, 369; Foot, *SOE in France*, 96–97.

59   *"hatted"*: Marks, *Between Silk and Cyanide*, 126.

59–60 *Carte's own men . . . Frager . . . security was nonexistent*: HS 9/648.4.079, UK National Archives. "I refused to work with him," Odette said during her debriefing on May 12, 1945, "as his security was so bad it was just not safe." Ibid. See also Cookridge, *Inside S.O.E.*, 168. ("His disputes with Henri Frager . . . reached a paroxysm of hostility.")

60   *bringing Peter and Carte to London*: Cookridge, *Inside S.O.E.*, 168; see also Foot, *SOE in France*, 224–25.

60   *location one of Carte's men found*: HS 9/648.4.057 and 9/648.4.079, UK National Archives.

60   *Per the SOE standards*: SOE's training manual stated that, to ensure the safety of the incoming craft, "Rising ground and hills should be ten miles away." Rigden, *How to Be a Spy*, 147.

60   *"My dear Raoul"*: Tickell, *Odette*, 143–44.

61   *"Your papers!"*: Churchill, *Duel of Wits*, 253.

61n   *Of the thirty-eight . . . 42 percent*: Foot, *SOE in France*, 414–18. SOE women who would not return from France were: Yvonne "Jacqueline" Rudellat (died in Belsen, April 1945), Andrée "Denise" Borrel (executed at Natzweiler, July 1944), Vera "Simone" Leigh (executed at Natzweiler, July 1944), Noor "Madelaine" Inayat Khan (executed at Dachau, September 1944), Cecily "Alice" Lefort (died or executed at Ravensbrück, early 1945), Diana "Paulette" Rowden (executed at Natzweiler, July 1944), Eliane "Gaby" Plewman (executed at Dachau, September 1944), Yolande "Yvonne" Beekman (executed at Dachau, September 1944), Madeleine "Solange" Damerment (executed at Dachau, September 1944), Denise "Ambroise" Bloch (executed at Ravensbrück, early 1945), Lilian "Nadine" Rolfe (executed at Ravensbrück, early 1945), and Violette "Louise" Szabo (executed at Ravensbrück, early 1945). See Buckmaster, *They Fought Alone*, 282–99.

62   *five-foot-high ridge*: Ibid., 256. Odette determined that the Germans had ploughed the field to create the hazard. HS 9/648.4.057 and 9/648.4.079, UK National Archives.

62   *"Where are the 1,600 meters" . . . the airman*: Churchill, *Duel of Wits*, 256–59. Odette remembered that the field had been chosen by a woman living in Manosque. HS 9/648.4.057 and 9/648.4.079, UK National Archives.

63   *"December Moon" . . . Arles*: Churchill, *Duel of Wits*, 261; HS 9/648.4.057
      and 9/648.4.079, UK National Archives.

63   *SOE procedure*: Rigden, *How to Be a Spy*, 150.

63   *"You're an odd"*: Churchill, *Duel of Wits*, 262.

64   *"It's a long story" . . . "Marianne's seven"*: Ibid., 263–64.

64   *Marseille . . . rue St. Bazil*: HS 9/648.4.080 and KV 2/164 (18a), UK
      National Archives.

64   *looked like a ruffian . . . Kiki*: HS 9/648.4.080, UK National Archives.

65   *20 Quai St. Pierre*: Cookridge, *Inside S.O.E.*, 169.

65   *"Michel"*: Churchill, *Duel of Wits*, 265.

65   *To beat a Control check*: An example of beating a Control check is
      best illustrated by an incident experienced by Philippe de Vom-
      écourt, one of three brothers who had joined SOE at the outset of
      the war. He had been stopped at a routine check in Vierzon during
      1943, and a German officer said to him, "Excuse me, but would you
      please step off the train? We just want to check one or two things."
      Philippe went with the soldier into a small office and was told to
      have a seat.
          "What are you doing?" a Wehrmacht lieutenant asked.
          "Doing? Why I'm an inspector of the railways, and I work for the
      Gestapo," Philippe answered, reciting his cover. "Here, look at my
      identity papers, it's all there."
          The lieutenant went through the papers, muttering to his associ-
      ate. "Do you speak German?" he asked.
          "I'm sorry, I speak English, but I don't speak German." Philippe
      was lying, of course.
          The lieutenant said to his assistant in German, "But I'm sure
      he's the right man. He will be shot, just like his brothers." The lieu-
      tenant's eyes, however, never left Philippe's.
          Philippe made no show of emotion or understanding; a deadpan
      face waiting to get his papers back so he could be on his way. The
      lieutenant turned to his aide. "No, his name's de Vomécourt, but he
      can't be the right one. The man we're looking for does speak Ger-
      man, but this one didn't understand what I said."
          He told Philippe that they'd have to check with Paris, and
      Philippe was ushered to a holding room containing some thirty peo-
      ple. Paris would confirm that he was, in fact, the man they were
      looking for, so he had to think fast. He noticed the pattern: a guard

would come into the room and call out a name, like in a doctor's office, and the person would be escorted to another location.

Minutes later the guard began calling out a dozen names, and Philippe said "Yes" and followed the group out. When the queue turned left, following the guard, Philippe turned right for the exit and caught an incoming train going in the opposite direction. Philippe de Vomécourt, *Army of Amateurs*, 98–100.

65   *duty officer*: Churchill, *Duel of Wits*, 268.

CHAPTER 6: THE KISS

66   *SOE handbook was clear*: Rigden, intro., *How to Be a Spy*, 109.

66   *"Where the devil"*: Churchill, *Duel of Wits*, 267.

67   *"I turned on a few"*: Ibid., 268.

67   *"Deux et trois"*: Ibid., 268. Tickell, *Odette*, 151, has a different code: *"Le ciel est gris."*

67   *rescue team . . . train*: Churchill, *Of Their Own Choice*, 103–4.

68   *"I know the very"*: Churchill, *Duel of Wits*, 269–70.

69   *"An admirable performance"*: Ibid., 270.

69   *Grand Hôtel Nord Pinus . . . Amphitheater . . . theater . . . St. Trophime*: Ibid., 270–71.

70   *Côtes du Rhône . . . "Pon-soir, Mademoiselle"*: Tickell, *Odette*, 148–50. Peter Churchill does not have this story in his account of December 1942 in *Duel of Wits*. However, the temerity of Odette in the piano story is in accord with a similar action in Churchill's account of the confrontation with the German general on the train. *Duel of Wits*, 269.

71   *"Deux et trois font cinq"*: Churchill, *Duel of Wits*, 275; Tickell, *Odette*, 151 (with *"Le ciel est gris"*).

72   *"And you will come"*: Churchill, *Duel of Wits*, 276.

73   *"I have listened to"*: Ibid., 277.

73   *The only Hudson*: Foot, *SOE in France*, 73.

73   *SOE's only Lysander*: Ibid.

73   *Bassillac*: Peter Churchill and Jerrard Tickell cover this operation in detail. *Duel of Wits*, 299–312; *Odette*, 154–63.

74   *arm in arm*: Ibid.

75   *"Les femmes sont"*: Churchill, *Duel of Wits*, 300, 304; Tickell, *Odette*, 157.

75 *temperature was now in the low teens*: Peter Churchill recorded that the temperature was 10 degrees below zero, Celsius, or 14 degrees Fahrenheit. *Duel of Wits*, 311.

75 *"Keep an eye"*: Ibid., 307.

76 *"Put out those lights"*: Ibid., 308; Tickell, *Odette*, 160.

76 *German Shepherd*: Tickell, *Odette*, 161; Churchill, *Duel of Wits*, 313. Tickell provides the dog chase from Odette's point of view (identifying it as a police dog), while Churchill identifies the breed as Alsatian, the British name for German Shepherd.

CHAPTER 7: PEARL OF THE FRENCH ALPS

77 *"Frizi, Frizi!"*: Tickell, *Odette*, 162.

77 *"I wonder how"*: Churchill, *Duel of Wits*, 310.

78 *the Domino*: Ibid., 311; Tickell, *Odette*, 162. Churchill and Tickell both track the morning, although the latter's account seems slightly embellished.

78 *four Gestapo*: Churchill, *Duel of Wits*, 312; Tickell, *Odette*, 163.

79 *"Eugene"*: Churchill, *Duel of Wits*, 313–14; Tickell, *Odette*, 164–65; Cookridge, *Inside S.O.E.*, 169.

79 *Gisèle*: Churchill, *Duel of Wits*, 313–14; Cookridge, *Inside S.O.E.*, 169.

79 *Corsican croupier named René Casale*: Cookridge, *Inside S.O.E.*, 152.

80 *Faverges . . . Hôtel de la Poste*: Churchill, *Duel of Wits*, 315.

80 *"You should have" . . . "Good God!"*: Tickell, *Odette*, 165–66.

80 *thirty-five-pound transceiver . . . B Mark II*: Foot, *SOE in France*, 95.

81 *As always*: Churchill, *Duel of Wits*, 317.

81 *mid-January and headed to the Alps*: HS 9/648.4.080, UK National Archives.

81–82 *they began with . . . resolute . . . her strength*: Churchill, *Duel of Wits*, 317.

82 *first Allied raid into Germany*: Dear and Foot, *Oxford Companion to World War II*, 1330.

82 *Stalingrad . . . Kursk*: Ibid.

82 *"Pearl of the French Alps"*: So nicknamed by French geographer Raoul Blanchard, a professor of geology at the University of Grenoble (and later, Harvard University) and the founder of the Alpine Geography Institute, Grenoble, France.

82 *Venice*: The canals produced by the Thiou River, which runs through the center of Annecy, bear a distinct resemblance to the Italian city.

83 *St. Jorioz . . . Hôtel de la Poste*: HS 9/648.4.080, UK National Archives.

83 *new identity cards*: Ibid. Odette identifies Marsac as "Muriel." Churchill, *Duel of Wits*, 318.

83 *Monsieur Guy Lebouton*: Cookridge, *Inside S.O.E.*, 170.

83 *"These are my friends"*: Tickell, *Odette*, 170–71; Churchill, *Duel of Wits*, 319–20. Tickell's and Churchill's accounts of the meeting with the Cottets vary slightly but otherwise confirm the event and details.

83 *Marsac rattled off his group*: Churchill, *Duel of Wits*, 320. See also HS 9/648.4.080, UK National Archives; Cookridge, *They Came from the Sky*, 80; and *Inside S.O.E.*, 175.

83 *Paul . . . Talloires*: HS 9/648.4.080, UK National Archives; Cookridge, *They Came from the Sky*, 80. Odette mentions in her debriefing on May 12, 1945 (HS 9/648.4.080) that Frager was "living at Montan" on the opposite side of Lake Annecy. This area, however, is called Talloires, so Montan may have been the name of the hotel or villa.

84 *medical certificate*: HS 9/648.4.080, UK National Archives.

84 *OVRA . . . district office in Annecy*: Cookridge, *They Came from the Sky*, 81.

84 *Seythenex . . . Faverges*: HS 9/648.4.080, UK National Archives; Churchill, *Duel of Wits*, 321–22.

84 *"Another little trick"*: Churchill, *Duel of Wits*, 323.

85 *radio direction finding*: See, generally, Foot, *SOE in France*, 41, 96–97, 149, 193, 287, 330; Cowburn, *No Cloak, No Dagger*, 156–57.

85 *107 . . . 31 were executed*: See Appendix 2 of Buckmaster, *They Fought Alone*, 282–99.

85 *fifteen to seventeen words*: Cowburn, *No Cloak, No Dagger*, 155.

85 *a capital crime*: Ruby, *F Section SOE*, 70.

85 *IF YOU PUT . . . "You can send"*: Churchill, *Duel of Wits*, 323.

86 *Marseille, Lyon, Nice . . . forty new drop zones*: Cookridge, *Inside S.O.E.*, 171.

86 *tall, thin . . . twenty-six . . . facial lines . . . hunted*: 9/648.4.079, UK National Archives; Bleicher, *Colonel Henri's Story*, 86–87; Foot, *SOE in France*, 327.

86 *Bardet had been arrested . . . Riviera . . . Aix-en-Provence*: Foot, *SOE in France*, 245.

86   *"I don't like that"*: Churchill, *Duel of Wits*, 323. "I was not taken by him," Odette said at her debriefing on May 12, 1945, "and the men certainly did not like him. Marsac alone thought he was a good man. I told Raoul I did not think it was any good having a man like that." HS 9/648.4.080, UK National Archives.

86   *"I've got a complicated"*: Bleicher, *Colonel Henri's Story*, 73–74.

86   For details of the elaborate setup and arrest at Café Jacques, including the various players, see Cookridge, *Inside S.O.E.*, 173–75, and *They Came from the Sky*, 78. See also Henri Frager's debriefing in London in November 1943, wherein he describes a Russian, Nicola Posniakov, who appeared to be involved in the plot. KV 2/2127.2 (2A), UK National Archives. Frager guesses correctly that it was not the Russian who set the trap. During his debriefing that year in October, Arnaud identifies the man as "Nicholas de Paris." KV 2/2127.2 (1y).

87   *"We know next to"* . . . *"Do everything"*: Bleicher, *Colonel Henri's Story*, 74–76.

87   *Café Jacques*: Cookridge, *Inside S.O.E.*, 175, and *They Came from the Sky*, 78.

CHAPTER 8: GRAND DUKE

88   *"Two umbrellas have"*: Buckmaster, *They Fought Alone*, 69.

89   *wife and two of his daughters*: Foot, *SOE in France*, 225.

89   *Tournus . . . Cammaerts*: HS 9/648.4.080, UK National Archives; Churchill, *Duel of Wits*, 321–39. Odette stated in her debriefing of 12 May 1945 (HS 9/648.4.080) that this pickup occurred on March 14, which is incorrect; March 14 was the original date ordered by Baker Street (Churchill, *Duel of Wits*, 327) but the Lysander failed to show, and the pickup was rescheduled for the night of March 22–23. See also Cookridge, *They Came from the Sky*, 73.

89   *"If they think"*: Churchill, *Duel of Wits*, 327.

89n2   *DONKEYMAN*: Ibid.

89n2   *"JEAN MARIE" circuit*: See, for example, Cookridge, *They Came from the Sky*, 169.

89n3   *the lieutenant was also a Cambridge*: Cookridge, *They Came from the Sky*, 77.

90   *"Au revoir"*: Ibid., 328.

91   *Georges Duboudin*: Ruby, *F Section SOE*, 71; Buckmaster, *They Fought Alone*, 288; Foot, *SOE in France*, 227.

91   *Cammaerts's . . . one car . . . Paris*: Foot, *SOE in France*, 227 (citing Cammaerts's final report after the war). Cookridge, who consulted Cammaerts for his *They Came from the Sky*, has the car going to the local station and Cammaerts and Marsac entraining from there to Paris (76).

91   *doctor's authorization*: Foot, *SOE in France*, 227.

91   *Roger stayed with Marsac*: Cookridge, *They Came from the Sky*, 76, and *Inside S.O.E.*, 178.

91   *two million francs and a pistol*: KV 2/2127.2 (5a), UK National Archives; Foot, *SOE in France*, 227.

91   *meeting . . . Champs-Élysées . . . afternoon*: Bleicher, *Colonel Henri's Story*, 75–76; KV 2/2127.2 (2a), UK National Archives; Cookridge, *They Came from the Sky*, 78, and *Inside S.O.E.*, 175.

91   *"Can't you control"*: Churchill, *Duel of Wits*, 342–43.

92   *FOR ARNAUD STOP*: Ibid., 343.

92–93 *Monsieur Gaston . . . Claire . . . handkerchief*: Bleicher, *Colonel Henri's Story*, 74–77; Cookridge, *Inside S.O.E.*, 174–75.

93   *"Messieurs, mesdames!"*: Bleicher, *Colonel Henri's Story*, 77. The date of Marsac's arrest is shown as 23 March 1943 at KV 2/164 (18a), and March 24 at KV 2/2127.2 (2A), UK National Archives. Adolphe Rabinovitch (cited with his operational name, "CATALPHA") confirmed the cafe arrest details as he heard them in his SOE debriefing on 1 October 1943 KV 2/2127.2 (1y), UK National Archives. Odette confirms details of the arrest as she heard them (believing with Arnaud that the arrests were a Gestapo operation) from Lejeune in St. Jorioz later that month, and notes that she and Peter had warned Marsac not to go to Paris. HS 9/648.4.081, UK National Archives.

93   *Lucienne Frommagot*: Her code name was Suzanne, KV 2/2127.2 (1x and 1y); Churchill, *Duel of Wits*, 344; Cookridge, *Inside S.O.E.*, 175.

93   *flat in the rue Vaugirard*: Cookridge, *They Came from the Sky*, 78, and *Inside S.O.E.*, 178.

93   *"Sorry to startle" . . . "I'd better"*: Cookridge, *They Came from the Sky*, 79.

93   *"Not one of us" . . . Voltaire . . . Hôtel de la Plage*: Ibid., 79–80.

94   *safe house in Cannes . . . the address*: HS 9/648.4.027 (Peter's letter

to Colonel Perkins on June 4, 1946, wherein he states: "she sent him . . . to a safe house in Cannes"); HS 9/648.4.064 (Odette's debriefing on May 12, 1945, wherein she states that she "had sent ROGER to a safe place in which to lie low" on April 13, 1943); HS 9/648.4.082 (Odette's debriefing on May 12, 1945, wherein she states: "The day before the operation I sent ROGER (Cammaerts) to a safe place in the South of France"), UK National Archives. Also, Cammaerts states in his affidavit for Odette's George Cross award on 20 November 1945 that only she knew of his address in Cannes. HS 9/648.4.042, UK National Archives. However, in a report dated January 16–18, 1945, Cammaerts mentions that Arnaud had sent him to the safe house. Foot, *SOE in France*, 490n63. Furthermore, after Bleicher arrested Odette and Peter, Arnaud refused to return to London (as Buckmaster had suggested) until he could personally warn Cammaerts (Marks, *Between Silk and Cyanide*, 283); Arnaud, of course, would need the address in Cannes where Cammaerts was staying to make this personal visit. The discrepancy is easily resolved by piecing together the logistics and meetings: since Cammaerts met with both Odette and Arnaud in St. Jorioz—apparently together—it appears that Odette and Arnaud *together* sent Cammaerts to the safe house.

94   *"Bleicher," he said, "we must get"*: Bleicher, *Colonel Henri's Story*, 77.

94   *three days . . . refused to talk*: Cookridge, *Inside S.O.E.*, 175. Note that Cookridge interviewed Hugo Bleicher after the war.

94   *"the Hitler system"*: Bleicher, *Colonel Henri's Story*, 78.

94   *6 percent and 9 percent . . . SOE training*: Rigden, intro., *How to Be a Spy*, 151 ("The Party is and will remain a minority of the German people; it consists of between 4 and 6 million [of a German population of 70 million] members. Membership was closed in 1933, soon after Hitler's advent to power."). See also HS 7/55 and HS 7/56, UK National Archives (containing the SOE syllabus lectures).

94   *"I cannot believe"*: Bleicher, *Colonel Henri's Story*, 78.

94   *Hugo confirmed that it didn't*: Before and after his own arrest, Bleicher always contended that he was anti-Nazi. KV 2/164 (18a), UK National Archives. While the assertion was self-serving, it apparently was true. After the war, MI5's Ian Wilson concluded: "Bleicher is believed to be an expert at his work and a relatively humane man— he had no love for the Nazis." KV 2/164 (2B).

94   *notorious and hated Gestapo*: The Abwehr, the intelligence arm of the military, was throughout the war in competition with, and hostile to, the Gestapo and SD, Nazi Party Intelligence. After the war, British Intelligence confirmed that Bleicher did, in fact, try to prevent captured agents from being mistreated by the Gestapo. In addition, he and his Abwehr superiors treated these agents as prisoners of war rather than as spies—who could be executed under international law. KV 2/164 (18a), UK National Archives. One British agent, C. J. Parke, interrogated and turned by Bleicher, testified to Hugo's "distrust of, and repugnance for the Gestapo and even the SD," and stated that Bleicher made "scathing remarks" about them. KV 2/2127.2 (14D). During his debriefing in London in 1943, Henri Frager told British Intelligence that Bleicher had confided that there was a "struggle to the death" between the Abwehr and the Gestapo. KV 2/2127.2 (1z). See also the comment by Major Wethered, one of MI5's regional security liaison officers, on November 19, 1943: "another example of the known feud existing between the Abwehr and the SD." KV 2/2127.2 (3a), UK National Archives.

    Finally, see Bleicher's remarks in his memoir: "We had daily brushes with the S.D. and its gangs . . . It would be a distortion of history if we did not mention the conflict between the S.D. and the Military Intelligence . . . [a]s my Abwehr service and the S.D. were on hostile terms." Bleicher, *Colonel Henri's Story*, 52, 63. At one point, Bleicher wrote, the conflict went so far that some Resistance men, "with Abwehr agents backing them, shot up several S.D. men in the sporadic clashes that followed." Ibid., 63.

95   *"Is it possible"*: Bleicher, *Colonel Henri's Story*, 78.

95   *In room 13 of the Hôtel Bergerac . . . one million francs*: Ibid., 79.

95–96 *"My dear Marsac" . . . "The precondition for"*: Ibid., 80–82. Bleicher's ruse of planning to escape with Marsac is confirmed at KV 2/164 (18a), UK National Archives.

96   *"I will work for"*: Bleicher, *Colonel Henri's Story*, 82–84.

97   *letters . . . Roger Bardet*: Ibid., 84; KV 2/164 (18a) and KV 2/2127.2 (11A, 10A, 9A), UK National Archives.

97   *"You are to be"*: Bleicher, *Colonel Henri's Story*, 85. See also KV 2/164 (12a), UK National Archives.

97   *fortyish, six feet . . . brown eyes . . . strong . . . elephant-like steps*: KV 2/2127.1 (unpaginated, but appearing at the beginning of P.F. 600,

861) and KV 2/2127.2 (15a), UK National Archives. In all descriptions of Bleicher from SOE and Resistance agents, there was one common trait: "strong."

97   *something about him*: HS 9/648.4.060 and HS 9/648.4.081, UK National Archives.

97   *Les Tilleuls*: Jerrard Tickell, *Odette*, 186; HS 9/648.4.081, UK National Archives.

97   *"Lise, there is"*: Tickell, *Odette*, 186–87; HS 9/648.4.060 and HS 9/648.4.081, UK National Archives. The accounts of the first meeting between Odette and Hugo Bleicher differ. By Bleicher's recollection, he doesn't confront Odette during lunch at the Hôtel de la Poste; instead of going directly to find Odette, he claims he went to visit Mrs. Marsac, who suggested the hotel as a good lunch spot. While there, Bleicher writes, he overheard a woman chiding someone about security and the chef said, "Oh, that is Lise, the Englishwoman, who came over from London with our new wireless operator. She is in charge here now and interferes all the time." *Colonel Henri's Story*, 88–89. Bleicher states that he doesn't see Odette again until he arrests her on April 16. The cable from Odette to London, however, suggests that Hugo did in fact meet her at the luncheon. Churchill, *Duel of Wits*, 344. Hugo's interest in capturing a British aircraft—or defecting—occurs again when he suggests a similar plan (requesting a Lysander) to Peter after returning from visiting the Fols. Peter Churchill, *Spirit in the Cage*, 95.

98   *wintry smile, glanced hard at Odette*: HS 9/648.4.060 and HS 9/648.4.081, UK National Archives.

98   *"Mademoiselle Lise?"*: Tickell, *Odette*, 187.

98   *slight Belgian accent*: KV 2/2127.1, UK National Archives.

CHAPTER 9: LIFELESS

99   *from Marsac*: HS 9/648.4.081, National Archives. Bleicher, in his account, does not mention showing the letter to Odette (*Colonel Henri's Story*, 86–88), but that he did is confirmed by Arnaud's debriefing on 1 October 1943 at KV 2/2127.2 (1y), and Odette's debriefing on 12 May 1945 at HS 9/648.4.081, UK National Archives. Note that Roger Bardet's code name was CHAILLAN, although Tickell refers to him as "Jules." Note also that Bleicher states that

he, Hugo, had suggested to Marsac that the escape plot required Bardet's participation, thus prompting Marsac's letter to Roger. Tickell, however, appears to have erroneously assumed that Odette had suggested Bardet's meeting with Marsac in Fresnes (a meeting which she opposed adamantly).

99   *recognized the handwriting*: HS 9/648.4.060 and HS 9/648.4.081, UK National Archives.

99   *"Je benerais le jour"*: Ibid.

99   *"It was I who arrested"*: Tickell, *Odette*, 188.

99   *for Henri and Marsac to escape*: HS 9/648.4.060, 9/648.4.061, and 9/648.4.081, UK National Archives.

100   *"What do you want"*: Tickell, *Odette*, 189.

100   *"Mozart's Magic Flute"*: Ibid., 190. Odette does not know that Bleicher's first dream was to be a concert pianist, or that his lifelong passion was classical music.

101   *April 10*: The sequence of events between April 10 and 15, 1943, differs slightly in almost every account. See Bleicher, *Colonel Henri's Story*, 86–92; Churchill, *Duel of Wits*, 344–46; Tickell, *Odette*, 187–95; KV 2/164, Arnaud's account at 2/2127.2 (1y), and Odette's account at HS 9/648.4.081–.082, UK National Archives.

101   *Odette met with Bardet . . . Arnaud*: HS 9/648.4.060, 9/648.4.081, and 9/648.4.082, UK National Archives.

101   *shoot the bloody traitor*: Churchill, *Duel of Wits*, 347. In Arnaud's account at KV 2/2127.2 (1y), he met with Bardet and Riquet and tried to persuade them not to return to Paris. When they insisted on doing so, Arnaud "lost his temper and threatened to shoot them." Apparently, after they left and Odette told him that Bardet had given up their hideout address to Bleicher, Arnaud decided to make good on his threat.

101   *"Jean, my dear"*: Bleicher, *Colonel Henri's Story*, 90. The meeting of Bleicher, Marsac, and Roger Bardet is also confirmed in Odette's testimony at HS 9/648.4.081–.082, UK National Archives.

102   *a plane*: Bleicher remembered asking for *two* aircraft (*Colonel Henri's Story*, 90), while in all other accounts, it is a single plane. See, for example, KV 2/164 (18a), UK National Archives.

102   *Marsac . . . rather die in a concentration*: Cookridge, *Inside S.O.E.*, 176.

102   *"Do you really believe"*: Bleicher, *Colonel Henri's Story*, 91.

102   *Bardet returned . . . told Odette*: HS 9/648.4.081–.082, UK National Archives.

103   *go back to Paris*: Tickell, *Odette*, 192.

103   *dead for seven months . . . automaton . . . locust*: Churchill, *Duel of Wits*, 343.

104   *FROM LISE STOP . . . "I think it"*: Ibid., 344.

104   *"I want to go"*: Ibid.

105   *HENRI HIGHLY DANGEROUS*: Ibid., 345.

105   *Talloires . . . Glaieulles*: HS 9/648.4.082, UK National Archives.

105   *Mont Semnoz*: Odette recalled that London had suggested Semnoz and asked if it would provide a suitable landing site. HS 9/648.4.061 and HS 9/648.4.081, UK National Archives. However, the cable from Baker Street and Peter's specific mention of looking at the Michelin map with Major Buckmaster to find the location of the site selected by Odette and Arnaud seem to refute the notion. Churchill, *Duel of Wits*, 345.

105   *"Well, will it do?" . . . "But it's a hell"*: Tickell, *Odette*, 193.

105   *one hundred yards*: Churchill, *Duel of Wits*, 347.

106   *"Oh. One more thing"*: Tickell, *Odette*, 193.

106   *morning of April 15*: Churchill, *Duel of Wits*, 346. The sequence of events differs by a day or so with various accounts, although all place the arrest on April 16. HS 9/648.4.005 and .007, UK National Archives. Arnaud stated at his SOE debriefing on 1 October 1943 that he reconnoitered the Semnoz field on April 11 (KV 2/2127.2 (1y), UK National Archives), yet, on this date, Roger Bardet was in Paris meeting with Marsac and Bleicher, and Odette had not yet sent her message to London. In addition, he places Peter arriving on the fourteenth, but Peter states that he left London at ten thirty on the night of April 15. Churchill, *Duel of Wits*, 346. Odette, in her debriefing on May 12, 1945, stated that she heard the BBC broadcast on April 14 and that they arrived to the drop zone at 12:10 A.M. on April 15. HS 9/648.4.061 and HS 9/648.4.082, UK National Archives.

106   *"Struth!"*: Churchill, *Duel of Wits*, 345.

106   *submarine insertion*: Peter was inserted into France on 1 January 1941 by the British submarine HMS *P36*. Eight hundred yards from the coast of Cannes, he left the sub and paddled ashore in a canoe. Churchill, *Of Their Own Choice*, 70–72.

106   *"This mountaintop"*: Churchill, *Duel of Wits*, 346.

107   *aou . . . eou . . . aou*: Ibid., 349.

107   *"Le scarabée d'or"*: Tickell, *Odette*, 194; Churchill, *Duel of Wits*, 348, 350. See also HS 9/648.4.082, UK National Archives.

107 *"Why aren't you ready?"*: Churchill, *Duel of Wits*, 350.

108 *Jean and Simone*: The Cottets joined Odette and Arnaud for Peter's reception on Semnoz. HS 9/648.4.027–.028, UK National Archives.

108 *"Look! I remember"*: Churchill, *Duel of Wits*, 351.

108 *"Look, Arnaud!"*: Ibid., 352.

108 *"Oh, God"* . . . *"When you have"* . . . *"Here it comes!"*: Ibid., 353.

109 *"Oh, God!"* . . . *"I can't"*: Ibid., 354.

109 *"Bonfire ahead"*: Ibid. See also HS 9/648.4.082, UK National Archives.

110 *"Hallo, Lise"* . . . *"Pierre"* . . . *everything a man could*: Churchill, *Duel of Wits*, 356–57.

110 *abandoned inn*: HS 9/648.4.082, UK National Archives.

110 *dynamite*: HS 9/648.4.061, UK National Archives.

110 *Sten gun . . . Colt automatics*: Churchill, *Duel of Wits*, 358.

111 *"Lise, Lise"*: Ibid., 360.

CHAPTER 10: THE BEAM

112 *"What are we"*: Churchill, *Duel of Wits*, 360.

112 *shattered vertebra*: Churchill, *Spirit in the Cage*, 232.

112 *eight o'clock . . . changed . . . bus to Annecy*: HS 9/648.4.082, UK National Archives.

112–13 *"You should have"* . . . *"I still think"*: Tickell, *Odette*, 195–96.

113 *Faverges to meet with Arnaud . . . over dinner*: HS 9/648.4.082, UK National Archives.

113 *Tom Morel*: Ibid. Odette specifically mentions going to contact "Simone," who apparently was to pass word to Morel.

113 *eleven o'clock*: HS 9/648.4.062 and HS 9/648.4.082, UK National Archives. The arrest at the hotel on 16 April 1943 is confirmed by all parties, although the details and dialogue differ slightly. See Bleicher, *Colonel Henri's Story*, 97–99; Churchill, *Duel of Wits*, 361–62; Tickell, *Odette*, 197; KV 2/164 (18a), KV 2/2127.2 (2A, 1y), HS 9/648.4.005, and HS 9/648.4.007, UK National Archives. Some SOE files indicate that the arrest date was April 17 because Bleicher and his team arrived at the Hôtel de la Poste after eleven o'clock on the night of the sixteenth but would not have left with Peter and Odette until after midnight, now April 17. See HS 9/648.4.008 and HS 9/648.4.012. KV 2/2127.2 (1y and 2A) for Arnaud's account of

events given to SOE in October and November 1943. Note that MI5 uses Arnaud's operational name—CATALPHA—for its extract from the SOE debriefing. See also Buckmaster, *They Fought Alone*, 296.

113 *small . . . large hat . . . pale*: KV 2/2127.2 (1y), UK National Archives.

113 *le Belge was downstairs asking for her*: HS 9/648.4.062, 9/648.4.064, 9/648.4.082, and KV 2/2127.2 (2A, 1y), UK National Archives; Churchill, *Duel of Wits*, 361.

113–14 *tall blue-eyed . . . Gestapo . . . jumpy*: HS 9/648.4.062, 9/648.4.064, and 9/648.4.082, UK National Archives.

114 *scarf with his hat*: Ibid.

114 *She wondered if*: Ibid.

114 *offered his hand*: HS 9/648.4.082, UK National Archives.

114 *"I think a lot of you" . . . "I don't care"*: HS 9/648.4.062 and HS 9/648.4.082, UK National Archives. Odette's quote was rendered from the prose of her report.

114 *"You have done a very"*: HS 9/648.4.064 and HS 9/648.4.082, UK National Archives.

114 *"Don't try to"*: Churchill, *Duel of Wits*, 361; HS 9/648.4.062, UK National Archives.

114 *felt the thing jabbing her spine*: HS 9/648.4.062, HS 9/648.4.064, and HS 9/648.4.082, UK National Archives. The "thing," of course, is a gun.

114 *Peter's door*: The accounts of sleeping arrangements is slightly inconsistent. While Odette has she and Peter staying in the same room (HS 9/648.4.062 and 9/648.4.082, UK National Archives), Peter and Hugo Bleicher both recorded that they had separate rooms. Churchill, *Duel of Wits*, 361–62; Bleicher, *Colonel Henri's Story*, 98. The discrepancy may be resolved by Bleicher's description ("I ceased to watch Odette and looked into the room next door"): two separate rooms but with an adjoining-party wall door, left open.

114 *"There is the Gestapo"*: HS 9/648.4.062 and HS 9/648.4.082, UK National Archives.

114 *Henri, the tall blond, and an Italian*: HS 9/648.4.065, UK National Archives; Churchill, *Duel of Wits*, 362.

114 *"What's your name?" . . . "Chambrun"*: Churchill, *Duel of Wits*, 362.

115 *in and out of his pocket*: HS 9/648.4.062, HS 9/648.4.065, and HS 9/648.4.082, UK National Archives.

115 *smiled . . . conveying a hundred*: Churchill, *Duel of Wits*, 363.

115 *"Do you want to go"*: HS 9/648.4.065, HS 9/648.4.005, HS

9/648.4.062, and HS 9/648.4.082, UK National Archives; Bleicher, *Colonel Henri's Story*, 99; Churchill, *Duel of Wits*, 363.

115 *surrounded by soldiers . . . gun in hand*: HS 9/648.4.065, UK National Archives.

115 *Peter's wallet . . . under the seat*: HS 9/648.4.062, 9/648.4.065, and 9/648.4.082, UK National Archives; Churchill, *Duel of Wits*, 363–64. Bleicher's account of the arrest is revealing in that not only was he unaware of the complicity of Jean and Simone, but also that he missed Odette's retrieval and hiding of Peter's wallet. *Colonel Henri's Story*, 97–99.

115 *Alpini barrack . . . Annecy*: HS 9/648.4.012, HS 9/648.4.062, and HS 9/648.4.065, UK National Archives; Churchill, *Spirit in the Cage*, 10.

115 *"Take good care"*: Churchill, *Spirit in the Cage*, 11. In Bleicher's account, he does not travel with the Italians to the barracks. *Colonel Henri's Story*, 99.

115 *Odette . . . squeezed*: Churchill, *Spirit in the Cage*, 11.

116 *office with a camp bed*: Churchill, *Duel of Wits*, 364; HS 9/648.4.065, UK National Archives.

116 *Sten gun, pistols, ammunition, crystals*: Churchill, *Spirit in the Cage*, 10.

116 *whatever the cost*: Churchill, *Duel of Wits*, 364 ("She vowed she would shelter me and save my life by every available means.").

116 *Arnaud swung by the Hôtel de la Poste*: KV 2/2127.2 (1y), UK National Archives.

116 *Roger had telephoned Bleicher*: Cookridge, *Inside S.O.E.*, 178–79. Contrary to Cookridge's suggestion, however, Bardet had no contact with London and could not have known that Buckmaster had rejected Bleicher's plane pickup idea.

117 *"Your plan to penetrate"*: Ibid., 179–80.

117 *suitcase to hide*: HS 9/648.4.027, UK National Archives.

117n1 *Hans Josef Kieffer*: Ibid. See "Staff of the Gestapo and Sicherheitsdienst in Paris" in the photograph section between pages 304 and 305.

118 *Operation North Pole*: See, generally, Hermann J. Giskes, *London Calling North Pole: The True Revelations of a German Spy*. Giskes was the Abwehr major in charge of the operation.

118 *"Jacques"*: Philippe de Vomécourt, *Army of Amateurs*, 129.

118 *"no longer recognizable"*: Marks, *Between Silk and Cyanide*, 20.

118 *April 18 . . . lengthy—and therefore dangerous—message . . . Cammaerts*: Ibid., 283.

119 *wallet . . . 70,000 francs*: Churchill, *Spirit in the Cage*, 11. Peter's recollection of the amount in his wallet was 30,000 francs in *Duel of Wits* (363), and the information lost varies slightly in his two accounts.

120 *silent kill*: For background on Fairbairn and the silent kill, see Loftis, *Into the Lion's Mouth*, 161–65. See also Langelaan, *Knights of the Floating Silk*, 66–67; Dourlein, *Inside North Pole*, 81; Millar, *Maquis*, 22; Foot, *S.O.E.*, 84; Rigden, *How to Be a Spy*, 5, 15–16, 361, 367.

CHAPTER 11: THEY WILL SEND FOR YOU

121 *Peter parried the charge*: Churchill, *Spirit in the Cage*, 13–14. Peter's life was undoubtedly saved due to SOE's specific training in bayonet defense. See the SOE training manual on "Defences against a rifle and bayonet." Rigden, intro., *How to Be a Spy*, 370.

121 *"Assistenza! Assistenza!"*: Churchill, *Spirit in the Cage*, 14.

122 *"Double the guard"*: Ibid., 15.

122 *"Let me have"*: Ibid., 15–16.

122 *"Your husband is" . . . "Why?"*: HS 9/648.4.066, UK National Archives. Odette's quoted response is rendered from the prose of her report.

123 *"You are very strong"*: Ibid.

123 *"Now do you feel"*: Churchill, *Spirit in the Cage*, 17.

123 *168 containers*: Ibid., 18.

123 *He wept*: Ibid., 18.

124 *Carabinieri wielding Schmeissers*: Churchill, *Spirit in the Cage*, 21.

124 *passionate love notes*: "Raoul sent messages as a man would to a woman he loved, and this appealed to the Italians." HS 9/648.4.066, UK National Archives.

124 *handcuffed . . . Peter's condition . . . face*: HS 9/648.4.066, UK National Archives.

124 *one finger . . . wondered if he had been tortured*: Ibid.

124 *oasis of happiness*: Churchill, *Spirit in the Cage*, 21. See also HS 9/648.4.067, UK National Archives ("Source did everything she could during the journey to raise his spirits and succeeded").

125 *"I know that you"*: Churchill, *Spirit in the Cage*, 22.

125 *Arnaud and Roger . . . save them*: HS 9/648.4.067, UK National Archives.

125   *each would lay down*: Ibid.

125–26 *the extent of his admiration*: Churchill, *Spirit in the Cage*, 23.

126   *"We know all about"*: Ibid.

126   *"It was I"*: Ibid., 25–26. Peter Churchill's account of exactly when Odette told the Italian guards that Peter was related to Winston Churchill, and that they were married, differs from the accounts of Bleicher and Tickell. Churchill's account—in general and on this matter—appears the more reliable. Ironically, Churchill records that the Gestapo knew his real name at the time of his arrest (*Duel of Wits*, 362), but Peter and Odette assumed—apparently correctly— that the Italians in Grenoble had not been informed of his real name. *Spirit in the Cage*, 23, 25. In addition, while Peter remembered their stay in Grenoble as being ten days, Odette recalled it as a week. HS 9/648.4.067, UK National Archives.

127   *"I was your wife"*: Churchill, *Spirit in the Cage*, 26. Exactly when Peter and Odette began holding themselves out as husband and wife is unsettled, as Odette recalls a different date. In her debriefing on May 12, 1945, she testified that they began operating as a married couple as early as November 1942, soon after she arrived: "All this time she was living with RAOUL at the Villa Augusta and they were working as husband and wife." HS 9/648.4.057, UK National Archives.

127   *"If I ever get the chance"*: Churchill, *Spirit in the Cage*, 26.

128   *Turin . . . Nice . . . villa . . . Toulon*: HS 9/648.4.067 and HS 9/648.4.068, UK National Archives; Churchill, *Spirit in the Cage*, 28–29.

128   *rue d'Antibes . . . Provence . . . garrigue*: Churchill, *Spirit in the Cage*, 30–31.

128   *May 8*: HS 9/648.4.068, UK National Archives.

128   *"Bonjour, mon Pierre"*: Churchill, *Spirit in the Cage*, 31.

128   *Colonel Henri greeted . . . apology*: HS 9/648.4.068, UK National Archives.

129   *underground passage . . . carried Odette's luggage*: Ibid.

129   *smoked and talked . . . polite*: HS 9/648.4.069, UK National Archives.

129   *"I don't like some"*: Ibid. This quotation and some of this dialogue exchange between Odette and Henri has been rendered from the narrative of Odette's debriefing officer, who alternated between quotations and narrative in recording her story in May 1945.

129   *"I don't like seeing"* . . . *"Of course you don't love"*: HS 9/648.4.068, UK National Archives. In Odette's SOE report upon her return to London in May 1945, the British officer debriefing her refers to her as "Source," and to Peter as "Raoul," one of his cover names. To avoid confusion in the text, I have replaced "Raoul" with "Peter" in these quotations.

129   *dangerous*: HS 9/648.4.069, UK National Archives.

129–30   *"You are making"* . . . *"Peter is a very"*: HS 9/648.4.068, UK National Archives.

130   *He realized that she knew*: HS 9/648.4.069, UK National Archives.

130   *anything he could do for her*: Ibid.

130   *Cell 108 . . . plaster walls*: Tickell, *Odette*, 202, 207–8; HS 9/648.4.069, UK National Archives.

131   *"Quand j'etais"*: Tickell, *Odette*, 211.

131   *"Lise, I am"*: Tickell, *Odette*, 202. For a summary of Odette's initial days at Fresnes, and her meetings with Henri and distrust of him, see HS 9/648.4.069, UK National Archives.

131   *"You are not the sort"*: HS 9/648.4.069, UK National Archives.

131   *"I remember how"*: Tickell, *Odette*, 202.

132   *negotiating with a psychiatrist*: HS 9/648.4.069, UK National Archives.

132   *"Does the possibility"* . . . *"I have no bargain"* . . . *"You are a mother"*: Tickell, *Odette*, 203–4.

133   *Fresnes version of*: It appears that Odette and Peter received the same rations: coffee (Tickell, *Odette*, 207; Churchill, *Spirit in the Cage*, 43), soup, and bread. *Spirit in the Cage*, 36–37, 44.

134   *Henri Peulevé . . . shot . . . spoon*: Foot, *SOE in France*, 350; Buckmaster, *They Fought Alone*, 295.

134–35   *"What would you say"* . . . *"I'm sorry to see"* . . . *"You'll be interrogated"*: Churchill, *Spirit in the Cage*, 38.

134   *manacled and chained*: Pierre de Vomécourt ("Lucas") and Lily Carré ("La Chatte," "Victoire"), both of whom Hugo Bleicher arrested and imprisoned at Fresnes, were at times chained by their feet. Vomécourt, who was incarcerated at Fresnes for eighteen months, spent half of that time manacled and chained by his feet. Philippe de Vomécourt, *Army of Amateurs*, 92. Similarly, after Carré was convicted of treason and sentenced to death by the French, she was chained by her feet. Carré, *I Was "the Cat"*, 199–200.

135 *"Arrange for me" . . . High Life cigarettes*: Ibid., 39.

135 *"But how do you"*: Tickell, *Odette*, 213.

135–36 *"If you choose" . . . "Tell me"*: Ibid., 214.

137 *"Then why do you"*: Ibid.

CHAPTER 12: TICK, TICK

138 *"Why don't you" . . . "I could order"*: Tickell, *Odette*, 215.

138 *Henri asked if there was anything*: HS 9/648.4.069, UK National Archives.

139 *"That one means . . . 'no showers'"*: Ibid., 216; Imperial War Museum (IWM), Oral History, interview with Odette Marie Céline Sansom, produced October 31, 1986, catalogue number 9478, Reel 3.

139 *no contact with anyone*: IWM, interview with Odette Sansom, October 31, 1986, catalogue number 9478, Reel 3.

139 *pangs of hunger . . . measured his cell . . . exercise*: Churchill, *Spirit in the Cage*, 46.

139 *waves of strength . . . enough for two*: Ibid., 47.

139 *Gestapo . . . putting their best man*: Ibid.

140 *immaculate . . . suit . . . blouse*: Ibid.

140 *Peter looked awful . . . looked pale*: HS 9/648.4.070, UK National Archives.

140 *POW*: Ibid.

140 *two-hour interlude*: Peter recalled that Henri had given them only fifteen minutes (Churchill, *Spirit in the Cage*, 48), but in Odette's debriefing on May 12, 1945, she indicated that it was two hours. HS 9/648.4.070, UK National Archives.

140 *a precious milestone*: Churchill, *Spirit in the Cage*, 48.

141 *Rodion Romanovitch*: Fyodor Dostoyevsky, *Crime and Punishment*, 455.

141–42 *time to invoke . . . gave thanks . . . Lord's Prayer*: Churchill, *Spirit in the Cage*, 49–51.

142 *"Tribunal!"*: Tickell, *Odette*, 218; Churchill, *Spirit in the Cage*, 52.

143 *"Bon courage"*: Churchill, *Spirit in the Cage*, 53.

143 *"You see, Mr. Churchill"*: Churchill, *Spirit in the Cage*, 53–54.

143 *"Reconstruction of offense"*: Rigden, intro., *How to Be a Spy*, 84.

143n *Sonderführer Ernst Vogt*: Cookridge, *Inside S.O.E.*, p. 11 of photographs (following p. 304 of main text).

144 *"The Gestapo's reputation"*: Ibid., 85.

144   *"I don't think you"* . . . *"Ever seen"*: Churchill, *Spirit in the Cage*, 54.

144   *"Never"* . . . *"What do you take"*: Ibid., 55.

145   *"What's the idea"* . . . *"On December 24th"*: Ibid., 56.

146   *meat, potatoes, and gravy* . . . *sleepy*: Tickell, *Odette*, 219.

146   *eau de Cologne*: Ibid.

146   *"Tribunal!"*: Ibid.

146   *"Lise, you wasted"*: Ibid., 221.

147   *"Have a look"*: HS 9/648.4.070, UK National Archives. Odette's report of her interrogations and the order of questions appears to be dischronologized on pages 13 (HS 9/648.4.069) and 14 (HS 9/648.4.070), perhaps due to the interviewing officer's confusion as to the sequence of events. The report seems to indicate, for example, that Odette was interrogated before she was registered at Fresnes. Likewise, the report suggests that she was tortured before introductory questions were asked.

147   *"My father was killed"*: HS 9/648.4.070, UK National Archives (quotation rendered from the interviewing officer's narrative).

147   *"Are you doing"* . . . *"A pity"*: Ibid.

147   *"No. Except, perhaps"*: Ibid. Rendered from the interviewing officer's narrative.

147   *three questions . . . Arnaud . . . Roger*: HS 9/648.4.069, UK National Archives; Tickell, *Odette*, 221. The Gestapo's demands for the whereabouts of Arnaud and Roger—and Odette's refusal to supply such—are confirmed throughout Odette's SOE file. See, for example, HS 9/648.4.009 and HS 9/648.4.042, UK National Archives. See also Imperial War Museum (IWM), Oral History, interview with Odette Marie Céline Sansom, produced October 31, 1986, catalogue number 9478, Reel 1. In this interview, Odette notes that because of her silence, the Germans never found Arnaud or Roger. [Arnaud was later captured, but only upon returning to France after visiting London.] This statement is confirmed by Cammaerts's affidavit on 20 November 1945 at HS 9/648.4.042, UK National Archives.

147   *"We will see"*: Tickell, *Odette*, 221.

147   *she was the only one*: HS 9/648.4.018 and HS 9/648.4.042, UK National Archives. See also "safe house in Cannes" note in chapter 8 regarding Arnaud's possible knowledge of Roger's hideout, as well

as HS 9/648.4.027, HS 9/648.4.064, and HS 9/648.4.082, UK National Archives.

148 *"I am aware"... "I resent your hands"*: Tickell, *Odette*, 222.

148 *red-hot fire iron scorched her skin*: This torture is confirmed throughout Odette's SOE file. See, for example, HS 9/648.4.009, HS 9/648.4.012, HS 9/648.4.018, and HS 9/648.4.069, UK National Archives. Odette also discussed the burning of her back and ensuing toenail torture in her 1986 interview for the Imperial War Museum. (IWM, interview with Odette Sansom, October 31, 1986, catalogue number 9478, Reel 1.) Her physician after the war, Dr. Markowicz, also bore witness to the scar on her back and her missing and deformed toenails. HS 9/648.4.019, UK National Archives.

149 *L tablet*: Tickell, *Odette*, 96. See also Marks, *Between Silk and Cyanide*, 60.

149 *"My colleague here... There are those"*: Tickell, *Odette*, 223.

149 *standard procedure with torture*: Foot, *SOE in France*, 50.

150 *Cammaerts... safe house in Cannes*: HS 9/648.4.042, UK National Archives.

150 *French and young—maybe twenty-eight—and exceedingly handsome... teeth... lashes*: HS 9/648.4.069, UK National Archives; IWM, interview with Odette Sansom, October 31, 1986, catalogue number 9478, Reel 1. The Germans were clever, Odette felt, in that they always tried to get someone of the victim's own nationality to conduct the torture so that Germans could never be charged with abuse. IWM, interview with Odette Sansom, October 31, 1986, catalogue number 9478, Reel 1.

CHAPTER 13: THE BLACK HOLLOW

151 *toenail*: This torture is confirmed throughout Odette's SOE file and medical records. See, for example, HS 9/648.4.009, HS 9/648.4.069, and HS 9/648.4.019, UK National Archives. Odette also discussed this torture in her 1986 interview: Imperial War Museum (IWM), Oral History, interview with Odette Marie Céline Sansom, produced October 31, 1986, catalogue number 9478, Reel 1.

151 *"Now would you"*: Tickell, *Odette*, 223.

152 *the Nazis preferred*: IWM, interview with Odette Sansom, October 31, 1986, catalogue number 9478, Reel 1.

152 *"Well, Lise" . . . "Conversationally"*: Tickell, *Odette*, 223–24.

153 *"Nothing of the sort" . . . "finger-tips" . . . "The Major"*: Ibid., 225; IWM, interview with Odette Sansom, October 31, 1986, catalogue number 9478, Reel 1.

154 *Father Paul Steinert . . . chaplain*: HS 9/648.4.077, UK National Archives.

154 *"You will please"*: Tickell, *Odette*, 226.

154–55 *"You've been to" . . . "Then there is"*: Ibid., 230, 232.

155 *"Can't you understand" . . . "It's sufficient"*: Churchill, *Spirit in the Cage*, 63.

155 *"Though the SOE"*: Malcolm Muggeridge, *The Infernal Grove*, 174.

156 *"My dear Henri" . . . "Marsac" . . . "Just give me"*: Churchill, *Spirit in the Cage*, 63–64.

156 *"These are for you"*: Ibid., 65.

157 *"I've just come" . . . "My profession has"*: Ibid., 71–72.

158 *the battle of faith*: Ibid., 73.

158 *"How is it, mon Père" . . . . . . "Man's needs"*: Ibid., 83–84.

159 *He who has not*: Ibid., 85. Peter mistakenly has this verse within "Mignon," but it comes from the poem that generally precedes it, "Wer nie sein Brot" (roughly, "Who never gets his bread").

159 *four guards . . . talking*: HS 9/648.4.070, UK National Archives.

159 *"Liar"*: Tickell, *Odette*, 233.

159 *slapped Odette twice*: Tickell, *Odette*, 234, has the guard hitting Odette with a brush, but Odette testified at her debriefing on 12 May 1945 that the guard slapped her twice. HS 9/648.4.070, UK National Archives.

159 *fatherly . . . midfifties, grey*: HS 9/648.4.071, UK National Archives.

159–60 *captain apologized . . . anything he could do*: HS 9/648.4.070 and HS 9/648.4.071, UK National Archives.

160 *"I am, of course, responsible"*: Tickell, *Odette*, 237.

160 *parcel . . . ginger biscuits*: HS 9/648.4.071, UK National Archives; Tickell, *Odette*, 237.

160 *Trude*: HS 9/648.4.071, UK National Archives; Tickell, *Odette*, 240.

160 *books and more parcels*: HS 9/648.4.071 and HS 9/648.4.073, UK National Archives.

160 *summoned to Avenue Foch . . . Miss Herbert and Madame Lechene*: HS 9/648.4.071, UK National Archives.

160   *Emile*: HS 9/648.4.071 and HS 9/648.4.072, UK National Archives. Emile was SOE agent George Millar. See, generally, Millar, *Maquis*. See also Buckmaster, *They Fought Alone*, 294; Foot, *SOE in France*, 327, 337.

161   *"Yes, we have met"*: HS 9/648.4.072, UK National Archives.

161   *"You must understand"*: Ibid.

161   *"What about Fresnes"*: Ibid.

161   *They'd both be dead*: Ibid.

CHAPTER 14: VIENNESE WALTZES

162   *"Can you tell me"* . . . *"Hess"*: HS 9/648.4.072, UK National Archives.

162   *"I went to a beautiful"*: Imperial War Museum (IWM), Oral History, interview with Odette Marie Céline Sansom, produced October 31, 1986, catalogue number 9478, Reel 2. See also HS 9/648.4.073, UK National Archives.

163   *"I would be very distressed"*: Tickell, *Odette*, 242.

163   *"Lise, I would very much"*: Ibid.

164   *"You asked me that"*: Ibid., 242–43.

164   *"Monsieur Fol has"*: Churchill, *Spirit in the Cage*, 90.

164   *"Now, Pierre"*: Ibid., 92.

165   *rue Pergolèse . . . apartment 56*: KV 2/2127.2 (14B), UK National Archives.

165   *Henri's flat . . . bathe . . . Suzanne*: The entire outing and stop by Bleicher's flat to freshen up before the Fol luncheon is confirmed in both Churchill, *Spirit in the Cage*, 92–94, and Bleicher, *Colonel Henri's Story*, 105–6.

165   *8 bis Chaussée de la Muette*: HS 9/648.4.073, UK National Archives; Churchill, *Spirit in the Cage*, 93; Bleicher, *Colonel Henri's Story*, 105.

166   *"Now your turn"*: Churchill, *Spirit in the Cage*, 93; Bleicher, *Colonel Henri's Story*, 106 ("[W]e sat around . . . playing the piano.").

166   *Hugo Bleicher's greatest ambition*: Tickell, *Odette*, 179.

166   *his talent was immense*: Bleicher's personnel file with British Intelligence records that he was a "[v]ery good pianist." KV 2/2127.1, UK National Archives.

167   *"I've got a transmitter"* . . . *"A pity, Henri"*: Churchill, *Spirit in the Cage*, 95.

168   *"I've decided"*: IWM, interview with Odette Sansom, October 31, 1986, catalogue number 9478, Reel 2.

168   *gland on the side*: HS 9/648.4.076, UK National Archives.

168   *175 grams . . . bread . . . cabbage soup*: Tickell, *Odette*, 243; Christopher Burney, *Solitary Confinement*, 16 (specifying that it was cabbage soup).

168   *minimum to keep one alive*: Burney, *Solitary Confinement*, 16 ("But it never kept us more than barely alive.").

168   *On October 15 the captain of the guard . . . two fellow prisoners*: HS 9/648.4.073, UK National Archives.

168   *number 337 . . . Simone Hérail*: Hérail's affidavit (French original and English translation) for Odette's personnel file can be found at HS 9/648.4.035–.041, UK National Archives.

168   *"her health was seriously"*: HS 9/648.4.038, UK National Archives.

169   *"at no moment"*: Ibid.

169   *Lucienne Delmas*: HS 9/648.4.074, UK National Archives.

169   *wireless set . . . news from England*: HS 9/648.4.073 and HS 9/648.4.074, UK National Archives.

169   *gland . . . size of a grapefruit . . . pleurisy*: Churchill, *Spirit in the Cage*, 232.

169   *captain requested . . . Gestapo refused*: HS 9/648.4.076, UK National Archives.

170   *"Frau Churchill, I must"*: Tickell, *Odette*, 246.

170–71   *"Pierre, Pierre" . . . "Can you see"*: Churchill, *Spirit in the Cage*, 102.

171   *Bardet . . . Vera Leigh*: Foot, *SOE in France*, 263–64, 415.

172   *November 11 . . . summoned again to Avenue Foch*: HS 9/648.4.074, UK National Archives.

172   *a car*: In Odette's statement on May 12, 1945, she is held at Avenue Foch until evening and taken to the car from there. HS 9/648.4.074, UK National Archives. In her 1986 account, she stated that it was from Fresnes that she was taken to the Arc de Triomphe. IWM, interview with Odette Sansom, October 31, 1986, catalogue number 9478, Reel 1.

172   *"Since you are"*: IWM, interview with Odette Sansom, October 31, 1986, catalogue number 9478, Reel 1. See also HS 9/648.4.074, UK National Archives ("You are French and would like to see the Arc de Triomphe.").

172   *"Look well, Frau Churchill"*: Tickell, *Odette*, 248.

172   *"You like what you"*: IWM, interview with Odette Sansom, October 31, 1986, catalogue number 9478, Reel 1.

173   *"Frau Churchill"*: Tickell, *Odette*, 227.
173   *"Madame Churchill"*: Ibid., 228; IWM, interview with Odette Sansom, October 31, 1986, catalogue number 9478, Reel 1.
173   *"condemned to death"*: HS 9/648.4.012, UK National Archives.
173   *For which country*: IWM, interview with Odette Sansom, October 31, 1986, catalogue number 9478, Reel 2.
173   *"Gentlemen, you must"*: Tickell, *Odette*, 228. See also HS 9/648.4.072, UK National Archives.

CHAPTER 15: ALL MY LOVE

174   *"Il est né"*: Tickell, *Odette*, 249.
175   *To Peter*: Churchill, *Spirit in the Cage*, 108.
175   *About three weeks later*: Tickell has the fingerprint episode occurring in September, while Peter Churchill records it as taking place in November. Diana Rowden, however, whom Churchill identifies as being at the event, was not captured until early November. That, coupled with the specific date of 8 February 1944 given by Odette at her debriefing on May 12, 1945 (HS 9/648.4.074, UK National Archives), suggests that her recollection is more accurate.
175   *rue de Saussaies, Gestapo headquarters*: HS 9/648.4.074, UK National Archives. See also Burney, *Solitary Confinement*, 1.
175   *"Frau Churchill, is it"*: Tickell, *Odette*, 242.
176   *"Diana Rowden"*: Churchill, *Spirit in the Cage*, 103; HS 9/648.4.075, UK National Archives.
176   *"Made in England"*: Churchill, *Spirit in the Cage*, 103.
176   *Odette's morale was*: Ibid., 104.
177   *"fourteen times"*: Ibid. Odette's fourteen interrogations are confirmed throughout her SOE file. See, for example, HS 9/648.4.008–.009, UK National Archives, Major General Colin Gubbins's formal recommendation for Odette's George Cross.
177   *"What do you mean?"* . . . *"Oh God!"*: Churchill, *Spirit in the Cage*, 105. Odette's scheme to deflect the heat off of Peter and onto herself is confirmed by Major General Gubbins's recommendation for the George Cross: "She also drew Gestapo attention off her Commanding Officer and on to herself by saying that he was completely incompetent and had only come to FRANCE on her insistence. She took full responsibility and agreed that it should be herself and not

her Commanding Officer who should be shot. By this action she caused the Gestapo to cease paying attention to her commanding Officer after only two interrogations." HS 9/648.4.008–.009, UK National Archives.

177   *message coded in a book*: Churchill, *Spirit in the Cage*, 107; Tickell, *Odette*, 249.

178   *"Frau Churchill won't"*: Churchill, *Spirit in the Cage*, 109.

178   *"I've got some"* . . . *"What do you"*: Ibid., 111.

179   *"Erik Hoffmeyer"*: Ibid., 118.

181   *"Frau Churchill"* . . . *"Has he been shot?"*: Tickell, *Odette*, 249–50.

182   *292 pilots . . . Big Week . . . Operation Argument*: Dear and Foot, *Oxford Companion to World War II*, 130–31, 253.

183   *February 27 . . . "Let them all come"*: Churchill, *Spirit in the Cage*, 123.

183   *Wagner's Ride of the Valkyries*: Richard Wagner was Adolf Hitler's favorite composer. As he wrote in *Mein Kampf*, 18: "My youthful enthusiasm for the Bayreuth Master knew no bounds. Again and again I was drawn to hear his operas." See also Albert Speer, *Inside the Third Reich*, 71, 107, 297; Charlotte Higgins, "How the Nazis Took Flight from the Valkyries and Rhinemaidens," *Guardian*, July 2, 2007; Clemency Burton-Hill, "Is Wagner's Nazi Stigma Fair?," BBC.com/culture, October 21, 2014. *Ride of the Valkyries* was often played at Nazi rallies.

CHAPTER 16: LILY OF THE VALLEY

184   *At midnight came*: Dietrich Bonhoeffer, *Letters and Papers from Prison*, 390–91.

185   *"How goes it?"*: Churchill, *Spirit in the Cage*, 124.

185   *"If you try any"*: Ibid.

185n   *Mensur, or "academic fencing"*: Loftis, *Into the Lion's Mouth*, 7–8.

185n   *Mark Twain . . . "led away drenched"*: Ibid., 7.

186   *Protective Custody Camp*: Reinhard Rürup, ed., *Topography of Terror: Gestapo, SS and Reichssicherheitshauptamt on the "Prinz-Albrecht-Terrain": A Documentation*, 99. See also Augustino von Hassell and Sigfrid MacRae, *Alliance of Enemies: The Untold Story of the Secret American and German Collaboration to End World War II*, 37.

186   *"preventive arrest"*: Heinz Höhne, *The Order of the Death's Head: The Story of Hitler's SS*, 196–99.

187   *Sonderbehandlung*: Rürup, 99, 106.

187   *"Is this my new"*: Churchill, *Spirit in the Cage*, 126.

187   *improved Odette's lot*: Ibid., 132.

188   *Kurt von Schuschnigg*: Dear and Foot, *Oxford Companion to World War II*, 974.

188   *"The slogan that"*: Nikolaus Wachsmann, *kl: A History of the Nazi Concentration Camps*, 100.

188   *Death's Head units*: Ibid., 101. For background on the SS, see Höhne, *Order of the Death's Head*.

188   *"There is a path to freedom"*: Wachsmann, *History of Nazi Concentration Camps*, 100.

188   *"There is a path to the SS"*: Ibid., 101.

188   *forty thousand*: Ibid., 628. Dear and Foot, *Oxford Companion to World War II*, 974, estimated the number at a hundred thousand, though Wachsmann's figure of thirty-five thousand to forty thousand seems more accurate, given his focus and meticulous research on the concentration camps.

188n   *Sachsenhausen . . . Bernhard*: Dear and Foot, *Oxford Companion to World War II*, 974. For details on Operation Bernhard, see Walter Schellenberg, *The Memoirs of Hitler's Spymaster*, 419–20.

189   *He thought of*: Churchill, *Spirit in the Cage*, 149.

189   *On May 12*: HS 9/648.4.077, UK National Archives.

189   *"I wanted to say"* . . . *"not very beloved"*: Tickell, *Odette*, 251. Angered by Father Paul's compassion and love for Fresnes prisoners, the Gestapo eventually forbade him from seeing male inmates. HS 9/648.4.077, UK National Archives.

190   *"Frau Churchill, I have"*: Tickell, *Odette*, 251. Amazingly, an identical scene was occurring simultaneously five hundred miles away, in Berlin. From his cell in the Tegel interrogation prison, German pastor Dietrich Bonhoeffer recorded his own struggle with the irony:

> *Who am I? They often tell me*
> *I would step from my cell's confinement*
> *calmly, cheerfully, firmly,*
> *like a squire from his country-house.*
>
> *Who am I? They often tell me*
> *I would talk to my warders*

> *freely and friendly and clearly*
> *as though it were mine to command.*
>
> *Who am I? They also tell me*
> *I would bear the days of misfortune*
> *equably, smilingly, proudly,*
> *like one accustomed to win.*
>
> *Am I then really all that which other men tell of?*
> *Or am I only what I know of myself,*
> *restless and longing and sick, like a bird in a cage,*
> *struggling for breath, as though hands were compressing*
> *my throat, yearning for colours, for flowers, for the voices of birds,*
> *thirsting for words of kindness, for neighbourliness,*
> *trembling with anger at despotisms and petty humiliation,*
> *tossing in expectation of great events,*
> *powerlessly trembling for friends at an infinite distance,*
> *weary and empty at praying, at thinking, at making,*
> *faint, and ready to say farewell to it all?*
>
> *Who am I? This or the other?*

Bonhoeffer, *Letters and Papers*, 347–48. See, generally, Eric Metaxas, *Bonhoeffer: Pastor, Martyr, Prophet, Spy*.

190 *Vera Leigh . . . Diana Rowden*: Foot, *SOE in France*, 414–16; Tickell, *Odette*, 252; Buckmaster, *They Fought Alone*, 292, 297.

190 *Vera Leigh . . . dress designer . . . 30 October*: Foot, *SOE in France*, 261, 264.

190 *Diana Rowden's arrest*: Ibid., 263–64. See also Rita Kramer, *Flames in the Field: The Story of Four SOE Agents in Occupied France*.

191 *Andrée Borrel, the first female*: Foot, *SOE in France*, 178. Borrel parachuted in close to Paris the night of September 24–25, 1942.

191 *"the best of us all"*: Ibid., 230. PROSPER circuit leader Major Francis Suttill wrote to Baker Street in March 1943: "Everyone who has come into contact with her in her work agrees with myself that she is the best of all of us."

191 *fearless contempt*: Foot, *SOE in France*, 280.

191 *Yolande Beekman*: Ibid., 99, 240, 324.

192 *Madeleine Damerment*: Ibid., 83, 302.

192   *Eliane Plewman*: Ibid., 229, 330–31, 378. See also Elizabeth Nicholas, *Death Be Not Proud*.

193   *"That is the work"*: Tickell, *Odette*, 254.

193   *"Where are we going?"*: Ibid., 255.

CHAPTER 17: THE BUNKER

194   *Something told him*: Churchill, *Spirit in the Cage*, 149.

195   *He thought of her*: Churchill, *Spirit in the Cage*, 149.

195   *Karlsruhe*: HS 9/648.4.012 and HS 9/648.4.077, UK National Archives.

195   *handcuffs*: HS 9/648.4.012, UK National Archives.

195n *"Poetic knowledge"*: A mother's certainty that something has happened to a child who is far away or who is in some kind of danger is no old wives' tale, some experts contend, but an aspect of poetic knowledge. It is a step beyond Aquinas's connatural knowledge—accumulated experience yielding a way of knowing placed deeply within the poetic. Rather, as one philosopher put it, it's a knowledge where the intellect is guided and directed by affective inclinations and dispositions of the will. See, generally, James S. Taylor, *Poetic Knowledge: The Recovery of Education*. See also Gerald Gutek, *Philosophical and Ideological Perspectives on Education*, 17 (citing philosopher Jacques Maritain).

196   *dehydrated mules' brains . . . animal blood*: Buckmaster, *They Fought Alone*, 73.

196   *306 messages . . . "Vilma vous dit oui"*: Ibid., 240–41.

196   *Maquis were dispatched*: Ibid., 244.

196   *"Well, Frau Churchill"*: Tickell, *Odette*, 256–57.

197   *July 6 . . . Natzweiler-Struthof . . . Dachau*: Foot, *SOE in France*, 414–16.

197   *July 18*: HS 9/648.4.077, UK National Archives.

197   *"Encore un peu"*: Tickell, *Odette*, 258.

198   *cage . . . iron mesh . . . five feet*: HS 9/648.4.012, UK National Archives.

198   *no water and no sanitation facility . . . two other women*: Ibid.

198   *Halle . . . prison attic*: HS 9/648.4.012, HS 9/648.4.013, and HS 9/648.4.077, UK National Archives.

198   *forty-odd Ukrainian women*: HS 9/648.4.012 places the number at forty-five, while HS 9/648.4.077 puts it at thirty-seven.

198   *Sanitation . . . dysentery . . . heat . . . sand*: Ibid.

198   *Gestapo . . . local police . . . struck her*: HS 9/648.4.012 ("Gestapo") and HS 9/648.4.077 ("regular police"), UK National Archives.

198   *On July 26 . . . Ravensbrück*: HS 9/648.4.077 and HS 9/648.4.013, UK National Archives.

198   *feared by every woman*: ten Boom, *Hiding Place*, 173 ("the notorious women's extermination camp whose name we had heard even in Haarlem").

198   *labor camp*: Jack Gaylord Morrison, *Ravensbrück: Everyday Life in a Women's Concentration Camp 1939–45*, ix, 12–13; Wachsmann, *History of Nazi Concentration Camps*, 98, 227. Ravensbrück was a labor camp (*Arbeitslager*) rather than an extermination camp (*Vernichtungslager*), which were all located outside of Germany.

198   *4,000*: Morrison, *Ravensbrück*, 16.

198   *more than 36,000*: ten Boom, *Hiding Place*, 181–82. Ten Boom states that her barracks contained 1,400, and the others, some 35,000.

198   *Poles . . . Germans . . . Jews . . . Russians*: Morrison, *Ravensbrück*, 86.

199   *133,000*: Dear and Foot, *Oxford Companion to World War II*, 929.

199   *40,000*: Wachsmann, *History of Nazi Concentration Camps*, 628. Dear and Foot, *Oxford Companion to World War II*, 929, cite a figure of up to 92,700, although Wachsmann's 30,000 to 40,000 appears more accurate, given the depth of his research.

199   *July 27*: HS 9/648.4.077, UK National Archives.

199   *two-mile . . . "Is there really"*: Ibid., 30–31.

199   *SS homes . . . fourteen-foot walls . . . towers*: ten Boom, *Hiding Place*, 173; Tickell, *Odette*, 261; Morrison, *Ravensbrück*, 31.

199   *valley . . . cinder . . . skull-and-crossbones . . . electrified*: ten Boom, *Hiding Place*, 173; Morrison, *Ravensbrück*, 32.

199n *Aufseherinnen . . . weibliche SS-Gefolge*: Morrison, *Ravensbrück*, 23–24.

200   *washroom . . . concrete floor*: Imperial War Museum (IWM), Oral History, interview with Odette Marie Céline Sansom, produced October 31, 1986, catalogue number 9478, Reel 2; Tickell, *Odette*, 262.

200   *Ravensbrück prisoner intake . . . naked . . . inspected*: ten Boom, *Hiding Place*, 175–76; Morrison, *Ravensbrück*, 32–35, 119.

200   *others committed suicide*: Morrison, *Ravensbrück*, 33.

200   *medical exam*: Ibid., 33–34; ten Boom, *Hiding Place*, 178.

201   *Sühren . . . Nazi Party . . . 1928 . . . SS three years later*: Tom Segev, *Soldiers of Evil: The Commandants of the Nazi Concentration Camps*,

71, citing the Fritz Sühren personnel file, Berlin Document Center Personnel File (SS Service Files); Wachsmann, *History of Nazi Concentration Camps*, 401.

201   *Sachsenhausen*: Segev, 71.

201   *Naujoks . . . winch . . . gallows*: Jerzy Pindera, *Liebe Mutti: One Man's Struggle to Survive in KZ Sachsenhausen, 1939–1945*, 71–72; Harry Naujoks, *Mein Leben im KZ Sachsenhausen, 1936–1942*.

201   *hard labor and starvation*: Morrison, *Ravensbrück*, 243.

201   *Dr. Karl Gebhardt . . . medical experiments*: Klaus Dörner, et al., eds., *The Nuremberg Medical Trial 1946/47: Guide to the Microfiche-Edition*, 91; Affidavit, Dr. Gerhard Schiedlausky (camp physician at Mauthausen, Ravensbrück, Natzweiler, and Buchenwald), NO-508, sworn on August 7, 1945, Holocaust Texts, http://madness-visible .blogspot.com/2011/06/no-508-affidavit-dr-gerhard.html; Morrison, *Ravensbrück*, 245–49.

201   *fearing legal repercussions*: Patricia Heberer and Jürgen Matthäus, eds., *Atrocities on Trial: Historical Perspectives on the Politics of Prosecuting War Crimes*, 136.

202   *sterilized . . . X-rays*: Morrison, *Ravensbrück*, 53; Vera Renouf, *Forfeit to War*, 303.

202   *"Sprechen Sie Deutsch?"*: Tickell, *Odette*, 265–66.

203   *Frau Schurer . . . Churchill name*: Ibid.; IWM, interview with Odette Sansom, October 31, 1986, catalogue number 9478, Reel 2.

203   *seventy-eight cells . . . written report . . . pregnant woman*: Morrison, *Ravensbrück*, 231–32.

203   *four and a half paces long by two and a half*: Ibid., 231 (citing a prisoner statement from the Guide to the Cell Building of the Ravensbrück Memorial).

203   *Margarete Mewes*: Tickell, *Odette*, 266.

204   *Bunker . . . pitch dark . . . food hatch*: HS 9/648.4.013, HS 9/648.4.077, and HS 9/648.4.078, UK National Archives; IWM, interview with Odette Sansom, October 31, 1986, catalogue number 9478, Reel 3; Tickell, *Odette*, 267; Churchill, *Spirit in the Cage*, 232. See, generally, Morrison, *Ravensbrück*, 231–33.

204   *coffee . . . bread*: Ibid., 267; ten Boom, *Hiding Place*, 174.

204   *turnip soup*: Tickell, *Odette*, 267; ten Boom, *Hiding Place*, 174; Morrison, *Ravensbrück*, 112 ("cabbage or turnip").

204–5 *"punishment room" . . . screams . . . strokes*: IWM, interview with

Odette Sansom, October 31, 1986, catalogue number 9478, Reel 2; HS 9/648.4.013, National Archives.

204–205 *caning . . . shackled . . . dress . . . blanket . . . twenty-five*: Morrison, *Ravensbrück*, 233 (citing testimony of Martha Wölkert, who received this punishment); Affidavit, Dr. Gerhard Schiedlausky, NO-508, sworn on August 7, 1945, Holocaust Texts.

205 *"elf . . . zwolf . . . dreizehn"*: Tickell, *Odette*, 268; HS 9/648.4.013, National Archives.

206 *Odette counted every*: IWM, interview with Odette Sansom, October 31, 1986, catalogue number 9478, Reel 2.

206 *the charrette*: Tickell, *Odette*, 264.

206 *leaf*: Starns, *Odette*, 103 (citing the *London Dispatch*, November 30, 1958).

206n *"the sounds of hell"*: ten Boom, *Hiding Place*, 177.

207 *"Yes, thank you"*: Tickell, *Odette*, 270; IWM, interview with Odette Sansom, October 31, 1986, catalogue number 9478, Reel 2.

207 *"you must take over"*: Starns, 103 (citing the *London Dispatch*, November 30, 1958).

207 *scabs . . . glands*: HS 9/648.4.013, UK National Archives.

207 *August . . . they were on full blast*: HS 9/648.4.013 and HS 9/648.4.078, UK National Archives; IWM, interview with Odette Sansom, October 31, 1986, catalogue number 9478, Reel 2; Churchill, *Spirit in the Cage*, 232.

207 *blanket . . . soaked it*: HS 9/648.4.013, UK National Archives.

207 *six days and nights . . . no food . . . inferno*: HS 9/648.4.013 and HS 9/648.4.078, UK National Archives.

207 *scurvy and dysentery . . . grapefruit*: Ibid.; Churchill, *Spirit in the Cage*, 232; Tickell, *Odette*, 271.

207 *Everything went black*: HS 9/648.4.013 and HS 9/648.4.078, UK National Archives. Odette passed out and was found unconscious on the floor by a guard. Ibid.; Churchill, *Spirit in the Cage*, 232.

CHAPTER 18: THE SLAUGHTER

208 *unconscious . . . semicoma . . . revived*: HS 9/648.4.013 and HS 9/648.4.078, UK National Archives; Churchill, *Spirit in the Cage*, 232.

208 *Dietrich von Choltitz*: See, for example, Hassell and MacRae, *Alliance of Enemies*, xix.

208 *"Permit me"*: Buckmaster, *They Fought Alone*, 261.

209 *"Have you any complaints?"*: Tickell, *Odette*, 271. See also HS 9/648.4.077, UK National Archives, regarding punishment in retaliation for the Allied invasion in southern France.

209 *Provence . . . little resistance*: Buckmaster, *They Fought Alone*, 253.

209 *"Peter Churchill and Odette"*: Ibid., 235–36.

209 *"You are aware"*: Tickell, *Odette*, 271.

209 *medical exams . . . nude*: ten Boom, *Hiding Place*, 178, 190.

209 *X-rays . . . tuberculosis . . . extermination . . . plates*: HS 9/648.4.013 and HS 9/648.4.078, UK National Archives; Imperial War Museum (IWM), Oral History, interview with Odette Marie Céline Sansom, produced October 31, 1986, catalogue number 9478, Reel 2, Reel 3. The recorded dates of Odette's treatments vary slightly—from August through October 6—in all probability due to her multiple visits to the camp hospital.

210 *dead within a few weeks*: HS 9/648.4.013 ("few weeks") and HS 9/648.4.078 ("two months"), UK National Archives.

210 *he needed insurance*: Ibid.

210 *injections . . . hair . . . vitamins*: Ibid.

210 *gland . . . grapefruit . . . operate*: HS 9/648.4.013, UK National Archives.

210 *Heinrich Himmler*: IWM, interview with Odette Sansom, October 31, 1986, catalogue number 9478, Reel 2.

211 *seven hundred . . . Vught*: ten Boom, *Hiding Place*, 169.

211 *November . . . Siemens factory*: Ibid., 185.

211 *December . . . new cell*: HS 9/648.4.013 and HS 9/648.4.078, UK National Archives.

211 *three months and eight days*: HS 9/648.4.013 and HS 9/648.4.078, UK National Archives; IWM, interview with Odette Sansom, October 31, 1986, catalogue number 9478, Reel 2 ("three months and eleven days").

211 *new cell . . . six yards*: HS 9/648.4.013, UK National Archives; IWM, interview with Odette Sansom, October 31, 1986, catalogue number 9478, Reel 2.

211–12 *ashes . . . hair . . . smell . . . screams*: Ibid. About this time, Corrie ten Boom watched an unusual proceeding while she was walking by the infirmary. A truck had backed up to the entrance, and some elderly patients were being helped in; weak and extremely sick prisoners followed, including several loaded from stretchers. Corrie grieved at what followed. The truck drove directly to the crematorium. Ten Boom, *Hiding Place*, 193.

212 *gas chamber*: Morrison, *Ravensbrück*, 289–91.

212 *January 12 . . . Prussia . . . Warsaw*: Dear and Foot, *Oxford Companion to World War II*, 1335.

212 *One in four . . . "death march"*: Wachsmann, *History of Nazi Concentration Camps*, 556; Morrison, *Ravensbrück*, 300–303.

212 *Himmler ordered . . . Johann Schwarzhuber . . . Dr. Richard Trommer*: Ibid., 288. See also Affidavit, Dr. Gerhard Schiedlausky, NO-508, sworn on August 7, 1945, Holocaust Texts, noting that Dr. Trommer was his replacement after he was reassigned to another camp.

212 *"Mittwerda" . . . 150*: Morrison, *Ravensbrück*, 290.

213 *"I heard moaning"*: Ibid.

213 *714,211 . . . 550,000*: Wachsmann, *History of Nazi Concentration Camps*, 627.

213 *1,500 . . . 4,500 . . . 6,000*: Morrison, *Ravensbrück*, 291, 294.

213 *"I could hear them"*: Tickell, *Odette*, 276; IWM, interview with Odette Sansom, October 31, 1986, catalogue number 9478, Reel 2.

213n1 *SS simply shot*: At Ravensbrück, prisoner Olga Körner witnessed forty-eight inmates being shot by SS guards. Morrison, *Ravensbrück*, 291.

213n1 *250 . . . Fürstengrube*: Wachsmann, *History of Nazi Concentration Camps*, 558.

213n1 *Palmnicken . . . Dachau*: Ibid., 560–61.

213n1 *1,300 infirm . . . Lieberose*: Ibid., 557.

213n2 *3,600 girls*: Wachsmann, *History of Nazi Concentration Camps*, 568.

213n2 *3,858*: Morrison, *Ravensbrück*, 294.

215 *"The town is"*: Bleicher, *Colonel Henri's Story*, 163.

215 *"You are a soldier"*: Ibid., 165.

215 *February 26 . . . Düsseldorf . . . March 7 . . . Remagen*: Dear and Foot, *Oxford Companion to World War II*, 1335.

215 *Austria . . . 30th . . . Danzig*: Ibid., 1336.

215 *April 4 . . . American and Canadian Red Cross*: Morrison, *Ravensbrück*, 296.

216 *April 9 . . . Königsberg*: Gen. Walter Warlimont, *Inside Hitler's Headquarters, 1939–45*, 513.

216   *the Elbe . . . Vienna . . . 13th*: Dear and Foot: *Oxford Companion to World War II*, 1336; Warlimont, *Inside Hitler's Headquarters*, 513; Michel, *Shadow War, Shadow War*, 381.

216   *Three days later . . . Zhukov*: Dear and Foot, *Oxford Companion to World War II*, 1301; Warlimont, *Inside Hitler's Headquarters*, 513; Michel, *Shadow War*, 381.

216   *Buchenwald and Dora*: Wachsmann, *History of Nazi Concentration Camps*, 577.

216   *April 15 he called a meeting*: Ibid., 579.

216   *Execute every prisoner*: Tickell, *Odette*, 277.

216n   *"There is no question"*: Wachsmann, *History of Nazi Concentration Camps*, 580.

217   *"Keep your chin up!"*: Churchill, *Spirit in the Cage*, 201.

217n   *Canaris and Oster . . . St. Anne's . . . Bonhoeffer and Niemöller*: Hassell and MacRae, *Alliance of Enemies*, 51.

218   *Prince Philipp . . . von Flügge . . . Innsbruck*: Ibid., 201–8.

218   *Fabian von Schlabrendorff*: See, generally, Rürup, *Topography of Terror*, 175–76.

218   *"I shall not be"*: Ibid., 204.

218n1   *Whose wife was killed*: Churchill, *Spirit in the Cage*, 203.

219   *"I'm sorry"*: Ibid., 210.

219–20 *Count Folke Bernadotte . . . Red Cross . . . four thousand*: Morrison, *Ravensbrück*, 297–99.

220   *walk to Malchow*: Ibid., 301–3.

220   *three thousand*: Morrison, *Ravensbrück*, 306.

220   *It was midnight*: Tickell, *Odette*, 277.

CHAPTER 19: STILL WARM

221   *"You will be"*: Tickell, *Odette*, 277.

221   *Black Maria for transport*: HS 9/648.4.013 and HS 9/648.4.078, UK National Archives.

221   *executed Mussolini*: Michel, *Shadow War*, 381.

222   *fourteen straight hours . . . Neustadt*: HS 9/648.4.013, UK National Archives.

222   *more were being executed at Neustadt*: Ibid.

222   *Münchof . . . no food*: Ibid. In her debriefing, Odette mentioned (or

the officer taking notes heard) that they had gone to "Malschoff." No such town exists, and it appears that she meant (or said) "Münchof," some twelve miles away.

222   *mown down by SS machine guns*: HS 9/648.4.013, UK National Archives; Tickell, *Odette*, 280.

222   *"What do you want?"*: Tickell, *Odette*, 280–81.

222   *"Adolf Hitler . . . is dead"*: Ibid.; Imperial War Museum (IWM), Oral History, interview with Odette Marie Céline Sansom, produced October 31, 1986, catalogue number 9478, Reel 2.

222   *"If Hitler should be"*: Churchill, *Spirit in the Cage*, 212.

223   *Execute all British*: Ibid., 214–15.

223   *May 1 . . . three in the afternoon*: HS 9/648.4.013, UK National Archives.

223   *"Ist Frau Churchill"*: Tickell, *Odette*, 281; HS 9/648.4.013, UK National Archives.

224   *head was shaved . . . "fresh"*: IWM, interview with Odette Sansom, October 31, 1986, catalogue number 9478, Reel 2.

224   *the other women . . . still warm*: Ibid.

224   *three cars . . . SS officers*: HS 9/648.4.013, UK National Archives.

224   *white Mercedes*: IWM, interview with Odette Sansom, October 31, 1986, catalogue number 9478, Reel 2. In Tickell's 1949 account (281), Sühren's Mercedes is black; however, in Odette's 1986 interview, she recalls that it was white.

224   *"Get out"*: Tickell, 282.

224   *von Schlabrendorff*: Churchill, *Spirit in the Cage*, 215–18.

224   *Kreisau Circle*: See, for example, William Shirer, *The Rise and Fall of the Third Reich: A History of the Third Reich*, 374.

224–25 *Canaris had sent him to England to warn Churchill*: Hassell and MacRae, *Alliance of Enemies*, 56.

225   *Gestapo tortured him*: Von Schlabrendorff's statement regarding his torture is set forth in Rürup, *Topography of Terror*, 174–76.

226   *"We are not out"*: Churchill, *Spirit in the Cage*, 218.

226   *"Where is your cousin?"*: Ibid., 219.

227   *arranged them in a pile and struck the match*: Tickell, *Odette*, 282.

227   *"In God's name" . . . Colonel von Bonin*: Churchill, *Spirit in the Cage*, 220.

228   *Pragser-Wildsee Hotel . . . stationed Kesselring's men*: Ibid., 221–22.

228   *Garibaldi . . . Attwood*: Ibid., 221–24.

229 *Red Army . . . Berlin . . . May 2*: Dear and Foot, *Oxford Companion to World War II*, 1301, 1336.

229 *"Do you want to"*: IWM, interview with Odette Sansom, October 31, 1986, catalogue number 9478, Reel 2.

229 *deserted wood to be shot*: HS 9/648.4.013, UK National Archives.

230 *"This is Frau Churchill"*: IWM, interview with Odette Sansom, October 31, 1986, catalogue number 9478, Reel 2; Tickell, *Odette*, 283.

230 *"No, if you don't mind"*: IWM, interview with Odette Sansom, October 31, 1986, catalogue number 9478, Reel 2; Churchill, *Spirit in the Cage*, 233; Tickell, *Odette*, 284.

230 *documents in Sühren's briefcase*: IWM, interview with Odette Sansom, October 31, 1986, catalogue number 9478, Reel 2; Churchill, *Spirit in the Cage*, 233.

231 *Footsteps*: Tickell, *Odette*, 285.

CHAPTER 20: PIERRE

232 *American soldiers arrived . . . Partisans*: Churchill, *Spirit in the Cage*, 224.

232 *May 4 . . . Lüneburg . . . May 7 . . . Reims . . . Berlin*: Dear and Foot, *Oxford Companion to World War II*, 1336; Warlimont, *Inside Hitler's Headquarters, 1939–45*, 517.

233 *Verona . . . May 9 . . . Naples . . . Lieutenant Colonel Hedin*: Churchill, *Spirit in the Cage*, 226–28.

234 *"You won't know"*: Ibid., 230–31.

235 *Queen Alexandra's Military Hospital*: Odette received treatment here as well as at St. Mary's Hospital in Paddington—the archive files suggesting that the Queen Alexandra's visit came first. See HS 9/648.4.044, UK National Archives.

235 *fifth vertebra*: Churchill, *Spirit in the Cage*, 232. See also Imperial War Museum (IWM), Oral History, interview with Odette Marie Céline Sansom, produced October 31, 1986, catalogue number 9478, Reel 3.

235 *severe anemia . . . injections . . . "intense general medicinal"*: HS 9/648.4.019, HS 9/648.4.026, and HS 9/648.4.032, UK National Archives.

235 *nervous tension and articular rheumatism*: HS 9/648.4.019, HS 9/648.4.026, and HS 9/648.4.032, UK National Archives.

236 *sepsis*: IWM, interview with Odette Sansom, October 31, 1986, catalogue number 9478, Reel 3.

236 *had killed . . . Reinhard Heydrich*: Höhne, *Order of the Death's Head*, 495.

236 *She would die*: In an interview with the *London Dispatch* on November 30, 1958, Odette stated: "I have had many operations since the war. Several times they have come to say good-bye because I was expected to die." Starns, *Odette*, 112. The SOE archive files do not mention Odette's sepsis or operations, although Peter wrote in 1946 (correspondence to Colonel Perkins on May 23 at HS 9/648.4.017, UK National Archives) and again in 1954 (*Spirit in the Cage*, 234) that Dr. Markowicz had saved her life (*see infra* and accompanying text), and medical correspondence on 8 November 1945 refers to her "severe illness last summer." HS 9/648.4.044, UK National Archives. Odette mentions her septic toe in her 1986 interview with the Imperial War Museum. IWM, interview with Odette Sansom, October 31, 1986, catalogue number 9478, Reel 3. See also HS 9/648.4.043, UK National Archives.

CHAPTER 21: HUNTING THE HUNTER

237 *aka Monsieur Jean, Jean Verbeck*: Hugo Bleicher's aliases can be found throughout KV 2/164 and 2/2127, UK National Archives.

237 *Sams . . . "the Order Service"*: Hugo Bleicher, *Colonel Henri's Story*, 167. For details of the hiding arrangement and persons involved, see KV 2/164 (4B), UK National Archives.

238 *May 31*: Bleicher remembered his arrest date as June 15 (*Colonel Henri's Story*, 168), but the official arrest report reveals the date to be May 31, 1945. KV 2/164 (unpaginated, but appearing between pages 7a and 7B).

238 *Dutch militia*: Bleicher remembered that the arresting party was composed of Dutch militia; the official arrest report, however, records that they were Canadian soldiers from "11 Cdn F S section," with the 1 Canadian Corps taking custody of Bleicher. It is likely, then, that a small band of Dutch militia—who knew of Bleicher's hideout—led the arrest and were backed by Canadian soldiers who had liberated the city. KV 2/164 (unpaginated, but appearing between pages 7a and 7B).

238 *Betrayal! . . . reverse of the medallion*: Bleicher, *Colonel Henri's Story*, 169.

239   *Camp 020:* For Bleicher's Camp 020 file, see KV 2/164, UK National Archives. In particular, see MI5's Ian Wilson's summary report of Bleicher and his work on page 2B.

239   *"The British Secret Service":* Bleicher, *Colonel Henri's Story*, 173–74. While Hugo didn't know it at the time, one of his interrogators was none other than F Section's Vera Atkins. "I was startled one morning to be visited by a very pretty young woman officer in uniform," he wrote later. "She turned out to have more aplomb than all the other officers put together. She boxed me in with astonishing ease and consummate tactics. Luckily my memory is good or she might well have put me in an awkward position. She seemed also to be quite tireless in her questioning and if the conducting officer had not felt hungry at lunch time and urged her to break off the interrogations, she would have kept me on tenterhooks for a great deal longer." Ibid., 174, 176.

239   *Walter Schellenberg:* Hugo wondered why Schellenberg was also not in solitary but, instead, was allowed to mingle with other prisoners. As the SD's foreign intelligence chief, had he not been aware of the Nazi atrocities? He had not, Schellenberg said during their dinners together. "Only later did I learn," Hugo wrote in his memoirs, "that as Chief of the Secret Service Schellenberg had done all he could to shorten the war." Bleicher, *Colonel Henri's Story*, 176.

Indeed, for more than two years Schellenberg had risked his own life in trying to convince Heinrich Himmler to separate from Hitler and seek peace with the West. At the end of 1944 Schellenberg initiated a meeting between Himmler and Jean-Marie Musy, former president of Switzerland, to discuss release of some prominent Jews in concentration camps, and to float peace feelers. In February 1945 Schellenberg brokered a similar meeting with the Swedish Red Cross's Count Bernadotte. Schellenberg pushed Himmler to discuss not only camp evacuations but also peace. Finish with Hitler, he urged, and finish the war.

"So you are demanding that I depose the Führer?" Himmler had asked.

"Yes," Schellenberg replied. "You still have enough higher SS leaders and you are still in a strong enough position to arrest him."

Himmler relished the notion of being the country's leader, but lacked the courage to pursue Schellenberg's plan.

See Höhne, *Order of the Death's Head*, 568, 570–71; Schellenberg, *Memoirs of Hitler's Spymaster*, 428–29, 433–54; Shirer, *Rise and Fall of the Third Reich*, 1114, 1116.

239   *A rumor . . . "Where is the plane"*: Bleicher, *Colonel Henri's Story*, 177.

240   *"Do you know me"*: Ibid., 178.

CHAPTER 22: FANNING THE DAMNED

241   *specialists*: HS 9/648.4.043, UK National Archives.

241   *Dr. T. Markowicz*: See HS 9/648.4.019, 9/648.4.026, and 9/648.4.032, UK National Archives.

241   *saved Odette's life*: Churchill, *Spirit in the Cage*, 234; HS 9/648.4.017, UK National Archives.

241   *nervous condition and anemia*: HS 9/648.4.019, UK National Archives.

241   *full disability pension*: Churchill, *Spirit in the Cage*, 234; HS 9/648.4.020, UK National Archives.

242   *$2,000*: Churchill, *Spirit in the Cage*, 234.

242   *He had escaped*: See "The Arrest of Fritz Suhren" (footage of Sühren's recapture) and accompanying description, Imperial War Museum, catalogue number MGH 617.

242   *Sühren and SS Sergeant Hans Pflaum*: "Wie ein SS-Mann aus Varel eine Agentin als Geisel ahm," *Nordwest Zeitung*, NWZOnline.de, April 30, 2015.

243   *"You arrested my"*: Bleicher, *Colonel Henri's Story*, 178–79.

243   *Lucas*: For details on Lucas (Pierre de Vomécourt) and Bleicher's arrest and subsequent involvement with him, see KV 2/164 (10B), UK National Archives; Carré, *I Was "the Cat"*, 130–50; Philippe de Vomécourt, *Army of Amateurs*.

243   *"Then Lucas will"*: Bleicher, *Colonel Henri's Story*, 178.

243   *"Have you had" . . . "You are not a convict"*: Ibid., 179.

243   *11 rue des Saussaies . . . French Ministry of the Interior*: Foot, *SOE in France*, 109.

244   *"I told you"*: Bleicher, *Colonel Henri's Story*, 180.

244   *"They were all truthful" . . . "Mon Dieu" . . . "The chief of"*: Ibid., 186–87.

245   *"Through him"*: Ibid., 129.

245   *almost tearful . . . prior August*: Foot, *SOE in France*, 361.

246   *"You should have" . . . "I am sorry"*: Cookridge, *Inside S.O.E.*, 369–70.

246 *"I often suspected"*: Ibid.

246 *"Promise me, Monsieur Jean"*: Bleicher, *Colonel Henri's Story*, 190.

247 *"So I went into"*: Ibid.

247 *"It was I who"* . . . *"like two souls"*: Ibid., 191.

248 *"Congratulations"* . . . *"The George Cross"*: Imperial War Museum (IWM), Oral History, interview with Odette Marie Céline Sansom, produced October 31, 1986, catalogue number 9478, Reel 3. Odette's George Cross was officially announced in the *London Gazette* on August 20, 1946.

248 *"I am going to stay"*: Starns, *Odette*, 113, citing an interview with Odette in the *Daily Telegraph*, August 21, 1946.

248 *"Mommy, is the George Cross"*: IWM, interview with Odette Sansom, October 31, 1986, catalogue number 9478, Reel 3.

249 *Member of the Order of the British Empire*: HS 9/648.4.002, .008, .010, .011, and .045–51, UK National Archives.

249 *promoted to lieutenant*: HS 9/648.4.055 and HS 9/648.4.056, UK National Archives.

249 *injections . . . guards . . . Lord Chamberlain*: Churchill, *Spirit in the Cage*, 235–36.

CHAPTER 23: COMPLETING THE LOOP

250 *"Madame, His Majesty"* . . . *"If you will kindly"*: Churchill, *Spirit in the Cage*, 236.

251 *Mrs. Sansom was infiltrated*: *London Gazette*, August 20, 1946; Churchill, *Spirit in the Cage*, 236–37.

251 *"I asked that"*: Churchill, *Spirit in the Cage*, 237.

253 *"Foreseeing that she would"*: Affidavit of Simone Hérail taken at Narbonne, France, on March 20, 1946. HS 9/648.4.038 and HS 9/648.4.039, UK National Archives.

253 *"mysterious"*: Imperial War Museum, "The Arrest of Fritz Suhren," catalogue number MGH 617.

253 *Sühren's guards*: Churchill, *Spirit in the Cage*, 234.

253 *screams of women*: London *Times*, December 17, 1946; Imperial War Museum (IWM), Oral History, interview with Odette Marie Céline Sansom, produced October 31, 1986, catalogue number 9478, Reel 2.

253 *General C. L. Stirling*: London *Times*, December 17, 1946.

254   *"Bleicher's methods"*: Buckmaster, *They Fought Alone*, 230.

255   *"It was generally conceded"*: Bleicher, *Colonel Henri's Story*, 191.

255   *"Bleicher has had"*: KV 2/164 (2B), UK National Archives. And from another report: "Bleicher . . . claims always to have been anti-Nazi . . . and to have struggled throughout the war to protect agents captured through his efforts from maltreatment at the hands of Amt. IV. There is a good deal of evidence to show that at least the latter part of this claim is to some extent justified. It is to the credit of Bleicher and his superior officers that the promises given to captured agents . . . have been carried out. He caused captured agents to be treated as Prisoner of War even in cases where, under international law, the Germans were entitled to impose the death penalty." KV 2/164 (10B), UK National Archives.

255   *"extremely nice and polite"*: KV 2/2127.1 (unpaginated, but see entry at 1943 in the fourth page of Bleicher's personnel file), UK National Archives.

255   *"There is no doubt"*: Buckmaster, *They Fought Alone*, 230.

EPILOGUE

257   *"There is no other"*: Imperial War Museum (IWM), Oral History, interview with Odette Marie Céline Sansom, produced October 31, 1986, catalogue number 9478, Reel 2.

257   *"Madam"* . . . *"this is"*: Ibid.

257   *Trude . . . had been a governess*: HS 9/648.4.044, UK National Archives; IWM, interview with Odette Sansom, October 31, 1986, catalogue number 9478, Reel 2.

257   *asked if she could work*: IWM, interview with Odette Sansom, October 31, 1986, catalogue number 9478, Reel 2; Churchill, *Spirit in the Cage*, 243.

257–58   *married the Fresnes guard captain*: Churchill, *Spirit in the Cage*, 243.

258   *"What happened to me"*: IWM, interview with Odette Sansom, October 31, 1986, catalogue number 9478, Reel 2.

258   *"No, never"*: Ibid., Reel 3.

258   *"They were in"*: Ibid., Reel 2.

258   *"There was nothing"*: Ibid., Reel 3.

259   *"No. Why?"*: Ibid.

259   *September 1946 Hugo Bleicher*: Cookridge, *Inside S.O.E.*, 371.

259   *Tettnang*: Churchill, *Spirit in the Cage*, 243; Cookridge, *Inside S.O.E.*, 371–72.

259   *le Belge and Roger Bardet . . . sentenced . . . released*: Churchill, *Spirit in the Cage*, 242; Cookridge, *Inside S.O.E.*, 372 (writing that Bardet was released in 1955).

259   *publication of Odette*: As occurs with many sensational stories, a few challenged the book's veracity. In *SOE in France*, M. R. D. Foot—who had interviewed neither Odette nor Peter Churchill (who later sued Foot's publisher for libel, and won)—writes that Tickell's account was "partly fictionalised" but "also accurate in parts" (411). In the 2000 reprint of William Mackenzie's *The Secret History of SOE* (1948), Foot (who provided the introduction and notes) reasserted the charge, writing that Odette became "a national heroine on appearance of film *Odette* based on Jerry Tickell's often inaccurate life of her with the same title" (252, note *). In *Odette: World War Two's Darling Spy*, Starns alleges twice that Tickell's authorized biography was "fictionalised" (12, 125).

However, neither Foot nor Starns cited examples in Tickell's biography where they thought the account was fictionalised. While Tickell's work is not error free, the book's accuracy was personally confirmed at the time by Odette and Peter, the individuals who knew the story best, and is corroborated in most places by SOE reports and interrogations now in the UK National Archives. Odette also wrote the foreword to the book and would continue to defend it years later. When asked if Tickell's biography was accurate or if any corrections needed to be made, Odette was unequivocal: "No. There are not. I think it was as it was . . . I'm sure that it's difficult for people to believe some part of it, but it did happen the way it did, and I can't alter the fact. I did survive, and I know I should not. I don't take any pride in that; it has nothing to do with me whatsoever." IWM, interview with Odette Sansom, October 31, 1986, catalogue number 9478, Reel 3. Peter would also vouch for the book's accuracy in his 1954 account of his own captivity, *Spirit in the Cage*: "Little by little, Odette told me her dreadful story. Since it has been accurately and sensitively told by Jerrard Tickell in his book *Odette* . . ." *Spirit in the Cage*, 232.

259 *Eppenschlag . . . Herbert Pakusch*: Hans von Begerow, "Wie ein SS-Mann aus Varel eine Agentin als Geisel ahm," NWZ online (Nordwest-Zeitung, Lower Saxony, Germany), April 30, 2015.

260 *Deggendorf . . . Rastatt . . . convicted . . . hanged*: Ibid.

261 *"Madame" . . . "I have no right"*: Churchill, *Spirit in the Cage*, 251.

261 *"In bringing Paul Steinert's"*: Ibid.

262 *the king and queen of England*: Footage from the premiere, including coverage of the king and queen, Odette, Peter, and Anna Neagle, can be seen at: www.youtube.com/watch?v=_giTVe5apbU.

263 *"It took her one year"*: IWM, interview with Odette Sansom, October 31, 1986, catalogue number 9478, Reel 3.

263 *Arnaud . . . Rawicz extermination camp . . . gassed*: Cookridge, *Inside S.O.E.*, 183.

264 *most highly decorated*: Australia's Nancy Wake received more total decorations (twelve), but five of those were campaign awards, and four were awarded more than twenty-five years after the war. Odette's George Cross and Member of the Order of the British Empire, however, were higher decorations than any received by Wake (both women received France's Chevalier de la Légion d'honneur, Odette in 1950, Wake in 1970). As such, Nancy Wake was World War II's most decorated woman, while Odette was the war's most *highly* decorated woman.

APPENDIX

267 *some alleged that Maurice*: In an article for the *Daily Mirror*, Buckmaster countered: "The penetration by the Germans in the summer of 1943 of the so-called 'Prosper' circuit was a serious setback to our operations . . . But it represented one success only—admittedly with grave repercussions and gave rise to a large number of arrests. It did not stop the progress of the French Section toward its objective: the constant harrying of the German forces and the stranglehold on the German economic machine in France." *Daily Mirror*, December 1, 1958; Starns, *Odette*, 132, citing TS 58/1160, UK National Archives.

267 *six members of the French*: Starns, *Odette*, 141. See also Cookridge, *Inside S.O.E.*, 163–64.

267 *"There was some trouble"*: HS 9/648.4.058, UK National Archives.

267 *Le Journal de la Villa Isabelle*: Cookridge, *Inside S.O.E.*, 163.

268 *ON LANDING IN FRANCE*: Ibid., 164.

268   *"The Baron and his wife"*: Ibid.

268   *three scandalous assertions*: Starns, *Odette*, 141.

268   *"She [Odette] pointed"*: Ibid., 142, citing the *Daily Telegraph*, November 24, 1958.

269   *"We signed the document"*: Ibid., 143, citing the *Daily Express*, November 24, 1958.

269   *"I have never known"*: Ibid., 143, citing the *Daily Telegraph*, November 24, 1958.

269   *"It is the most amazing"*: Ibid., 144, citing the *Daily Express*, November 24, 1958.

270   *letter . . . to Colonel Perkins*: HS 9/648.4.017, HS 9/648.4.018, HS 9/648.4.027, and HS 9/648.4.028, UK National Archives.

270   *I certify that on 17th*: HS 9/648.4.042, UK National Archives.

271   *"impeccably"*: Starns, *Odette*, 145, citing the *Daily Telegraph*, November 24, 1958.

271   *"What Churchill did"*: Ibid.

271   *Robert Knox . . . Sir Norman Brook . . . May 8*: T 350/11.001–.002, UK National Archives.

272   *"There seems to be no precedent"*: T 350/11.003, UK National Archives.

272   *"I have studied"*: T 350/11.004, UK National Archives.

272   *"In this further letter"*: T 350/11.005, UK National Archives.

273   *"I cannot think"*: CAB 103/573.001–.002, UK National Archives. The letter, dated April 20, 1965, was sent after Buckmaster reviewed the second galley proofs.

273   *SOE files had been lost or destroyed by fire*: Starns, *Odette*, 155, estimates that 85 percent of SOE files were destroyed by a fire at headquarters after the war. Foot, *SOE in France*, xi–xii, obliquely references the hurdle, noting in the preface of *SOE in France* that he had access to all relevant "surviving files of SOE."

273–74   *to not allow key agents a prepublication review*: Foot, *SOE in France*, preface, xii ("Since this book first appeared in April 1966 I have had further help . . . from former members of SOE.").

274   *"virtually unavailable" . . . "good agents kept"*: Foot, *SOE in France*, preface, x.

274   *"unpublished archives are"*: Ibid., xi.

274   *completed his original draft . . . 1962*: Ibid., x.

274   *invited libel actions*: TS 58/1155 (generally) and TS 58/1157 (regarding Odette in particular), UK National Archives.

274   *discussion of . . . galley proofs with Maurice Buckmaster*: Buckmaster reviewed the first set of galley proofs on January 1, 1965 (TS 58/1160.001, UK National Archives), and the second set from April 7 to April 20, 1965 (CAB 103/573.001, UK National Archives).

274   *"Buckmaster affirmed to have"*: Correspondence of E. G. Boxshall to Treasury solicitor F. N. Charlton, June 22, 1966, at TS 58/1160.001-002, UK National Archives. Boxshall's comment is somewhat cryptic, but suggests that Foot made the notation: "I have looked up the Notes on the Meeting with Col. Buckmaster which took place in your office on 1 January 1965 for the purpose of discussing the first edition of the galley proof. From these Notes I quote the following passage: Odette Sansom. Buckmaster affirmed to have been."

274   *"Peter Churchill was here"*: Buckmaster, *They Fought Alone*, 76.

274   *"Men like Peter Churchill"*: Ibid., 95.

274   *"Peter Churchill and Odette"*: Ibid., 235–36.

275   *Odette had made a grievous error*: It appears from the postwar SOE files that Odette offered an excuse during the discussion of Foot's book after its publication, suggesting that London instructed her to "play" Bleicher and leave the hotel on April 18. See correspondence of E. G. Boxshall to Treasury solicitor F. N. Charlton on 22 June 1966 at TS 58/1160.001–002, UK National Archives. The excuse was apparently refuted by Buckmaster and was directly contradicted by Tickell's authorized biography, wherein Odette agrees with Peter that she should have left the Hôtel de la Poste immediately upon receiving London's wire (Tickell, *Odette*, 195–96), and by Peter Churchill's account of the events, wherein he recorded only the cable for Odette to cut contact with Bleicher. *Duel of Wits*, 344–45.

275   *"Buckmaster was deeply"*: Marks, *Between Silk and Cyanide*, 283.

275   *"Odette opened the door"*: Bleicher, *Colonel Henri's Story*, 98.

275   *wherein he states that*: Churchill, *Duel of Wits*, 362 ("[S]he took the enemy to the room of the man . . . My door was opened.").

276   *"partly fictionalized"*: Foot, *SOE in France*, 411.

276   *"They were to be"*: HS 9/648.4.078, UK National Archives.

276   *"the tall thin man"*: HS 9/648.4.069, UK National Archives.

276   *"Mrs. O. Sansom has been"*: HS 9/648.4.019 and HS 9/648.4.026, UK National Archives.

276   *"I believe you expressed"*: HS 9/648.4.024, UK National Archives.

277 *fears of libel claims*: TS 58/1155 (generally) and TS 58/1157 (by Odette), UK National Archives.

277 *"I have been through"*: Starns, *Odette*, 158; TS 58/1160, UK National Archives.

277 *indemnity insurance*: Starns, *Odette*, 161.

277 *Goodman, Derrick and Co. . . . "The British government"*: Ibid., 164; TS 58/1160, UK National Archives. See also TS 58/1157.001, TS 58/1157.002, and TS 58/1157.003–.004, UK National Archives.

277 *Odette was compensated £646*: Starns, *Odette*, 168.

277–78 *met with Odette's attorneys . . . Foot agreed to make the changes*: See F. N. Charlton's "Mrs. Odette Hallowes" memo dated 15 June 1966 at TS 58/1157.005, UK National Archives.

278 *"There has been one"*: Starns, *Odette*, 170–71, citing the London *Times*, July 11, 1966, 13.

278 *his lawyers filed suit*: Peter was represented by Oswald, Hickson, Collier & Co. FO 953/2431.00002, UK National Archives.

278 *"Luxury was as"*: FO 953/2431.00004–.00005, UK National Archives.

278 *ordered to remove*: Michael Foot, in his preface for the revised *SOE in France*, wrote on September 4, 1967: "I have also taken this opportunity to modify a number of passages which gave some quite unintended personal offence [*sic*], and to make explicit a few points misunderstood by reviewers." *SOE in France*, xii.

BIBLIOGRAPHY

ARCHIVES AND OFFICIAL DOCUMENTS

Berlin Document Center (Bundesarchiv)

Churchill Archives Centre, Cambridge University

Geneva Convention: Laws and Customs of War on Land (Hague IV, October 18, 1907) and Convention Relative to the Treatment of Prisoners of War, Geneva (July 27, 1929)

Imperial War Museum, London

National Archives of the UK

Trial of the Major War Criminals Before the International Military Tribunal, Official Text, English Edition, Nuremberg

US Holocaust Memorial Museum, Washington, DC

BOOKS AND ARTICLES

Begerow, Hans von. "Second World War: How an SS Man from Varel Took an Agent as a Hostage." NWZ Online (*Nordwest-Zeitung*), last modified April 30, 2015, https://www.nwzonline.de/politik/nieder sachsen/mit-frau-als-geisel-freikauf-versucht-wie-ein-ss-mann-aus -varel-eine-agentin-als-geisel-nahm_a_27,0,1027734928.html.

Binney, Marcus. *The Women Who Lived for Danger: The Women of the Special Operations Executive*. London: Hodder and Stoughton, 2002.

Bleicher, Hugo. *Colonel Henri's Story: The War Memoirs of Hugo Bleicher,*

Former German Secret Agent. 2nd ed. Edited by Ian Colvin. London: William Kimber, 1954.

Bonhoeffer, Dietrich. *Letters and Papers from Prison*. Edited by Eberhard Bethge. 1953. Reprint, New York: Touchstone, 1997.

Boom, Corrie ten, with Elizabeth and John Sherrill. *The Hiding Place*. Grand Rapids, MI: Chosen Books, 1971.

Bristow, Desmond, with Bill Bristow. *A Game of Moles: The Deceptions of an MI6 Officer*. London: Little, Brown, 1993.

Brown, Anthony Cave. *Bodyguard of Lies: The Extraordinary True Story Behind D-Day*. New York: Harper & Row, 1975.

Buckmaster, Maurice. *They Fought Alone: The Story of British Agents in France*. London: Odhams, 1958.

Burney, Christopher. *Solitary Confinement*. New York: Macmillan, 1952.

Burton-Hill, Clemency. "Is Wagner's Nazi Stigma Fair?" BBC online, Culture, last modified October 21, 2014, www.bbc.com/culture/story /20130509-is-wagners-nazi-stigma-fair.

Carré, Mathilde-Lily. *I Was "the Cat": The Truth About the Most Remarkable Woman Spy Since Mata Hari—by Herself*. London: Souvenir Press, 1960.

Casey, William J. *The Secret War Against Hitler*. Washington, DC: Regnery Gateway, 1988.

Churchill, Peter. *Duel of Wits*. New York: G. P. Putnam's Sons, 1953.

———. *Of Their Own Choice*. London: Hodder and Stoughton, 1952.

———. *The Spirit in the Cage*. London: 1954. Reprint, Yorkshire, UK: Elmfield Press, 1974.

Churchill, Winston S. *The Second World War*. Vol. 2, *Their Finest Hour*. Boston: Houghton Mifflin, 1949.

———. *The Second World War*. Vol. 3, *The Grand Alliance*. Boston: Houghton Mifflin, 1950.

Cookridge, E. H. *Inside S.O.E.: The Story of Special Operations in Western Europe, 1940–1945*. London: Arthur Baker, 1966.

———. *They Came from the Sky*. New York: Thomas Crowell, 1967.

Cowburn, Benjamin. *No Cloak, No Dagger*. London: Jarrolds, 1960.

Crowdy, Terry. *Deceiving Hitler: Double Cross and Deception*. Oxford: Osprey, 2008.

Cunningham, Cyril. *Beaulieu: The Finishing School for Secret Agents*. London: Leo Cooper, 1998.

Dalton, Hugh. *The Fateful Years: Memoirs 1931–1945*. London: Frederick Muller, 1957.

Dalzel-Job, Patrick. *From Arctic Snow to Dust of Normandy*. 1991. Reprint, Oxford and Winter Springs, Florida: ISIS, 2001.

Deacon, Richard [Donald McCormick]. *Spyclopedia: The Comprehensive Handbook of Espionage*. New York: William Morrow, 1987.

Dear, I. C. B., and M. R. D. Foot, eds. *The Oxford Companion to World War II*. Oxford: Oxford University Press, 1995.

Delmer, Sefton. *The Counterfeit Spy: The Untold Story of a Phantom Army That Deceived Hitler*. New York: Harper & Row, 1971.

Doerries, Reinhard. *Hitler's Intelligence Chief: Walter Schellenberg*. New York: Enigma, 2009.

———. *Hitler's Last Chief of Foreign Intelligence: Allied Interrogations of Walter Schellenberg*. London: Frank Cass, 2003.

Dörner, Klaus, et al., eds., *The Nuremberg Medical Trial 1946/47: Guide to the Microfiche Edition*. Translated by Cath Baker and Nancy Schrauf. Munich: K. G. Saur, 2001.

Dorril, Stephen. *MI6: Inside the Covert World of Her Majesty's Secret Intelligence Service*. New York: Free Press, 2000.

Dostoyevsky, Fyodor. *Crime and Punishment*. 1867. Translated by C. J. Hogarth. Reprint, *Dostoyevsky*, London: Chancellor Press, 1994.

Dourlein, Pieter. *Inside North Pole: A Secret Agent's Story*. Translated by F. G. Renier and Anne Cliffe. London: William Kimber, 1953.

Dulles, Allen Welsh. *Germany's Underground: The Anti-Nazi Resistance*. 1947. Reprint, Boston: Da Capo Press, 2000.

Escott, Beryl E. *The Heroines of SOE: F Section: Britain's Secret Women in France*. Stroud, UK: History Press, 2012.

Fairbairn, W. E. *All-in Fighting*. 1942. Reprint, East Sussex: Naval and Military Press, 2009.

Fairburn, W. E., and E. A. Sykes. *Shooting to Live*. Edinburgh: Oliver and Boyd, 1942. Reprint, Boulder, CO: Paladin Press, 2008.

Foot, M. R. D. *S.O.E.: The Special Operations Executive, 1940–46*. 1984. Reprint, London: Mandarin, 1993.

———. *SOE in France*. London: Whitehall History, 1966.

Garby-Czerniawski, Roman. *The Big Network*. London: George Ronald, 1961.

Giskes, Hermann J. *London Calling North Pole: The True Revelations of a German Spy*. 1953. Reprint, Brattleboro, VT: Echo Point Books & Media, 2015.

Gutek, Gerald. *Philosophical and Ideological Perspectives on Education*. New York: Pearson, 2013.

Handel, Michael. *Strategic and Operational Deception in the Second World War*. Abingdon, UK: Frank Cass, 1987.

Hassell, Augustino von, and Sigrid MacRae, with Simone Ameskamp. *Alliance of Enemies: The Untold Story of the Secret American and German Collaboration to End World War II*. New York: Thomas Dunne Books, 2006.

Heberer, Patricia, and Jürgen Matthäus, eds. *Atrocities on Trial: Historical Perspectives on the Politics of Prosecuting War Crimes*. Lincoln: University of Nebraska Press, 2008.

Helm, Sarah. *A Life in Secrets: Vera Atkins and the Missing Agents of WWII*. New York: Anchor Books, 2005.

———. *Ravensbrück: Life and Death in Hitler's Concentration Camp for Women*. New York: Nan A. Talese/Doubleday, 2014.

Hemingway, Ernest. *A Farewell to Arms*. 1929. Reprint, New York: Scribner, 2014.

Higgins, Charlotte. "How the Nazis Took Flight from Valkyries and Rhinemaidens." *Guardian* (US edition) online, last modified July 2, 2007, www.theguardian.com/world/2007/jul/03/secondworldwar.musicnews.

Hinsley, F. H., with E. E. Thomas, C. F. G. Ranson, and R. C. Knight. *British Intelligence in the Second World War*. Vol. 1, *Its Influence on Strategy and Operations*. London: Her Majesty's Stationery Office Books, 1979.

———. *British Intelligence in the Second World War*. Vol. 3, Part 2, *Its Influence on Strategy and Operations*. New York: Cambridge University Press, 1988.

Hinsley, F. H., and C. A. G. Simkins. *British Intelligence in the Second World War*. Vol. 4, *Security and Counter-intelligence*. New York: Cambridge University Press, 1990.

Hitler, Adolf. *Mein Kampf*. Edited by Rudolf Hess. Translated by James Murphy. 1925. Reprint, Haole Library, 2015.

Höhne, Heinz. *The Order of the Death's Head: The Story of Hitler's SS*. Originally published in 1966 in German as *Der Orden unter dem Totenkopf*. Translated by Richard Barry. Reprint, London: Penguin Books, 2000.

Holt, Thaddeus. *The Deceivers: Allied Military Deception in the Second World War*. New York: Scribner, 2004.

Höttl, Wilhelm. *The Secret Front: Nazi Political Espionage, 1938–1945*. 1953. Reprint, New York: Enigma Books, 2003.

Howard, Michael. *Strategic Deception in the Second World War*. 1990. Reprint, New York: W. W. Norton, 1995.

Hoyt, Edwin P. *The Invasion Before Normandy: The Secret Battle of Slapton Sands*. New York: Cooper Square Press, 1999.

Jackson, Julian. "Vera Atkins" (obituary), *Guardian* (US edition) online, last modified July 5, 2000, www.theguardian.com/news/2000/jul/06/guardianobituaries.ianjack.

Jacobs, Peter. *Setting France Ablaze: The SOE in France During WWII*. Barnsley, UK: Pen & Sword Books, 2015.

Jones, R. V. *The Wizard War: British Scientific Intelligence, 1939–1945*. New York: Coward, McCann & Geoghegan, 1978.

Kahn, David. *Hitler's Spies: German Military Intelligence in World War II*. New York: Macmillan, 1978.

Klemperer, Klemens von. *German Resistance Against Hitler: The Search for Allies Abroad, 1938–1945*. New York: Oxford University Press, 1992.

Knightley, Phillip. *The Second Oldest Profession: Spies and Spying in the Twentieth Century*. New York: W. W. Norton, 1987.

Kramer, Rita. *Flames in the Field: The Story of Four SOE Agents in Occupied France*. London: Michael Joseph, 1995.

Ladd, James, Keith Melton, and Captain Peter Mason. *Clandestine Warfare: Weapons and Equipment of the SOE and OSS*. London: Blandford Press, 1988.

Langelaan, George. *Knights of the Floating Silk*. London: Hutchinson, 1959.

Leverkeuhn, Paul. *German Military Intelligence*. Translated by R. H. Stevens and Constantine FitzGibbon. New York: Praeger, 1954.

Levine, Joshua. *Operation Fortitude: The Story of the Spy Operation that Saved D-Day*. London: HarperCollins, 2011.

Liddell Hart, B. H. *History of the Second World War*. New York: G. P. Putnam's Sons, 1971.

Loftis, Larry. *Into the Lion's Mouth: The True Story of Dusko Popov—World War II Spy, Patriot, and the Real-Life Inspiration for James Bond*. New York: Berkley Caliber, 2016.

Lorain, Pierre. *Clandestine Operations: The Arms and Techniques of the Resistance, 1941–1944*. New York: Macmillan, 1983.

Macintyre, Ben. *Double Cross: The True Story of the D-Day Spies*. London: Crown, 2012.

Mackenzie, William. *The Secret History of SOE: The Special Operations Executive, 1940–1945*. London: St. Ermin's Press, 2000.

Maclean, Fitzroy. *Eastern Approaches*. 1949. Reprint, London: Penguin Books, 1991.

Marks, Leo. *Between Silk and Cyanide: The Story of S.O.E.'s Code War.* London: HarperCollins, 1998.

Masterman, J. C. *The Double-Cross System in the War of 1939 to 1945.* New Haven, CT: Yale University Press, 1972.

Metaxas, Eric. *Bonhoeffer: Pastor, Martyr, Prophet, Spy.* Nashville: Thomas Nelson, 2011.

Michel, Henri. *The Shadow War: Resistance in Europe, 1939–1945.* Translated by Richard Barry. New York: Harper & Row, 1972.

Millar, George. *Maquis: An Englishman in the French Resistance.* 1945. Reprint, London: Cassell, 2003.

Miller, Francis Trevelyan. *The Complete History of World War II.* Chicago: Readers' Service Bureau, 1947.

Montagu, Ewen. *Beyond Top Secret Ultra.* New York: Coward, McCann & Geoghegan, 1978.

Montgomery, Field Marshal Bernard. *Normandy to the Baltic.* Cambridge: Houghton Mifflin, 1948.

Morrison, Jack Gaylord. *Ravensbrück: Everyday Life in a Women's Concentration Camp, 1939–45.* Princeton, NJ: Markus Weiner Publishers, 2001.

Muggeridge, Malcolm. *Chronicles of Wasted Time.* Vol. 2, *The Infernal Grove.* New York: Morrow, 1974.

Murphy, Christopher J. *Security and Special Operations: SOE and MI5 During the Second World War.* New York: Palgrave Macmillan, 2006.

Naujoks, Harry. *Mein Leben im KZ Sachsenhausen, 1936–1942.* Cologne, Ger.: Röderberg, 1987.

Nicholas, Elizabeth. *Death Be Not Proud.* London: Cresset Press, 1958.

Ousby, Ian. *Occupation: The Ordeal of France, 1940–1944.* New York: Cooper Square Press, 2000.

Paine, Lauran. *German Military Intelligence in World War II: The Abwehr.* New York: Stein and Day, 1984.

———. *Mathilde Carré: Double Agent.* London: Robert Hale, 1976.

Peis, Günter. *The Mirror of Deception: How Britain Turned the Nazi Spy Machine Against Itself.* New York: Pocket Books, 1977.

Philby, Kim. *My Silent War: The Autobiography of a Spy.* 1968. Reprint, New York: Modern Library, 2002.

Pindera, Jerzy. *Liebe Mutti: One Man's Struggle to Survive in KZ Sachsenhausen, 1939–1945.* Edited by Lynne Taylor. Lanham, MD: University Press of America, 2004.

Renouf, Vera. *Forfeit to War.* Victoria, Can.: Trafford, 2002.

Richards, Brooks. *Secret Flotillas: Clandestine Sea Operations to Brittany, 1940–44*. London: HMSO, 1996.

Rigden, Denis. Intro. In *How to Be a Spy: The World War II SOE Training Manual*. Toronto: Dundurn Press, 2004.

Rothfels, Hans. *The German Opposition to Hitler*. 1947. Reprint, Regnery, 1963.

Ruby, Marcel. *F Section SOE: The Story of the Buckmaster Networks*. London: Leo Cooper, 1988.

Rürup, Reinhard, ed. *Topography of Terror: Gestapo, SS and Reichssicherheits-hauptamt on the "Prinz-Albrecht-Terrain": A Documentation*. Translated by Werner T. Angress. Berlin: Willmuth Arenhövel, 2006.

Schellenberg, Walter. *The Memoirs of Hitler's Spymaster*. 1956. Edited and translated by Louis Hagan. Reprint, London: Andre Deutsch, 2006.

Segev, Tom. *Soldiers of Evil: The Commandants of the Nazi Concentration Camps*. New York: McGraw-Hill, 1988.

Sherry, Norman. *The Life of Graham Greene*. Vol. 2, *1939–1955*. New York: Viking, 1994.

Shirer, William. *The Rise and Fall of the Third Reich: A History of the Third Reich*. New York: Simon & Schuster, 1960.

Speer, Albert. *Inside the Third Reich: Memoirs*. New York: Macmillan, 1970.

Stafford, David. *Secret Agent: The True Story of the Covert War Against Hitler*. Overlook Press, 2001.

Starns, Penny. *Odette: World War Two's Darling Spy*. Stroud, UK: History Press, 2009.

Taylor, James S. *Poetic Knowledge: The Recovery of Education*. Albany, NY: State University of New York Press, 1998.

Tickell, Jerrard. *Odette: The Story of a British Agent*. 1949. Reprint, London: Pan Books, 1976.

Vomécourt, Philippe de. *An Army of Amateurs: The Story of the SOE Resistance Movement in France, by One of the Three Brothers Who Organized and Ran It*. Garden City, NY: Doubleday, 1961.

Wachsmann, Nikolaus. *kl: A History of the Nazi Concentration Camps*. New York: Farrar, Straus and Giroux, 2015.

Warlimont, Gen. Walter. *Inside Hitler's Headquarters, 1939–45*. 1962. Translated from the German by R. H. Barry. Reprint, Novato, CA: Presidio Press, 1991.

West, Nigel. *The A to Z of British Intelligence*. Lanham, MD: Scarecrow Press, 2005.

————. *Historical Dictionary of World War II Intelligence*. Lanham, MD: Scarecrow Press, 2008.

————. *MI5: The True Story of the Most Secret Counterespionage Organization in the World*. New York: Stein and Day, 1982.

————. *MI6: British Secret Intelligence Service Operations, 1909–1945*. London: Weidenfeld & Nicolson, 1983.

————. *A Thread of Deceit: Espionage Myths of World War II*. New York: Random House, 1985.

Wighton, Charles, and Günter Peis. *Hitler's Spies and Saboteurs*. New York: Holt, Rinehart & Winston, 1958.

Wituska, Krystyna. *Inside a Gestapo Prison: The Letters of Krystyna Wituska, 1942–1944*. Edited and translated by Irene Tomaszewski. Detroit: Wayne State University Press, 2006.

Young, Gordon. *Cat with Two Faces*. London: Putnam, 1957.

INDEX